W9-BCC-641

TO ANALYZE DELIGHT

TO ANALYZE DELIGHT

A Hedonist Criticism of Shakespeare

Gary Taylor

NEWARK
University of Delaware Press

First published in the USA in 1985 by
Associated University Presses
440 Forsgate Drive
Cranbury, NJ 08512

Published in the UK in 1985
under the title
Moment by Moment by Shakespeare

Library of Congress Cataloging in Publication Data
Taylor, Gary.
  To analyze delight.

  Bibliography: p.
  Includes index.
  1. Shakespeare, William, 1564–1616 – Criticism
and interpretation.   I. Title.
PR2976.T27   1985   822′.33   83–40617
ISBN 0–87413–269–X

Printed in Hong Kong

Contents

List of Illustrations

Preface

This book began in frustration, the frustration engendered by reading a great deal of literary criticism, ancient and modern, very little of which had anything to do with the actual pleasure I derived from reading or seeing Shakespeare's plays. What seems to me a similar frustration with the inutility and cloudiness of much contemporary criticism has found recent expression in Richard Levin's *New Readings vs. Old Plays,* in G. K. Hunter's keynote address to the 1979 Shakespeare Association of America conference, in Harriett Hawkins's annual reviews for *Shakespeare Survey,* to mention only some of the more prominent manifestations which have happened to catch my eye or ear. But these reactions, however much I sympathize with them, do little to replace the edifice being torn down; they don't attempt to provide a more satisfactory or precise explanation of the real pleasure generated by the plays. What I have tried to do in this book, however vainly (in both senses), is to replace the modern emphasis upon interpretation with a kind of critical hedonism, the study of drama as a 'superior amusement'. When I began, years ago, I thought this a devastatingly original enterprise, which I would carry out with a suitably unanswerable panache. As the years pass I become increasingly conscious of my indebtedness to other approaches, and of the limits to my own panache. Every reader will perceive my indebtedness to 'new' criticism, to the theatrically oriented Shakespearian criticism of recent decades, to the several recent studies of audience response, to the critics and editors of the plays I discuss in detail.

If my general intellectual debts are immeasurable and unpayable, some of the more specific overdrafts can at least be publicly acknowledged. Richard Hardin and Margaret Arnold supervised the University of Kansas honours thesis from which this whole project sprang; Theodore Redpath nurtured it, with his usual sympathy and astuteness and great learning, for three years at Cambridge. During that time Peterhouse not only supported me with a studentship, but was especially generous in financing an extended stay at Stratford-upon-Avon; during which stay Terry Hands in particular, and the Royal Shakespeare Company generally, were very free with that most precious of commodities, their time. Anne Barton, Emrys Jones, John Banks, John Kerrigan, John Wilders, E. A. J. Honigmann, Michael Warren, M. C. Bradbrook and Philip Brockbank have all seen and much improved earlier versions of this book; and, though Peter Blayney and Peter Holland have not actually read it, the book is indebted in many places to the stimulation of their conversation. Nobby Clark and Mary White (of the Shakespeare Centre, Stratford-upon-Avon) searched tirelessly for a particular photograph which had apparently been lost (Plate 2). As for Stanley Wells, he has not only improved this book, by specific criticism and personal example, but made its completion possible, by showing confidence in me at a time when few others seemed willing to: without his providential intervention, it would be an inchoate chaos rotting in some drawer.

These debts are deep enough; but what I owe to Rebecca is of a different order of magnitude. Others have taught me art; she teaches me life. With her, life too has its moments.

G. T.

1 Passing Pleasures

Bad commentators spoil the best of books.
So God sends meat (they say), the devil cooks.
Benjamin Franklin
'Poor Richard' (1735)

Criticism too often consists in filtering out pleasure in the pursuit of meaning, in reducing poems to their lowest common denominator ('life vs. death'), in counting how many images had Lady Macbeth. I would rather analyse delight. Shakespeare was, as Dr Johnson complained, 'much more careful to please than to instruct'. His plays move and delight us still; I want to know how we are delighted, how we are moved, from unique moment to unique moment. For, though the pleasure of a single moment may depend upon the preparations of an hour, our pleasure remains a function of that lone moment. Therefore I am first interested in the immediacy of Shakespeare's art, not its unity. (Cardboard boxes have unity; unity does not make them interesting.) Or rather, I am interested in unity only in so far as it contributes to the pleasures of the single moment. Virginia Woolf said of Jane Austen that she was, of all great artists, the most difficult to catch in the act of greatness.[1] I want to catch Shakespeare in the act.

I should probably define delight, since it is the subject of this inquiry, but I shall content myself with a remark of Wittgenstein's: after inquiring whether a set of gramophone records was 'any good', on being told, 'it depends on what you mean by *good*', he retorted, tartly, 'I mean what you mean.'[2] One of my own primary experiences of art is that some works give me more pleasure than others, and that the works which give me more pleasure tend also to give other people more pleasure. I am intrigued to know why this should be so.

1

Consequently, although what follows is an attempt to analyse why certain moments in Shakespeare's plays give pleasure, I have not asked why the human mind should delight in fictions, or why it should take pleasure in the representation of murder or suffering or immorality, for these are questions about our responses to *all* works of a certain kind; the answers, even if I found them, need not be of much use in explaining why certain fictions or certain representations of murder please more than others, and it is these latter questions which interest me.

But I can only analyse *how* we are delighted if I can first establish *that* we are delighted. Initially at least, I must therefore restrict myself to cases beyond controversy, where the capacity to give pleasure is confirmed by an abiding and secure consensus, approaching unanimity. The selection of examples is therefore crucial; it is also necessarily arbitrary. I have chosen one scene from *Julius Caesar*, the character of Viola, the 1975 Royal Shakespeare Company production of *Henry V*, and one scene from *King Lear*.[3] The value and relevance of these examples should emerge as each is in turn discussed, but I ought perhaps to explain briefly the rationale behind this unlikely assortment and the order of its presentation; for, though the choice of examples is inevitably arbitrary, the choice of topics those examples serve to illustrate, and the order of those topics, is not. With *Julius Caesar*, by limiting myself to one acclaimed scene (the assassination), I can concentrate on describing, in detail, what in the language and action of that scene has given so many discrete, successive moments of pleasure to so many readers and spectators – while at the same time illustrating a variety of approaches to the analysis of response generally, and 'moments' particularly. The next two chapters expand on specific problems either raised by or not faced in this first analysis, problems which are fundamental to any sustained and convincing description of how we respond to Shakespeare's plays. With *Twelfth Night*, by limiting myself to a single character, I can concentrate on how Shakespeare creates such a fictive being, and on how readers and spectators respond to it. With *Henry V*, by limiting myself to a single production, I can observe and analyse the contemporary pleasure of a succession of living audiences, and thereby isolate and analyse differences between reader and audience responses in a play where those differences are especially striking. In the last chapter, on *King Lear*, I return to the method of the first, limiting myself to the detailed analysis of a single scene, but incorporating the more complex methods and conclusions of the two intervening chapters, in an attempt to describe how a dramatist controls emphasis and determines an audience's perspective, even while encouraging a latitude and complexity of response to individual moments.

What follows, then, is a study of response.[4] Two fundamental objections to any such study must be faced at the outset. The first is a repugnance, often unspoken, to the very notion of a dramatist 'manipulating' the responses of his audience. In part this repugnance arises from an unfortunate choice of verbs: in psychology and the sciences one does not normally speak of 'manipulation and response' but of 'stimulus and response'. The image of Shakespeare *stimulating* an audience is both more attractive and closer to common experience than the image, implicit or explicit in previous studies of response, of a man unscrupulously manipulating our passions to cheat our reason – a portrait likelier to conjure up Hitler's performance at the Nuremburg Rallies than Shakespeare's *Hamlet*. But of course, in so far as the dramatist decides when and when not to stimulate us, and what and what not to stimulate, he is to a large degree, consciously or not, manipulating our sympathies. But even this selection and ordering of stimulants can be seen in a much less sinister light, if regarded as symptomatic of the necessary schizophrenia of the artist himself. He knows what will happen when, and how; his audience will not. He must bridge this disparity in perspectives by imagining how the given moment will look to that other person, the spectator. That is, 'manipulating an audience' is an exercise in imaginative sympathy, the same sympathy which enables the dramatist to construct his characters. But this defence, too, is largely cosmetic. In truth, the notion of dramatist as manipulator disturbs precisely because it directly raises nasty questions about the morality of art, questions which most of us most of the time would prefer not to think about. 'Shakespeare like Hitler manipulates his audience, and tells lies. Shakespeare like Hitler occasionally tells the truth, but only in order to make his lies more persuasive. *Hamlet* is a fiction; that is, a lie.'

Fortunately, this is a work about the technique of art, not its morality; a student of response would be justified in retorting, as an artist himself might, that 'if this book disturbs your complacent moral equanimity, so much the better'. But, though such a defence may be justified logically, rhetorically it is likely to backfire. By flaunting the alleged immorality of the artist's technique, such a defence ensures that the ethical issue, instead of remaining decently dormant until the exploration of technique ends, nags continually at the reader's conscience.

In fact, I find nothing immoral, *per se*, in Shakespeare's manipulation of his audience. The very word 'manipulation' is itself an emotive and manipulative one; substitute 'guidance', and the entire moral climate changes. The same objection can be made to the word 'lie', invoked in the comparison with Hitler. The concept of lying usually presupposes an antecedent and determinable truth which is being consciously distorted. With *Hamlet*, there is no such antecedent truth; the presumption that one exists is merely the most fundamental manifestation of the documentary fallacy. Even in plays based upon historical events or peopled by characters with historical names, there is no pretence that the play dramatizes *exactly* what happened; where there is no pretence, there can be no deception. Even if some naïve spectator is misled, the misinformation supplied him by the play is of two morally distinct kinds. Misinformation about matters of detail is morally irrelevant, unless it contributes to a wholesale falsification of history in the interests of an ideology upon which auditors are expected to act, once they leave the theatre. This throws the issue of falsification away from the domain of fact into that of ideology: one judges the artist's 'morality' by the correspondence between 'the real world' and his model of it. His model will of course turn out to be deficient – like the models of philosophers, economists, political theorists, psychologists, historians, biologists, chemists and mathematicians. If Shakespeare is guilty of lying, so are the others. Indeed, in this sense every hypothesis is a lie, in so far as it is eventually proven to be an inadequate or incomplete description of the real.

A play is, I would argue, a hypothesis; more specifically, a hypothetical *model*. The notion of a model is valuable because it entails the notion of construction, which in turn usefully disposes of two difficulties. First, the dramatist's falsifications of detail can usually be described as attempts to overcome the limitations of his medium, in constructing the model; second, a model, while attempting to reproduce the features of an existing whole, is in itself a new and a real thing. The poet is a 'liar' and a 'maker', a fabricator.

Another fundamental objection has been levelled at all studies of response. How can one speak of 'audience response' when in fact every member of an audience responds differently? I have sought to anticipate this objection by choosing examples where a secure consensus exists, and by taking account, in my analyses, of the differences between kinds of audience, between spectator and reader, between Renaissance and modern. I have also tried to isolate areas where differences within an audience are likely, or even encouraged, to develop, and to explain how the dramatist allows such differences without endangering the larger movements of sympathy essential to his structure. Nevertheless, in one form or another the objection will no doubt continue to be made, and should be answered. The comedian, for instance, lives by making people laugh: if he is a good comedian, his audience will laugh when he wants it to laugh, and it will laugh collectively. Some will laugh louder and longer than others; a few, for a variety of reasons, will not laugh at all. But if a Catholic does not laugh at jokes about the Pope, which 999 other listeners find funny, then, though the Catholic's reaction may not be wrong, it is abnormal, and statistically insignificant. Likewise, an Elizabethan Puritan may not have been amused by the gulling of Malvolio. But the play was not designed for Puritans; it assumes, quite reasonably, that Puritans would not attend such plays at all. So every art selects its audiences.

The modern literary critic is like the seventeenth-century Puritan in that he quite often does not share the predisposition or perspective of the rest of an audience. In 1980, at the Nineteenth International Shakespeare Conference at Stratford-upon-Avon, the actor Patrick Stewart told the assembled Shakespearians that there were three kinds of audience: 'A normal audience; an audience with Peter Brook in it; and you lot'. I shall be almost entirely concerned, in the rest of this book, with the first of Stewart's categories – whereas most criticism of Shakespeare is, I think, geared to the assumptions of the third. Stewart himself was drawing upon an experience in 1978, when the Royal Shakespeare Company's small Other Place theatre was completely filled by Conference delegates for a performance of John Barton's production of *The Merchant of Venice*. Everyone in the cast agreed that it was the most unresponsive, hostile audience they had ever played to; they were astounded when that audience gave them a prolonged and spontaneous standing ovation. What bewildered the performers was the very intensity of the spectators' concentration: the assembled academics were like a massive vacuum cleaner, sucking up every detail of a sensitive and brilliant production, and yet radiating back no hint of their responses – a galaxy of individual black holes, which absorbed but did not reflect light. Without wishing to give this incident more symbolic significance than it will bear, it does seem to me indicative of the abnormality of the literary critic's responses.

The literary critic could be broadly distinguished from the ordinary playgoer and the ordinary reader by three traits ('caricaturistics'): the abnormal intensity of his attention, his abnormal familiarity with the text, and the abnormal strength of his preconceptions. The intensity of the critic's attention is customarily regarded as a virtue, as it enables him to perceive what others do not – including, perhaps, things he was never meant to perceive. The critic's abnormal familiarity with the text is partly a function of his abnormal attention, and partly the consequence of repeated readings or viewings. But the distinction between one's first experience of a play, and one's second, is arguably more important than that between Renaissance and modern audiences. The undoubted pleasure we derive from a return to that first experience, from the attempt to re-enact it, is nevertheless a pleasure subsequent and subsidiary, one oftener complicated by extraneous motives and more easily influenced by the opinions of others. In any case, if the initial contact did not please, we would never seek a second. Finally, the abnormal strength of the critic's preconceptions is a function of his abnormal familiarity with the text. Unlike the rest of the audience, the critic has often already decided (often rightly, no doubt) what the play means, and comes to the theatre to judge the fidelity of a performance to that ideal. Audiences on the contrary have come to the theatre, readers on the contrary have picked up a book, in order to be pleased; they want to enjoy what is offered; they are receptive. Author and audience share a negative capability; too often the critic does not (though, of course, many good critics do overcome their predispositions and preconceptions).

Like most elites, the literary bureaucracy has elevated its deficiencies into virtues. Being committed to the infinite production of new interpretations from a finite supply of raw materials, it will not admit that audiences do, or should, respond in unison. With a vested interest in maximizing and glorifying the differences between itself and the general public, it has inevitably stressed individual intellectual subtleties rather than a community of shared response. Its members tend to be intellectual elitists; Shakespeare, on the evidence of his plays, was not. The man who wrote 'Small have continual plodders ever won / Save base authority from others' books' can hardly be imagined as an apologist for literary critics. According to the critical ethic, the responses of a professor who has read the play ten times matter more than the responses of ten barristers or physicians who have not – although of course in the theatre the applause of the ten drowns the disgruntlement of the one. (Notice that this is not a difference in education or intelligence, but in profession; the presumed superiority would be even greater if the ten satisfied spectators were charwomen or lorry-drivers, who are *assumed* to be less intelligent.) Critics as a class are also inclined to glorify reading at the expense of performance, thereby discrediting theatrical competition, in the market place of interpretation. Admittedly, most Shakespearians would now admit the need to envisage a play in the theatre – though in practice this usually means reading books about performances, such as Marvin Rosenberg's *The Masks of King Lear*, its encyclopaedic account of ways the play has been performed enabling a critic to claim to know more than the actors themselves about Shakespeare in the theatre – and far more than any lay spectator, who will not realize, when Kent after tripping Oswald pushes him out, that this stage direction derives from Theobald, or, when Lear kneels to curse Goneril, that this business derives from Garrick, acting Tate's adaptation.

Of course, the critical uses of theatrical history needn't be so cynical or self-serving: there are critics who, on the basis of a wealth of personal theatrical experience, have developed a marvelously astute and seemingly instantaneous sensitivity to the details, nuances and subtleties of individual performances. Moreover, these details (which are sure to be missed by most spectators) obviously give such critics great and justifiable pleasure. That pleasure springs from a sensitivity to the quality of particular *moments*, the critic's discrimination having been sharpened and deepened by familiarity – usually personal, rather than merely historical – with the handling of that moment in other productions. This experience gives such theatrically minded critics a measure of the potency of particular moments, and this in turn qualifies them to judge whether a given production or performance realizes that potential, falls short of it, or even, at the best, revises upward the critic's own estimate of it.

But in making such judgements the critic has of course turned himself away from the text to its performance, away from contemplation of the essence toward evaluation of a particular manifestation of that essence. And in doing so he creates for himself displeasure as well as pleasure, for his constant and instinctive juxtaposition of the real with the ideal, the manifestation with the essence, will inevitably result in his being relatively disappointed by one thing or another: a disappointment which could not be felt by those spectators, Elizabethan or modern, who are encountering the play for the first time. To take an example: when I first saw the production of *Henry V* which will be analysed in Chapter 4, I was not familiar with the work of Alan Howard (who played Henry), and was consequently unaware of some of his limitations, of the extent to which many of his parts resemble one another, of the fact that certain elements of his performance relied on recurrent mannerisms. Having since seen that production many times, having seen the same actor in many other roles, I can well understand the complaints about his performance as Henry which have been voiced by some critics. But these complaints nevertheless seem to me largely irrelevant to an analysis of the pleasure which that production gave specta-

tors, for the complaints are essentially assertions that the
production might have been *better*, that it might have given
more pleasure (which may well be true); whereas I am
interested in describing and analysing the pleasure which it
did give. For the critic himself, of course, the sense of frustrated potential will to some degree offset the real pleasure
stimulated by the performance; but the ordinary playgoer –
and certainly the 'innocent' one – has no such sum of disappointment to subtract from the total of his joy, and is therefore
likely to go away more satisfied than the critic. Thus, to give
undue weight to the responses of literary critics, even those of
literary critics especially attuned to the theatre, would
seriously unbalance any description of the responses of the
total audience.

Critics are the most eloquent spectators, and presumably
sincere in describing their own responses. But when I speak of
an audience I exclude the critics in its midst. For the critic, it
seems to me, is often distinguished partly by his very refusal to
become part of an audience, to submit to the collective will.
The ambition of the academic is to elevate himself, by excep-
tional strength of mind, above the anonymity of the mass;
even in a crowd, he insists upon his individuality, upon the
intellectual integrity of his own responses. I will not say those
responses are wrong; indeed, that insistence upon spiritual
independence is in most respects a great virtue. But the
responses of such individuals are abnormal, and therefore (for
my present purposes) irrelevant.

I have so far treated rather cursorily an issue of fundamental
importance: the difference between our first and second
experience of a play. Let me take as an illustration Samuel
Beckett's *Play*, with its famous stage direction '*Repeat play.*'
What happens as we sit through this repetition of what we
have just seen? We notice things we did not notice or understand the first time; but equally, we lose interest in features
that have already been deciphered (particularly the plot).
Generally, we shift our focus from matters of structure to
matters of detail. Moreover, because we already know what is
happening, we focus on *how* it happens: knowing in advance
of the climactic 'wild low laughter' of the second woman, we
follow with particular interest her progress to insanity. We
focus upon causes, rather than events. In Beckett's case, this

preoccupation with causes has a further relevance, for we cannot help asking why the play is being repeated. We question the playwright's motives. Of course, as Shakespeare doesn't force us to return to his plays, we do not question *his* motives. Nevertheless, even in Shakespeare's case the repetition is motivated, but motivated by the reader or spectator, rather than the author. The reader or spectator, however, is unlikely to investigate his own motives, in the way he investigates Beckett's; yet those motives will in fact crucially influence his responses. To borrow a distinction from Piaget: in our first encounter we *accommodate* ourselves to an experience; by subsequent encounters we seek to *assimilate* that experience, to master it, to relate it to our other experiences and ideas (and prejudices), to incorporate it in our own system of concepts about the world.[5] It is not that our first encounter is passive, our second active; rather, we are dealing with two different kinds of activity. In the first, we tend to shape ourselves to fit the object. In the second, we tend to shape the object to fit ourselves.

In the second encounter, our attention to detail enables us to perceive subtleties that initially escaped us – though they may not have escaped the spectator next to us. Repetition also enables us clearly to perceive and relate details which at first did no more than contribute to a general impression. When, in a well-known experiment, a set of twelve numbers (in three rows of four) is flashed briefly on a screen, subjects can only recall an average of 4.3 numbers; but, when, after seeing the entire set, they are asked to recall the numbers in one specific row, they can recall three of the four. This means that they have seen nine of the twelve, for they can recall three of any four: nine numbers are available for recall, but in the time it takes to write down four numbers, the other five are forgotten.[6] This experiment might serve as a model of the relation between the spectator and the play. Into any given moment, Shakespeare compacts (let us say) twelve elements, but so quickly does the moment pass that no spectator, on a first encounter, can perceive more than nine – although *which* nine will vary from spectator to spectator. These nine factors all contribute to the spectator's impression of that moment, but five will be almost immediately forgotten, as another moment crowded with detail demands his attention. As the play proceeds, our memory of the details of individual moments will progressively deteriorate. But by returning to the play we can perceive elements we missed at first, and we can retain more, so that, after many readings or viewings, we could theoretically perceive all twelve elements simultaneously, and retain them for the duration of the play. In fact, this model will have to be modified. We pay closer attention to some moments than others; the dramatist can sometimes strongly discourage us from seeing certain elements; the theoretical goal, of complete perception and recall, is not only impossible but undesirable. These issues will be taken up in later chapters. But for the moment let us accept the model in this simple form, for some such simple form underlies the critic's assertion of the value and validity of repetition.

What happens when we apply this model to Beckett's *Play?* In the first encounter, all spectators will focus, more or less, on matters of structure. The dramatist can therefore largely determine which elements we see, and which we don't. But in subsequent encounters our focus dramatically and progressively shifts to matters of detail, and, as there is such a multiplicity of details (even in Beckett), the spectator must select from among them particular objects of attention. This process of selection will be far more subjective than in our first encounter, because any subsequent encounter is itself a motivated activity guided by increasingly personal goals. It is in these subsequent encounters that the biases and motives of the critic's profession may most seriously distort his perceptions, by guiding his selection of detail. But he will also be liable to another distortion. When we are forced to sit through a repetition of *Play*, we lose interest in features, like the plot, which we have already noticed and deciphered. The more often we return to a play, the less interested we are in such structural elements, until finally they become virtually invisible, through our attention to detail. This again has been demonstrated experimentally: we simply *stop seeing* things which do not interest us and do not alter.[7] We focus instead upon the changes in our own perceptions (the discovery of new subtleties) or upon changes in the object itself (the variants from production to production, as in Rosenberg's book).

Such are the uses, and dangers, of the critic's repeated encounters with the work of art. Of course, Beckett accelerates and accentuates the differences between a first and second viewing, by immediately juxtaposing them; the longer we postpone our return to a play, the smaller such differences may become. But the differences do exist, and most studies of response have been sabotaged by their failure to deal with those differences. We want both the impartiality of innocence and the subtlety of experience in our responses to the work of art. In this book I shall be almost entirely concerned with our initial responses. But in that category I include any subtlety which *could* be perceived in that first encounter.

The analysis of a single moment leads inevitably to an analysis of audience response; the analysis of response as inevitably leads, in turn, to the analysis of perception. But most studies of perception are based upon simple or static visual objects, and, though obviously of great relevance to an art critic such as E. H. Gombrich, such experiments are not obviously or necessarily relevant to the perception of Shakespeare. A recent essay illustrates these dangers. Norman Rabkin argues that *Henry V Q* resembles a famous a64iguous sketch (Figure 1), which at one moment looks like a rabbit, and at another like a duck, but which we always see as a rabbit *or* a duck, it being impossible to perceive both figures simultaneously. Thus, to some Henry is the mirror of all Christian kings; to others, a Machiavellian militarist.[8]

Figure 1   Rabbit/duck (from 'Die Fliegender Blätter')

Now, no analogy with this figure can explain the disparity between readers and spectators, which is a central fact in the critical history of *Henry V*: it is as though spectators consistently saw a rabbit, where readers consistently saw a duck. In the figure, every viewer will eventually see both rabbit and duck; this cannot be claimed of *Henry V*. But most important, the optical illusion requires but a single moment of perception: now you see rabbit, now you see duck. The ambiguity of the figure perpetually requires us to revise our interpretation, then instantly revise it again. *The observer cannot prevent the alternation of rabbit and duck.*[9] But Professor Rabkin demands that we maintain one view for the duration of the play; we are not required, but actually forbidden, to alter our perspective from moment to moment. Instead, we shall be permitted (or required) to take the other view when we return to the play, though we must then maintain it, again, for two or three hours. Professor Rabkin has treated a play as though it were a static object; he has treated three hours as though they were a single moment. Any adequate description of audience perception must take as its starting-point the simple fact that audiences respond to one moment at a time.

What follows is not a study of perceptual psychology, nor a study of the differences between critics and spectators, nor (even) a study of audience response. My subject is the pleasure of moments. As such, by definition, it is deprived of the two sorts of significance to which works of criticism usually aspire. It can make no claims about whole works, let alone about the corpus of a single writer or a whole age; it cannot consist of brilliant and subtle new interpretations, since its purpose is not to offer new insights, but to explain how everyone arrived at the old ones. What follows is, then, only a study of technique, only an exploration of transient but superlative pleasures.

2 *Julius Caesar*: The Noblest Moment of Them All

> *His real power is not shown in the splendour of parti-
> cular passages but by the progress of his fable, and the
> tenour of his dialogue; and he that tries to recommend
> him by select quotations, will succeed like the pedant
> in Hierocles, who, when he offered his house to sale,
> carried a brick in his pocket as a specimen.*
>
> Dr Johnson, 'Preface to Shakespeare'[1]

But a play is felt a brick at a time. Its parts are perceived not
simultaneously but one by one. Even at play's end, though we
have seen every part, only one is before us; the others are
present in memory only, and imperfectly. No one mind, not
even Shakespeare's, can contain *King Lear* in a single act of
perception. Furthermore, though all bricks are more or less
alike, all scenes, all speeches, all lines of poetry are not, but
vary in quality from marble to papier-mâché.

Johnson's house (metamorphosed into 'architectonics')
and Coleridge's tree ('organic unity') between them still
govern the assumptions of most critics; but neither metaphor
is particularly happy, for both are spatial, and the play is
temporal. Coleridge's description seems, to most of us, much
the more attractive, but as an analytical tool it boils down to
little more than a pseudo-scientific formulation of the common notion that one work 'comes alive' while another is
'dead'.[2]

> The form is mechanic when on any given material we
> impress a predetermined form not necessarily arising out of
> the properties of the material, as when to a mass of wet clay
> we give whatever shape we wish it to retain when hardened.

14

The organic form, on the other hand, is innate; it shapes as it develops itself from within, and the fullness of its development is one and the same with the perfection of its outward form. ... Nature, the prime genial artist, inexhaustible in diverse powers, is equally inexhaustible in forms. Each exterior is the physiognomy of the being within, its true image reflected and thrown out from the concave mirror. And even such is the appropriate excellence of her chosen poet, of our own Shakespeare.

On the one hand, 'mechanic', impressed, inappropriate, 'a mass of wet clay'; on the other, 'organic', 'innate', 'fullness', 'Nature', 'genial', and *our own* Shakespeare'. Between the denigration and the panegyric, however, little analysis takes place. Again,

I may take the opportunity of explaining what is meant by mechanic and organic regularity. In the former the copy must appear as if it had come out of the same mould with the original; in the latter there is a law which all the parts obey, conforming themselves to the outward symbols and manifestations of the essential principle. If we look to the growth of trees, for instance, we shall observe that trees of the same kind vary considerably, according to the circumstances of soil, air or position; yet we are able to decide at once whether they are oaks, elms or poplars.

Coleridge here says more about an artist's ideal relation to his predecessors than about the ideal structure of any single work of art: he contrasts servile imitation of a literary tradition with work shaped by the pressures of its own content and, equally, its own social and temporal context, the soil and air and position which affect the growth of individual trees, while never subverting the generic distinctions between them. One may agree with Coleridge that unimaginative plagiarism seldom produces great art, without being any the wiser about what does produce great art.

A play is of course not an organism; it is not literally alive. In the physical world organic unity is simply a complex and sophisticated system of subsystems, which are themselves, even in the most primitive organisms, extraordinarily complex; so that, if we apply this metaphor to works of literature, it tells us only to expect that the individual parts will be complex, and complexly related to each other. Organisms also move, as houses generally do not, and organisms grow, while houses are instead built. But Coleridge's phrase remains primarily an epithet of approval, usually a mere synonym for 'lively' or 'complex', or a vague authority invoked to justify the search for unsuspected and increasingly tangential 'patterns' in a given work; it does not provide a precise model or testable hypothesis about what the relation between the parts of a great play is or should be. Plays are in fact built, like houses; the appearance of growth is an illusion. Even the distinction between 'mechanic' and 'organic' unity tells us next to nothing, for the works of the Greek dramatists and Racine clearly have, despite Coleridge's nationalistic animadversions, an 'organic' coherence, as well as obeying certain mechanical rules, while the plays of Shakespeare also obey mechanical imperatives not properly understood in the early nineteenth century (the 'law of re-entry'; the size of Shakespeare's company; the nature of the theatrical space or spaces available to him).

Coleridge's metaphor legitimizes what Johnson's criticized: recommending Shakespeare by 'select quotations'. But these quotations may be, indeed should be, culled from diverse parts of the work: chosen in order to illustrate the 'essential principle' within, the 'law which all the parts obey', they must be as widely scattered as possible, if we are to demonstrate the all-pervading influence of any 'essential principle' we discern. We can therefore hope to understand a work only by imaginatively treating all its parts as coexistent and equivalent constituents of a thematic pattern, as tiles in a mosaic. In practice, then, Coleridge gives us tiles where Johnson offers bricks; both regard individual lines and speeches as parts of a structure, rather than as moments of a performance.

Neither Johnson nor Coleridge properly recognizes – or, at least, their metaphors fail to convey – that the relationship between elements of a performed play entirely depends on memory, and that memory itself depends in part on initial impact. In one very real sense a performed play is a 'show': it is pure appearance: what is not 'seen' (aurally or visually or intellectually) does not exist. In modern theatrical usage a 'show' is something with little or no working relation between its parts, each of which asks to be appreciated simply in and for itself: *Side by Side by Sondheim* called itself 'more of a show than a play', while *Sweeney Todd* clearly aspired to playhood. A play, so defined, differs from a show only in that the impact of its individual moments vitally depends upon our perception of their relationship with other moments, this perception of relation itself depending on whether we remember or recall an earlier moment or moments (or antici-pate a future one). If we imagine a show as a sequence of discrete illuminations, which appear and disappear without ever coexisting, then a play is a sequence of illuminations which persist, accumulate and overlap; which gradually fade, rather than merely disappear; and – this is fundamental – which fade at different rates, and vary in their initial bright-ness or magnitude. Whether the dramatist succeeds in creating the impression of what we call 'organic unity' thus depends upon his command of immediate perception and continued retention; consequently any description of the organizing principles of a dramatic work depends, finally, upon an understanding of the processes of human perception and memory. Moreover, such a description must concentrate on the individual illuminations themselves, the moments, Johnson's 'bricks' – how they make their impression upon us, and how they bid for relative emphasis, for intellectual and emotional longevity.

This definition might be taken to imply that Seneca and Oscar Wilde are the greatest of dramatists, and a great play simply a collection of priceless gems on a twopenny string. But I am not advocating a mediocre homogeneity of sparkle. In isolation, each of Wilde's witticisms or Seneca's sententiae is striking; put them one after another in any quantity and they quickly become (in my experience) somnolently dull. In isolation 'No cause, no cause' or 'Speak hands for me!' are hardly breathtaking; in place, each has, as we all know, immense power.

What is true of individual lines is true also of individual episodes or scenes, and this chapter will be devoted to an analysis of the impact of one such episode, almost universally admired: *Julius Caesar*, III.i, the so-called 'assassination scene'.[3] In fact, I shall confine myself almost entirely to the first seventy-seven lines, up to and including the moment when Caesar is actually killed. I cannot prove that this is a 'great' scene; but surely no one would deny that it has been a *successful* one.[4] I shall do no more than look at the seventy-seven lines in terms of three basic approaches to the analysis of our responses to a set of moments: first in terms of audience awareness (what we know and do not know in advance); secondly in terms of economy (the most effective use of a small number of stimulants); thirdly in terms of the relation between speech and action, or text and performance. What these three nets catch will obviously remain only a selection of the scene's moments; what they leave out is the subject of the rest of this chapter (in which I dwell on a single moment at some length) and the rest of this book.

The audience knows Caesar will be assassinated; three things it does not know. Popilius Lena is the first. The scene begins with the quick dismissal of the Soothsayer and Artemidorus, two threats to the conspiracy which have been painstakingly prepared, but which are now parried casually in ten lines. Two obvious and anticipated obstacles have thus been removed; the third comes unannounced and ambiguous. We and the conspirators are surprised into doubt, into intense and anxious attention to every movement on stage. We cannot hear what Caesar and Popilius Lena say; we can only watch their gestures and their faces; any minute everything could change. As it happens, nothing happens, and this danger too passes, but not before Shakespeare elicits our total, strained alertness.

We know Caesar will be assassinated; we do not know when. 'Casca, you are the first that rears your hand.' Casca therefore demands our attention. But Casca does not speak until just before he acts, and we do not know when he will act until he does. Shakespeare now escalates the attack on our nerves. After the whispered manoeuvrings of the conspirators comes Caesar's unconsciously ironic 'Are we all ready?'; then Caesar's slow encirclement by his kneeling enemies; Casca's silence; Caesar's long speech on his own constancy, where the irony hits a pitch it cannot long hold; then in rapid succession two more conspirators kneeling, the pace quickening, Caesar's voice rising, all accelerating to Casca's savage explosion. Here Shakespeare alters his source. In Plutarch, 'Metellus at length, taking his gowne with both his handes, pulled it over his necke, which was the signe geven the confederates to sette upon him.'[5] Plutarch thus allows us a moment's warning. Shakespeare gives us none, only sudden violence.

Admittedly, the assassination has not always been performed suddenly or even violently. In Kemble's 1817 production, in Stuart Burge's 1970 film (starring Gielgud as Caesar), in the 1977 National Theatre production (again starring Gielgud), Caesar was murdered slowly, formally, ritually – and on each occasion his assassination drew ridicule or involuntary laughter from the audience.[6] Shakespeare has spent considerable art in escalating the tension and emotional strain to the pitch of 'Speak hands for me!' That tension must be released explosively and at once, or it will be released in anarchic nervous giggling. Had Shakespeare meant to stress the slow formality of the act, he would surely have given it in contrast a prologue hurried and confused. Instead, the action and stage picture immediately before the murder are perhaps the most dignified and formal in the entire play.

We knew Caesar would be assassinated; only now, in the moment after he falls, do we and the conspirators realize that we do not know what will happen next. Caesar is not a long time dying, nor is his corpse immediately given the conventional eulogy, and the deed so long awaited is over almost before it begins. Its violence – Antony later says that their 'vile daggers / Hacked one another in the sides of Caesar' – answers our emotional need by releasing the heightened tension, yet its very rapidity must make it seem something of an anticlimax, and perhaps for that very reason Kemble and Gielgud sought to prolong it. (Indeed, any production committed to Caesar's domination of the play will be loath to allow his death to be anything less than monumental.) But the vacuum of this anticlimax has its purpose. Into it come the Senate's panic and the conspirators' confusion, and only then, after chaos is let loose and Antony again recalled, does the scene rise to exhilaration and ritual. Shakespeare first gives us ceremony, then its interruption (the murder, the confusion afterwards), then its unexpected return.

> Stoop, Romans, stoop,
> And let us bathe our hands in Caesar's blood
> Up to the elbows, and besmear our swords.

Physical violence is not enough. The conspirators are murderers, they must seem murderers, and to make them murderers in our imaginations as in fact Shakespeare paints them with blood, as he will later paint Macbeth (and Lady Macbeth).

This is of course a complex and potent moment in its own right; but in relation to Caesar's murder the important fact about this washing of hands in blood is that, like Antony's eventual eulogy over the body, it does *not* immediately follow the killing. If it did, no one would think the killing an anticlimax, but neither would we think the conspirators bewildered by success or unready for the future. The remainder of this scene, the Forum scene, arguably the remainder of the play, compensate for that initial sense of anticlimax, demonstrate that the physical act, so swiftly and so easily done, is a beginning not an end. And the anticlimax can convey or arouse an inarticulate intellectual unease as well: the conspirators have satisfied their aspirations, but the fulfilled aspiration does not itself satisfy.

The physical act – the one thing which we know in advance *will* happen – obviously organizes our perception of the whole scene. Intellectually, it creates the immediate irony of so many of Caesar's individual statements, thereby not only making these lines themselves more complex but also decisively colouring our view of the character as a whole; it also makes us fleetingly conscious of alternative possibilities (What if Caesar had read the message from Artemidorus? What if Popilius Lena had warned Caesar? What if Antony had stayed behind? What if Caesar had repealed the banishment?), so that the foreknown conclusion is seen as the product of a series of individual but interacting motives, causes, decisions. None of this will determine our emotional response to Caesar himself, or his death; we can regard his ignorance as derisory, or as tragic; we can take the combination of contingencies resulting in his death as evidence that the death was avoidable, or that it was fated. It is, I think, generally true that such ironies, such 'discrepancies of awareness', are in themselves emotionally neutral, though critics often speak as though they offered decisive proof of one interpretation or another.[7] In fact how we respond to the irony itself depends on our predispositions toward the character or the world of the play, predispositions which affect and incorporate that irony, but cannot themselves be determined by it.

In saying that an audience 'knows' Caesar will be assassinated I have perhaps overstated the case, and thereby underestimated the contribution of this particular expectation to the organization of the scene. After the portents and conspiratorial machinations, and in watching a play called *The Tragedy of Julius Caesar*, even the playgoer most innocent of history must strongly expect that Caesar will be assassinated in the course of this scene. Moreover, for an experienced playgoer the accumulation of ironies in the scene itself will create very strong expectations that the scene will culminate in their confirmation. On the other hand, one does not generally expect the death of the title character to occur only halfway through a literary work, and the beginning of the scene, at least, seems deliberately to arouse and flirt with our residual uncertainties about whether this will indeed be Caesar's final hour. The first part of the scene thus depends in part on the tension between what we think we know and a series of things we don't know (how Caesar will respond to the Soothsayer and Artemidorus) or don't expect (Popilius Lena). After this introduction, however, Shakespeare intrudes no more false alarms; he has played the uncertainty for what it was worth, and the scene from then on relies wholly on our confident expectation that Caesar will soon be assassinated.

Creating individual sparks of irony, illuminating undeveloped possibilities, highlighting the moments and movements which counter our strong but not yet certain expectation – in all these ways the anticipation of Caesar's death helps to establish a hierarchy of emphasis in the scene, to direct our perception of which acts and utterances are most important. It is, for instance, partly this expectation which makes the actual death of Caesar the climax of this half of the scene, and this half of the play; even more important, in satisfying that expectation the act itself becomes satisfying, regardless of our ethical or emotional reaction to it. (I may here seem to be contradicting myself, for I have just said that the conspirators' success is anticlimactic and unsatisfying; but I am in fact talking about two theoretically and I think actually distinct moments. The killing itself satisfies, as the emotional and physical and formal climax of the movement; it is only immediately after that one feels vaguely let down.)

The economy with which Shakespeare achieves such effects – exploiting expectation to make some moments seem more important than others – can be seen in the first ten lines.

> *Caesar.* The Ides of March are come.
> *Soothsayer.* Ay, Caesar, but not gone.
> *Artemidorus.* Hail, Caesar! read this schedule.
> *Decius.* Trebonius doth desire you to o'er-read,
>   At your best leisure, this his humble suit.
> *Artemidorus.* O Caesar, read mine first, for mine's a suit
>   That touches Caesar nearer. Read it, great Caesar.
> *Caesar.* What touches us ourself shall be last served.
> *Artemidorus.* Delay not, Caesar, read it instantly.
> *Caesar.* What, is the fellow mad?
> *Publius.*   Sirrah, give place.

The opening couplet is so famous and so disarmingly simple that one is inclined to credit history rather than Shakespeare. Shakespeare however has done three things. Here is the same exchange as given in two of his possible sources, North's *Plutarch* and *The Mirror for Magistrates:*

> Caesar going unto the Senate house, and speaking merily to the Soothsayer, tolde him, The Ides of March be come; So be they, softly aunswered the Soothsayer, but yet are they not past.

> (Quod I) the Ides of Marche bee come, yet harme is none.
> (Quod hee) the Ides of Marche be come, yet th'ar not gone.[8]

Shakespeare first cuts it to the bone; he leaves no superfluous word. Happily, this economy also produces a neat couplet, the Soothsayer mirroring Caesar's metre while contradicting his meaning. Shakespeare also places this exchange at the head of the scene, so that 'The Ides of March are come' emphatically and ominously stand as the first words of Caesar's last scene. In fact, as both the Soothsayer and Artemidorus proclaim their intention to find a good place before the procession arrives, and there 'wait' for Caesar, the scene can, and sometimes very powerfully does, begin with the two of them alone on an otherwise empty stage, silently waiting, in their different ways, for Caesar.

Equally important, the position of the Soothsayer's warning, at the start of the scene, allows the conversation to be effectively broken off. To the Soothsayer's rejoinder history does not record a reply, and yet Shakespeare's Caesar clearly hears it: the preceding scene, and the vocative 'Caesar', make it obvious that the Soothsayer would not speak his warning as an aside (though he usually and properly does speak it, as Plutarch says, softly). History as anecdote, in Plutarch's manner, may offer us such snatches of conversation without worrying overmuch about what was said before or after, but Shakespeare must get us into this dialogue and out of it again as naturally as possible. He gets us into it by starting his scene with Caesar's characteristic decision to speak to the Soothsayer, before he is spoken to; he gets us out again by interrupting before Caesar can answer. 'Hail, Caesar! read this schedule.' The two famous lines are thus, by Shakespeare's handling of 'the tenour of his dialogue', memorably isolated without seeming in any way tacked on. And the simple juxtaposition of Artemidorus and the Soothsayer has its own rewards: the irony of one wellwisher interrupting another, then being himself interrupted by Decius; the sense that the play's pace is being forced forward; the contrast between the Soothsayer recognized and addressed by Caesar, and Artemidorus clamouring for attention; the contrasts of four different voices in four lines.

Shakespeare's preparation of the Soothsayer is his third and greatest improvement on the sources. The second scene of Act I, which introduces him, is itself one of the play's most brilliant. 'Caesar!' That first cry tells us nothing; it only interrupts. For five lines, while everyone on and off stage listens for his voice again, the Soothsayer remains silent. Then 'Beware the Ides of March'. This famous warning is spoken three times within six lines, phrased identically each time. All around Caesar is a cluster of voices, amplifying his orders, feeding him information, and to us they are voices only, unattached as yet to Casca or Cassius or Brutus; they exist only as extensions of Caesar. The Soothsayer and Caesar himself alone have independence. The Soothsayer calls Caesar, instead of waiting to be called, like the others; for five lines and more he ignores Caesar's questions, instead of leaping to answer at the first word from the great man's mouth, like Antony and Calphurnia. Finally, as they will again in Act III, Caesar and the Soothsayer occupy the centre of a crowded stage; they face. 'Beware the Ides of March.' He is warning incarnate. Shakespeare does not permit him the confusions of a personality; he can only cry the name, and speak the message.

The Soothsayer appears again to speak with Portia just before the assassination scene, so that we expect him at the Capitol. On his first appearance, when we did not expect him, his intrusion was startling; at the Capitol, where we do expect him, Shakespeare dispenses with him in two short lines. This too is startling. Into twelve syllables Shakespeare packs his accumulated power and meaning and menace.

Artemidorus is treated, in this scene at least, with similar economy. (The brief scene which introduces him, II.iii, is hardly very impressive in itself, its sole and apparent function being preparation for the assassination scene; even by comparison with similar one-character information scenes, like that of the Scrivener in *Richard III*, III.vi, the writing is flat.) To Caesar and to us Artemidorus must convey urgency. He conveys it by his interruption of the Soothsayer, his interjections and short sentences, his vocative 'Caesar' (five times repeated within four lines). These qualities are of course the more remarkable alongside the leisurely formality of speech in Decius Brutus and Caesar himself. But the man's very urgency, and his appeal to self-interest, Caesar finds distasteful. By line 10 Artemidorus too is dismissed. His presence, however, lingers. His intervention makes it clear that someone has betrayed the details of the conspiracy, and this gives added menace to the ambiguous words of Popilius Lena. The whispering of the conspirators stands out in the wake of his clamouring, as does their fawning and deceit in the wake of his useless bold sincerity. Caesar may even continue to carry, unread, the roll Artemidorus gives (or tries to give) him here, thereby sustaining this particular irony till the actual moment of his death.

Equally economical is the magnification of Brutus, the conspirator in whom we are most interested. Shakespeare establishes his ascendancy in ten words.

> What, Brutus?

> Doth not Brutus bootless kneel?

> *Et tu, Brute?*

All Caesar's, all questions, all incredulous. By such simple means Shakespeare creates the special relationship between Caesar and Brutus, making Brutus the moral focus of the event.

But Caesar is murdered not by Brutus but by them all. In this scene as perhaps nowhere else in the play, ensemble asserts itself.

> *Cassius.* Trebonius knows his time; for look you, Brutus,
>   He draws Mark Antony out of the way.
> *Decius.* Where is Metellus Cimber? Let him go
>   And presently prefer his suit to Caesar.
> *Brutus.* He is addressed. Press near, and second him.
> *Cinna.* Casca, you are the first that rears your hand.

In six lines, every conspirator speaks or is spoken of, creating an immediate impression both of their numbers and of the prearranged coordination of their actions. After Antony's exit, Caesar is surrounded by men we know hate him. Later, immediately after the assassination, we are again made conscious of the conspirators as a group, but there to entirely different effect. There, in rapid succession, we hear all six voices, in broken lines and short speeches picking up another's suggestion or contradicting it, speaking often at cross purposes, improvising. Instead of confirming and enacting a plan known beforehand to all, they follow no plan, six different plans. Immediately after the assassination the

ensemble serves to suggest confusion, fear and the expectation
of revenge, while the calm and forethought of Brutus make
themselves the more felt by contrast. But before the assassination Shakespeare uses the same plurality of actors to suggest a
community of intent.

The community of the conspirators contrasts most forcibly
of course with the isolation of Caesar. Caesar is soon to be
murdered, and murdered as Hector and Coriolanus are, in
ambush by a group. Even were he the monster some critics
and some productions claim him to be, his two long speeches
here, and the final appeal to Brutus, suggest that Shakespeare
means us to be more than mildly interested in him at this
juncture. The two long speeches are singularly cold. But being
long and cold does not make them uneconomical or inept: as
an attack on the hypocrisy of the conspirators, as ironic
commentary, as a defence of the rule of law ('preordinance
and first decree', 'by decree is banished'), they contribute
fundamentally to our intellectual and emotional response.
After many brief speeches by many voices, their mere length
impresses us; it also screws up the tension. From Caesar's
entrance till Cimber begins his suit, events move with dizzy-
ing rapidity: the Soothsayer, Artemidorus, Popilius Lena, the
whispered final arrangements of the conspirators. Now,
though, the action moves with an almost unbearable slow-
ness, at what we surely all feel to be the penultimate moment
of Caesar's life.

Important as the mere bulk of these speeches is, though, it is
their detailed content which sustains our intellectual attention, the individual complexity of moments such as 'I must
prevent thee, Cimber.' Prevent the speech, prevent the plot?
We do not yet even know what Cimber's suit is; Caesar,
apparently so unknowing, here knows more than we do.
When he speaks of 'such rebel blood', he is ostensibly referring to his own, but the phrase could easily be aimed at the
conspirators. When he says he will not let their 'low-crooked'
(or 'low, crooked') curtsies warp his judgement, does he mean
that he sees through their hypocrisy, or only that he will not
grant their suit? As it happens, he means only the latter, so
that in immediate retrospect the ambiguity becomes only an
irony, directed against himself. But the initial frisson surely
exists – as does the fact that Caesar rejects the conspirators'

suit, initially at least, by claiming that to do otherwise would be to let personal prerogative overturn legislative decree. The conspirators are thus ostensibly urging him to do the very thing they assassinate him to prevent. But then Caesar's stubbornness itself is made to seem the exercise of an excessive personal power. How many of these ironies any individual spectator perceives is immaterial; like the twelve numbers on the screen, they are all there, all on the surface, all springing from immediate juxtapositions and expectations visible to everyone.

But, even granting the effectiveness of all this, the speeches do not move us. They do not incite us to sympathy. Caesar's speeches are cold; but then so is the whole scene. It is difficult actively to feel for a group. We sympathize with Brutus certainly, to a greater or lesser degree. But who loves Cinna, or Metellus? If we are distant from both sides, the ostensible subject of their dispute here makes us more so. What do we care for Publius Cimber? We have never heard of him; we shall not hear of him again. Cimber is an excuse for contention, a topic which cannot itself interest us, a topic therefore which cannot distract us from the impending assassination, from the irony of history and the hypocrisy of its participants. Caesar's speeches, even Caesar's death, arouse primarily an intellectual attention – and an intellectual attention deprived of the possibility of resolution, because the crucial information which would allow us to judge the issues, the actual rights and wrongs and details of the banishment of Publius Cimber, have been deliberately withheld. *'Et tu, Brute?'* moves us as it does partly because it is the first personal expression in a consistently impersonal sequence.

The power of that line, itself the most famous moment in the scene, can only be fully appreciated if seen in the context of the larger problem of the relation between text and performance. This scene as read is only marginally less effective than this scene as acted; but this equivalence, which is of course by no means necessary or inherent in dramatic texts, is in itself remarkable, and worth some attention. Shakespeare's reputation has since the Restoration always rested, and continues to rest, largely on the power of his plays as reading-texts. Critics may argue – justifiably, in my opinion – that the plays can only be fully appreciated in and through performance, but the fact remains that many people who have never seen them performed satisfactorily, or at all, have derived immense pleasure from merely reading them. If we imagine individual works of literature as experiments conducted on the reading and playgoing public, then the assassination scene of *Julius Caesar* is an experiment which succeeded with both groups, whereas *Henry V* (say) has had more success with the playgoing than the reading public, and *Troilus and Cressida* or *Antony and Cleopatra* (say) more success with the latter than the former. Criticism, it seems to me, should take some interest in explaining the disparity of these results.

The Popilius Lena episode raises most of the relevant issues. From Plutarch, Shakespeare took only Popilius's brief remark to Cassius. As Plutarch's Popilius speaks to Cassius and Brutus both, Cassius need not tell Brutus what has happened; the panic of the conspirators, and the calm of Brutus, are conveyed in Plutarch by gesture and facial expression alone. The conspirators, reasonably enough, are afraid to speak to one another before the assassination.[9] Gesture and facial expression alone might tell the story as well in the theatre as on the page, but Shakespeare does not rely on them. He gives acts words. He does so partly, I think, for simple clarity. This is what perceptual psychologists call redundancy. Of course, critics might call it redundancy too, but the critic uses the word disparagingly, as the psychologist does not, for the psychologist knows that the rapidity and security of all perception depends on redundancy, on a multiplicity of information directing us to a single conclusion.[10]

Redundancy is particularly necessary in the theatre. In film, the camera directs and focuses our attention for us: the BBC Television Shakespeare (1978) could give us a close-up of Brutus, Cassius and Casca at this crucial moment (see Plate 1). But in the theatre we must each select from a wide visual field what we consider most important, and, though a variety of conventions helps guide this selection, perceptually we remain freer agents. Moreover, in a theatre, particularly one such as the Globe, each spectator has a different perspective on the visual field (the stage), and these perspectives can significantly affect what one sees and what seems prominent. In such circumstances, a dramatist can rarely entrust his narrative to details of facial expression and gesture alone, because he cannot control the visual attention of his audience (at least, not in a scene as crowded as this). But, though he cannot ensure that every spectator will see the same things, he can presume they will hear the same things; he overcomes their visual individuality through their aural community. The Popilius Lena episode depends on confusion of purpose, and such scenes are apt to confuse the audience more than the characters, unless the situation is made unmistakably clear. Shakespeare makes it so. But a film could do so through gesture alone, and so might a modern theatre, by means of lighting, and even the Globe might have managed, if Shakespeare had insisted. But Shakespeare through language achieves more than narrative clarity. In Plutarch, Caesar and Popilius speak; the conspirators are silent. In the theatre as in life, one naturally turns to watch the person speaking. By having the conspirators speak, by preventing us (and them) from hearing what Caesar and Popilius say, Shakespeare ensures that we see the episode from the conspiratorial viewpoint; that is, Shakespeare determines our perspective. He also by such means markedly contrasts their whispering with the clamour of Artemidorus. He also accelerates rather than slows the scene, giving us a hurried interchange of speeches in place of a pause (which would be necessary to ensure that we noticed the stage business, if for no other reason). He also reinforces the ascendancy of Brutus and Cassius, for, though presumably all the conspirators react, only they speak, and they decide. He also furthers the characterization of Cassius, for, though Cassius might speechlessly put his hand on his dagger, and though Brutus might speechlessly restrain him, it would be difficult speechlessly to convey Cassius's intent, when he reaches for that dagger, to use it on himself, not Caesar. In short, by adding language where action alone would suffice, Shakespeare simultaneously makes for better theatre and a more satisfactory reading text.

The episode with Popilius, and particularly the dialogue surrounding it, also facilitates the transition from outside to inside the Capitol, a transition obviously required by the progress of the scene, though its actual execution has much exercised the ingenuity of editors and producers. Several things are happening between line 12 ('Come to the Capitol') and line 31 (when Caesar as it were convenes the Senate). Artemidorus and/or the Soothsayer probably leave the stage; though they might conceivably remain, it was their presence which established the 'street' locale in the first place, and by leaving they would help take that locale with them – as in other Elizabethan scenes where the character 'leaving' remains onstage, while those 'staying' vacate it. While they are leaving, Popilius Lena draws Cassius apart, then joins Caesar. This means that Cassius and Popilius must stop to speak while Caesar is presumably still moving away; then, when Popilius goes to join the now stationary Caesar, Brutus moves to question Cassius, and then speaks aside to Casca ('Casca, be sudden, for we fear prevention'). This means that three of the conspirators must now have formed a distinct group downstage, where they can be overheard by the audience, while Caesar and Popilius (and most of the rest of the others, presumably) are upstage, where we can see but not hear them. This gives us three distinct but related movements, at the moment of transition to the Capitol: Artemidorus and the Soothsayer off, Cassius (first with Popilius, then with Brutus and Casca) downstage, Caesar and the rest upstage. At the same time, two other 'entries' are probably occurring upstage. Though the Folio text does not call for the entry of Senators, here or at the beginning of the scene, they are clearly addressed immediately after the assassination ('People and Senators, be not afraid'); as, according to the Folio directions, only one Senator is present who does not participate in the

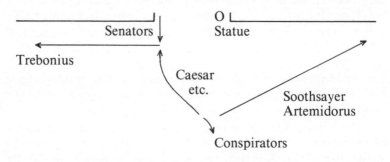

Figure 2   *Julius Caesar*, III.i. 12–26

assassination, editors have reasonably inferred that more are needed, and that the natural place to introduce them is here, during this transition to the Senate locale – especially as we have been told earlier that the Senate waits for Caesar. Consequently, while Caesar and his train are moving upstage, at least a couple of mute Senators are probably entering from upstage, to welcome him. These four sets of movements collectively create the impression of a change of locale; Popilius, and the dialogue about Popilius, is crucial, not only in initiating the downstage movement which complements Caesar's upstage move, but also in distracting our primary attention away from the change of place, onto the ambiguous threat to the conspiracy. The combination of movements also makes it all the more necessary that the conspirators' reactions be verbally expressed, rather than merely shown: with so much other movement on the stage, the risk of any audience overlooking a merely visual moment of panic obviously increases. When combined with and clarified by the words, however, the variety of movement on stage at this crucial juncture itself increases the sense of uncertainty and confusion.

All this may seem like an exercise in imaginative (or fanciful) blocking, but all the key movements seem to me clearly implied by the text, though editors usually give readers very little help in reconstructing them. When Trebonius leads Antony away, the downstage group of conspirators move upstage to position themselves in front of Caesar, and Caesar turns front to address the whole stage and audience. Only at this final point are we clearly in the Senate, the sleight-of-place having been achieved with masterly economy, happening without our being at any one moment ever actively conscious of it, while our attention is distracted by a series of individual dramatic movements. Editors, or directors eager for an impressive setting for the Capitol scene, make this scene-change awkward, by transforming a gradual and multi-faceted transition into a distinct and immediate act, an isolable 'moment' that was never intended to be there.

I have said that two 'entries' contribute to this transition, and I meant by this not the two or more Senators but the Senators and the statue of Pompey. After Caesar is killed we are told that he 'on Pompey's basis lies along'; later Antony confirms that he was killed in front of Pompey's statue. Some sort of statue, or at least a pedestal, thus seems necessary, later in the scene. It must therefore 'enter' at some point, and though this would be easiest if it could be 'discovered' – which could probably be done in the Globe – in fact the same effect could be achieved simply by having the Senators open the large central doors as they come on, leaving them open for the duration of the scene, with the statue visible just inside. (This would mean, incidentally, that Caesar should be killed upstage, whereas the modern theatrical instinct is to get him downstage; and this literal difference in distance makes some difference to our metaphorical and emotional distance from the act.) The statue's discovery would thereby be partly covered by the entry of the Senators and by the group of characters moving upstage with Caesar; the property would become part of the scene as unobtrusively as the locale itself changes.

But the statue's unobtrusiveness depends upon our not knowing the play in advance, since anyone who has seen the play before, or read it, will immediately recognize that this is the statue of Pompey, and that Caesar must be killed in front of it. Shakespeare conspicuously does not tell us this in advance, for the very reason that to do so makes us awkwardly conscious of the blocking of the assassination itself. In modern productions those familiar with the play are, almost inevitably, painfully aware of the efforts of director and cast to make sure that Caesar winds up dead on the right spot. When it first appears, to an innocent audience the statue is simply a prop which helps identify and dignify the setting; only after the assassination do we realize that it is very particularly the statue of Caesar's old enemy.

In the Popilius Lena episode, and the change of locale associated with it, the use of language where mere action would apparently suffice proves on closer examination to be essential to the successful communication of the action. In the assassination itself, on the other hand, Shakespeare surrenders to stage business. He even cuts two speeches found in Plutarch. He does not clutter the act with arias of poetry, as many verse dramatists would. Nevertheless, the murder begins and ends with words. But though 'Speak hands for me!' and 'Et tu, Brute?' are both justifiably famous, both could be

cut, as the information they convey the action conveys well
enough, without any of the confusions which made speech
necessary to the Popilius episode.

Shakespeare could simply have written '*They stab Caesar;
Casca first, Brutus last.*'[11] At least in Casca's case, this might
be thought preferable. For, though no director would dare cut
Casca's line, more often than not it plays awkwardly, creating
a pause when the tension demands there be none, and thereby
wrongfooting the climax, so that in its frustration the audience
releases the energies of its tension in hostile impatience with
the actor – which will be exacerbated further if, in the effort to
ensure that Casca strikes Caesar from behind,[12] the director
perpetrates the absurdity of not permitting Caesar to turn to
Casca, of not permitting the soldier Caesar to turn and face, at
least momentarily, the man addressing him in that unmistakably hostile tone, of not permitting Caesar to turn to Casca
though he has turned to each of the others as they spoke. The
fault here is not Shakespeare's but the actor's. When he says,
'Speak hands for me!', Casca should (I think) kneel with the
rest, his clasped hands raised in supplication; from those
clasped hands comes the flash of a blade, and Casca leaps at
Caesar. However the moment is staged, the ambiguity of
Casca's line must be preserved, for only the ambiguity allows
the climax. It gets Casca into position for the kill. His words
are themselves the final escalation of the tension, the climax
coming immediately afterward, in the flash of the blade,
which in retrospect defines Casca's meaning.

But, even if we grant that Casca's line contains an ambiguity and an idea (violence as self-expression) which a stage
direction would probably sacrifice, I doubt whether the same
claim could be made for Caesar's: the sense of personal
betrayal and subsequent surrender could easily be communicated without words. Why then did Shakespeare write those
words, when stage directions could have communicated his
intention, and communicated it more naturally, in the context
of such an assassination? Or rather – since I am less interested
in Shakespeare's motives than in the consequences of his
decision – does the use of dialogue, instead of gesture, contribute to the pleasure readers and/or spectators take in this
moment? I think it does, and for two reasons, both connected
with the preservation of pleasure.

It is far easier to identify objects and phenomena, or to re-
create them in memory, if we have names for them.[13] 'Speak
hands for me!' and '*Et tu, Brute?*', by giving us 'names' for a
complex theatrical experience, enable us to recall that experience (and the pleasure associated with it) at will. Moreover, the remnant of the original pleasure which we are thus
able to recall encourages us to repeat the original and full
experience: to see the play again, to read the book. Casca's
and Caesar's lines can serve as such 'names' partly because of
their brevity, partly because of the intensity of the actors'
emotions as they speak them, partly because of their innate
aesthetic excellence (the product of a variety of rhetorical
properties). But to a degree the mind will actively *seek* names
for an experience, and, the more powerful the mental energies
aroused, the more insistent that search will be. Hence the
difficulty of explaining in purely aesthetic terms the power of
so many of Shakespeare's most famous lines. Frequently, the
lines themselves seem simple or commonplace, but serve as
receptacles for retention of the energies created by the whole
scene. Casca's and Caesar's lines here are probably examples;
so are Cordelia's lines in the reunion with Lear ('And so I am,
I am'; 'No cause, no cause'). Although a wordless assassination or a wordless reunion might well be as exciting or as
moving in the theatre, they would not, even in the theatre,
provide us with such means for retaining (during the play, and
beyond it) that excitement or that emotion, nor with such
incentives to seek it again. Moreover, even in the theatre, the
words serve the function of locating the emotion, providing it
with a specific cue, so that the audience responds in unison.

In the case of '*Et tu, Brute?*' this naming function is particularly obvious. The phrase did not originate with Shakespeare:
it appears in its Latin form at least four years before, is translated into English in *The Mirror for Magistrates* (1587), and
may have been first used dramatically as early as 1582.[14] As
Francis Gentleman objected, why should Caesar, who speaks
English in the remainder of the play, suddenly revert to Latin
here?[15] One can hardly claim that 'You too, Brutus?' would be
any less *affecting*, as a personal statement; it would certainly
be more natural. But for its first audience the line already
worked, as it does today, as a recognized sign, an allusion,
'what Caesar actually said when he was actually killed', its

very unnaturalness in an English-speaking context increasing
its distinction and validity as a sign. How much the allusion
also depended, even for that first audience, on the memory of
other theatrical renderings, we cannot know; but certainly, for
modern audiences, it has become not only 'a quotation', by its
familiarity distancing us from the event even while confirming
its historical authenticity, but also, in the psychologist's sense,
a 'name' for the whole complex moment, a paradigm of
betrayal.

The reading-text of a play represents the effort of an author or
a culture to preserve, as best it can, the full pleasure of the
original performances, to make that pleasure available in part
to those who have not seen the play performed at all, and
thereby to provide a perpetual incentive for further performances, to satisfy the unfulfilled desire created by the written
text. But often, when I read a play, the more stage directions
the less pleasure; the closer the description of performance,
the farther the experience of reading is removed from the
experience of performance. Plays seem the most anonymous
of poems; they seem to act themselves – until the playwright
intrudes. Every stage direction can interrupt the illusion,
reveal the playwright behind the character, recall the gap
between page and performance. (This is why Dover Wilson's
stage directions are often so irritating.) The gap between page
and performance of course exists, but the cost of overcoming
it often turns good scripts into bad narratives. If directions are
few and simple – entrances, exits – the reader may digest the
information they supply quickly and without thought. '*They
stab Caesar*': colourless, anonymous, formulaic. Anyone
could have written it; it hardly seems written at all.

Three modern examples may help clarify the principle at
issue. The detailed description of a set, at the beginning of an
Ibsen text, is discomfiting because it wildly misrepresents our
experience of the play. When the curtain rises, we immediately perceive a certain kind of room, and from this room we
vaguely infer social or personal traits. But the director does
not spotlight each piece of furniture in turn; he does not ask us
to consider them individually or in any specific order, but

only to scan them cursorily, enough to derive from them a general impression. Later, certain details of the set may be pointed out by the characters, or we may notice them as our eyes wander in one of our inevitable moments of inattention, and when we do notice them we may then appreciate their significance or fitness. Ibsen's text falsifies the actual pleasure of his plays by giving these details in a single authorial lump, before we have any but the vaguest interest in them: a single oppressive lump of seemingly undigested naturalism.

But Beckett also begins plays with descriptions of the set, and his texts often contain proportionally more stage directions than Ibsen's, yet they read as well as they play; indeed, one may feel there is little point in playing them at all, so precisely does the text define and control the pleasures of performance. But in Beckett's plays we are not confronted by a room, or a recognizable place with evident social implications, but instead with a structured and select set of objects, which require our individual attention. Beckett's text describes these objects – and his characters too are objects – in precise, terse and repetitive terms: that is, Beckett creates his own formulaic language. The stage directions are as exactingly written as the dialogue. Moreover, these formulaic descriptions are overwhelmingly paratactic, reproducing for the reader a succession of moments in the theatre, wholly controlling the disposition of time, even to the marking of pauses, so that only rarely are dialogue and stage direction simultaneous, being instead departmentalized in the theatre as on the page; therefore the distinction on the page between italic and roman type reproduces a theatrical schizophrenia of speech and act. If the stage directions intrude a reminder of the author's control, that too serves Beckett's purpose, to suggest the mechanization and determinism of his world. Beckett's text thus conveys, far more accurately than Ibsen's, the experience and pleasure of performance.

Shakespeare's stage directions do not positively misrepresent the theatrical experience (like Ibsen's), nor do they reproduce or fix it in minute detail (like Beckett's). Instead, by their very paucity and abbreviation, they incite the reader to imaginative collaboration.

She clasps hands to breast, closes eyes.
Lips move in inaudible prayer, say ten seconds.

They stab Caesar.

Beckett tells us exactly what happens; he warns us against embellishment. Shakespeare, by the very inadequacy of his approximation, demands our participation – and does so not only occasionally with stage directions, but perpetually, as the dialogue infers simultaneous or antecedent acts which are not otherwise specified (as in the transition from street to Senate). This imaginative collaboration only increases the desire of readers to see the plays performed, and of actors and directors to perform them, whereas with Beckett one can feel excluded from the work, that nothing remains to be done. (Beckett's later plays are like masques, designed for performance, but for *one* performance, specific and perfect.) Shakespeare's stage directions do, at chosen moments, remind us of the gap between page and performance. They ask us to fill it – as Edwin Booth did in having Cassius pull Caesar from the throne, stab him and then throw him over to Brutus; as Macready did in having Cassius stab Caesar repeatedly; as Phelps's Brutus did in his 'burst of exultation' after the death of Caesar; as Joseph Papp did in creating 'a devastating hush as Caesar spun silently from one conspirator to another, the only sound his grunts as they stabbed him'; as Trevor Nunn did in dressing the conspirators in white gowns which, when spattered with blood, looked like butchers' aprons (or surgeons' gowns).[16] As often elsewhere, Shakespeare's text here asks for the energies of a reader's imagination at the very moment when, in the theatre, the energies of a prolonged tension are suddenly released, physically; so that the reader may spend the energies of that tension in the exercise of imagination, at the very moment when the actors absorb into themselves the energies of an entire audience, for the expression of a violent and relieving act.

Against both Beckett and Shakespeare can be set a stage direction typical of another modern dramatist, Eugene Ionesco: '*He either kisses or does not kiss Mrs Smith.*' This, from *The Bald Soprano*, like many of Shakespeare's texts creates a performance option, an ambiguity, but Ionesco does so in a different manner and for a different purpose. Ionesco's direction increases rather than diminishes the discrepancy between the reader's and the spectator's experience, for the reader is aware of the option, while the spectator sees only one version or the other. For Shakespeare, even the reader or spectator who is aware that a moment might be played more than one way usually assumes that Shakespeare *intended* one treatment or the other, and even for those who make no such assumption, who recognize the impossibility of legislating the 'proper' choice, the impression created by Shakespeare's ambiguity is of freedom, not caprice; of living potency, rather than mechanical absurdity. Ionesco, by framing his direction in this way, asserts that whether Mr Martin does or does not kiss Mrs Smith makes no difference, and that human actions are completely unpredictable. Shakespeare, on the other hand, *asserts* nothing; it is partly for this reason that his characters seem independent creatures, rather than puppets. (Ionesco of course wants them to seem puppets.) Rather than announce that human conduct is unpredictable, Shakespeare forces *us* to predict it; he leaves gaps, which we fill in, often so unconsciously that we never realize a choice has been made, or fail for years to see that any alternative exists. If, on the other hand, we are conscious of making a choice, we become conscious too of the characters' doing so; we are forced to act, just as they are. And which of the options we choose, consciously or not, *does* make a difference. Of course, the choice makes some little difference, even in Ionesco, however the author may try to deny it: if Mr Martin does kiss her, the audience responds to an action, but if he does not, they do not respond to the absence of an action which they had no reason to expect (unless he *starts* to kiss her, and then stops himself). But Ionesco's either–or does not stimulate us to re-evaluations of the whole character, in a way that Shakespeare (as I shall try to show in the next chapter) often does; for Ionesco's characters have no character to re-evaluate.

Shakespeare's plays of course vary in the kind and number of stage directions they contain, these variations arising largely from the different uses to which different manuscripts were put, and the contrast between Renaissance and modern texts in this respect is obviously in part a function of changed theatrical circumstances. But the preceding generalizations

nevertheless seem to me valid as descriptions of the differences in the reading-experience created by the usual treatment
of directions in these four authors. Whether Shakespeare ever
intended such effects, the form in which his text was trans-
mitted has produced them, and will continue to do so. I am
concerned, again, with consequences, not intentions.

I have called the text of a play an attempt to preserve the
pleasures of performance. But it is also, clearly, an attempt to
preserve the author's intentions. Through the text, we feel we
make direct contact with the author, having dispensed with
the distorting subjectivity and imperfection of his theatrical
interpreters and intermediaries. But the objectivity of the text
is illusory;[17] print is itself a medium, with its own limitations
and conventions. Language, being by nature sequential,
cannot properly express simultaneity, a fact which creates
grave perplexities for editors. When the text says, *Enter A, B,
C and D,* does it mean that they should enter in that order, or
together? All the features of Ibsen's set are simultaneously
present when the curtain rises, but he must in the text list
them one by one. When, in the second scene of *Julius Caesar*,
the text tells us that Brutus and Cassius and a Soothsayer enter
with Caesar, the text misrepresents the play, for, though
Brutus and Cassius indeed enter, in the theatre we do not
know and are not meant to know who they are; nor are we
meant to anticipate the Soothsayer's presence in the crowd;
nor, when a voice cries 'Caesar!', are we meant to know whose
voice. The text is not only sequential but also analytic; performance is by contrast capable of both simultaneity and
synthesis. We trust the text as a final repository of the author's
intentions only because its distortions are systematic; they can
be anticipated, defined and thereby neutralized. The distortions of any one performance are instead haphazard and
unpredictable, caused not by the limitations of the medium
but by the intervention of individuals with intentions of their
own, which can contradict or obscure those of the author. The
play *Julius Caesar* thus exists, in its perfect state, only in the
human mind, for we must reconstruct it from elements necessarily imperfect.

There is, as it happens, a famous and important textual crux in this scene, one which is immediately pertinent to many of the issues raised by a criticism based upon individual moments, upon audience or reader response. In the Folio text at III.i.47 Caesar says, 'Know, Caesar doth not wrong, nor without cause / Will he be satisfied'; but, according to the testimony of Ben Jonson, on two occasions, as originally written and performed the lines read, 'Caesar did never wrong, but with just cause, / Nor without cause will he be satisfied'.[18]

Before proceeding to literary we must first make a (brief) foray into textual criticism. From an editorial point of view, the question is simply whom (or what) to believe: Ben Jonson or the First Folio? This situation would be familiar enough to classical scholars, who often emend their literary manuscripts on the authority of early quotations from the work in question – if the source of the quotation seems to have had access to a more authoritative text than the one which has survived. On the first occasion, as is well known, Jonson was citing this particular line as a striking example of a more general fault (Shakespeare's never having blotted a line, when he should have blotted a thousand).[19]

> His wit was in his own power; would the rule of it had been so too. Many times he fell into those things could not escape laughter: as when he said in the person of Caesar, one speaking to him: 'Caesar thou dost me wrong' – he replied: 'Caesar did never wrong, but with just cause', and such like, which were ridiculous.

As Dover Wilson pointed out, Jonson gave a specific context for the line, so that his account of it could be verified. Any neoclassicist critic could (and Jonson's successors did) find plenty of examples of equally absurd lines in Shakespeare, without having to invent one; if such a critic did feel a need to invent something particularly atrocious, he need hardly have been so superfluously specific about the whereabouts of the nonexistent blemish. Jonson's second allusion is even more difficult to dismiss, depending as it does not upon an assertion that Shakespeare wrote this ludicrous line, but upon a mere allusion to it, in *A Staple of News* (1626).

EXPECTATION. I can do that too, if I have cause.
PROLOGUE. Cry you mercy, *you never did wrong, but with just cause.* (Induction, 34–5; Jonson's emphasis)

This allusion cannot prove that Shakespeare wrote the line in question; but, unless someone wrote it, and unless it had been publicly performed, Jonson could hardly expect anyone to get the joke. Given that Jonson's earlier statement specifically attributes the line to Shakespeare, this second reference argues very strongly that *Julius Caesar* must at some stage have been performed with the line in question substantially as Jonson reports it.[20]

It thus seems to me that Jonson's testimony cannot, in this case, be credibly dismissed.[21] The Folio text, on the other hand, could be the victim of editorial tinkering (or even simple compositorial or scribal error). It remains possible that Shakespeare himself revised the line, under Jonson's influence; but it is also possible that Shakespeare *added* the four words, as an inspired afterthought.[22] The line as reported by Jonson certainly represents Shakespeare's intention *at some stage*, and may represent his only or final intention.

Jonson's critique of the line records an individual response to a particular moment; as such, it is one of our few surviving eyewitness reactions to the minutiae of Shakespeare's text. Equally important, it illustrates an obvious potential danger in any criticism based upon responses to particular moments – the danger of taking the moment out of context. Jonson points to the line in isolation and asserts, 'this statement is ridiculous'. Jonson's response to the statement is in fact a genuine and valid one; his mistake lies in assuming that his own response cannot, or should not, have been intended by the author: and this mistake arises, in part, from a failure to relate this moment to others. The line must have been meant to be paradoxical. The paradox depends in part on the ambiguity of *doth wrong*, which can mean either 'perform an act which is morally wrong' or 'do someone an injury': a politician can, indeed often will, wrong a particular individual (as Caesar does Publius, as Brutus does Caesar) while asserting and believing that he has good cause ('the sanity and health of the whole state', as Laertes puts it) for doing so. I need hardly add that this is the ethical crux of the whole play. And, as I have already said, this is the very moment in the scene when our attention is most focused upon the intellectual content of the dialogue, upon nuances of irony and unexpected meaning.

But I suspect that Jonson's real difficulty was less the line itself than the fact that Caesar spoke it, and that Caesar should not say something ludicrous in the final moments before his assassination, in a work which pretends to be his tragedy. Jonson clearly found the line not simply illogical but actually risible: he cites it as evidence that Shakespeare did not always govern his 'wit', therefore falling into things which 'could not escape laughter' and were 'ridiculous'. The potential or actual risibility cannot, I think, be denied; but at least two things can be said in its defence, more particularly in defence of putting the line in Caesar's mouth. First, the word 'Caesar' is itself crucial to the statement's resonance, standing as it did as an accepted and hallowed personification of the temporal and political order: 'Give unto Caesar what is Caesar's. . . .' But second, and much more important, the line encapsulates in its extremest form our continuing central difficulty with the character of Caesar throughout the play: that he is both magnificent and pompous, regal and risible. Throughout the play's stage history, the problem has usually been solved by portraying him either as a ranting buffoon (for most of the eighteenth century, apparently) or as a figure of superhuman classical grandeur, good or evil. The text itself, it seems to me, calls for something considerably more difficult: both. The problem for the actor here resembles that facing Beatrice and Benedick, who are nowadays often judged on whether they succeed in controlling an audience's inclination to laugh at the line 'Kill Claudio': an actor of Caesar could be judged on whether he can incorporate 'Caesar doth not wrong, but with just cause' into his performance, without either sacrificing its absurdity *or* provoking derisory laughter. The author has, at this critical moment, left it to the actor to manipulate successfully the audience's response.

The particular problem here, of combining dignity with comic frailty or absurdity, is of course a fairly familiar one, at least in Shakespeare – Polonius being the obvious parallel. The link between Polonius and Caesar is also, as is well known, one of the few for which we have good contemporary authority: for Polonius tells Hamlet (played by Burbage) that in his own youth he played Caesar, and was killed by Brutus (also played, almost certainly, by Burbage); soon after, Hamlet kills Polonius. *Hamlet* is the most openly topical of Shakespeare's plays in its admission of contemporary theatrical allusions; *Hamlet* and *Julius Caesar* were not only close to one another in date of composition, written by the same man and performed by the same company; they could also, in the Elizabethan repertoire system, have often been performed in the same week, or even on alternate days. In these circumstances it is very difficult to dismiss the implication that the same actor created the roles of both Julius Caesar and Polonius.

Others have noted this, but usually in connection with the passing frisson it lends the exchange in the latter play;[23] it seems more important to me as evidence that Shakespeare's company (and so presumably Shakespeare) recognized the similarity in the technical demands made by both roles, and solved the problem by entrusting both to the same actor. This chain of inference need not involve the assumption that each of Shakespeare's fellow actors was capable of only one kind of role. It merely recognizes that all actors, even the greatest, do some things better than others, and that casting decisions are largely based upon past performance, so that the serio-comic juggling-act which is Polonius (which has defeated most actors) might naturally have been entrusted to an actor who had recently proven himself in the related juggling-act which is Caesar.[24] This in turn suggests that the difficulties which post-Restoration actors and critics have felt in their own responses to Caesar were also felt and/or anticipated by both the author and the actor who first played the role. And this difficulty with the whole role is exactly Jonson's difficulty with the single line 'Caesar doth not wrong, but with just cause'. More particularly, that line carries the larger problem into the assassination scene – the scene in the Roman Senate, where we know that a pivotal historical act is about to occur, where our expectations of grandeur and tragic dignity are at their highest.

What an observer sees and how he responds to it are obviously related to what he expects. The technical problem created by this line, and Caesar in general, seem to me the dramatist's own response to the problem created by his audience's expectations – here, expectations of unalleviated tragic grandeur, historical magnitude, classical dignity. The conflicting views of Caesar in classical and Renaissance political thought, which have been explored and exploited by modern scholars, also must have influenced audience expectation; but these expectations increased the dramatist's freedom, allowing him to adopt, allude to, or combine whichever of the pre-existing (and hence recognizable) interpretations of the historical Caesar appealed to him. In contrast, the shared expectation of Caesar's importance and greatness instead restrict the dramatist's options, or at the least seriously complicate his task. How is a dramatic fiction to live up to an audience's idea of a man as legendary as Julius Caesar? There are, broadly, only two alternatives: either to create a suitably sublime style and a sequence of impressive dramatic acts, or to resist expectations by deflating the characters to normal human size (or less). Shakespeare faced this problem most acutely in *Julius Caesar, Troilus and Cressida* and *Antony and Cleopatra*; in portraying the Homeric heroes he resorted to wholesale deflation, but in the two Roman plays he relied upon a combination of deflation and sublimity. The unique style of all three plays, which has been often remarked upon, can be seen as a direct reaction to the problem of excessive audience expectation.

I think everyone would agree that Shakespeare managed the combination of grandeur and frailty, magnificence and risibility, much more successfully in *Antony and Cleopatra*; but what matters for the moment is that this diffuse but real expectation of grandeur shapes our responses to *Julius Caesar*, and this scene in particular, as clearly as our knowledge that Caesar will be assassinated, that Artemidorus and the Soothsayer will try to warn him, that Casca will strike the first blow. For in this scene alone does Caesar satisfy our Caesarian expectations. On his first appearance, in I.ii, he says very little, his heroic stature being conveyed largely by reflection, in the attitudes of others toward him; after his exit (having, as we know or strongly suspect, misjudged the Soothsayer), we hear Cassius's unflattering description of his infirmities; he then returns again, briefly, with an accurate character sketch of Cassius himself, but also with a pointed allusion to his own partial deafness, and the defensive pomposity of 'I rather tell thee what is to be feared / Than what I fear; for always I am Caesar.' After he goes we hear Casca's mocking description of his offstage conduct, culminating in an epileptic fit. In II.ii we see him not as a statesman but as a henpecked husband; he wavers, is at his most pompous, gives in, then changes his mind – and changes it under the influence of what we know to be cynical flattery. We see him gulled by his own arrogance. As yet, then, we have seen little or nothing of the scale of figure we expect (though modern actors and directors usually do their best to supply this deficiency, by inflating these earlier scenes as best they can). Only here, just before his assassination, does Caesar appear primarily as a statesman, using a grand but not markedly inflated or inappropriate style, speaking at length and with poetic authority on specifically political issues (rather than passing out instructions for a footrace, or explaining his preference for fat companions). This is his noblest moment.

I recognize that the tone of Caesar's speeches in this scene, and how we should respond to them, remain matters of critical controversy, and that the roots of that controversy extend far beyond this scene; consequently I cannot, here, rely on any real consensus of response. The greater length of Caesar's speeches here, their political content, their occasion, are matters of fact, as it were; we can say with some confidence that in these respects at least Caesar is here most Caesarian. And these matters of fact clearly impinge directly on our reactions to Caesar's rhetoric: what seems appropriate in the Roman Senate seems less so in a bedroom, spoken to his wife by a man in his dressing-gown. But tone is subject to interpretation, and raises larger questions about the nature of dramatic character, about style (particularly a high or oratorical style), about memory. For instance, when Caesar says 'I am constant as the Northern star', does an audience (or any significant minority of an audience) remember the vacillation of II.ii, and judge Caesar's statement accordingly? If it does not, why not? Partly because the sentiment satisfies our inchoate expectation of a larger-than-life Caesar; partly because we are 'distracted' by the more immediate and glaring irony, that this assertion of superhuman constancy is spoken by a mortal whom we expect to die at any moment. But these *ad hoc* excuses fall well short of a full or fully convincing explanation: the selective amnesia which affects an audience's interpretation of any given moment is central to an understanding of dramatic unity and structure, and of the differences between audiences and readers. 'I am constant as the Northern star' seems to me a kind of rhetoric which works in the theatre more easily than on the page, and which I shall discuss at some length in the chapter on *Henry V;* but for the moment I can do no more than assert this.

My purpose in raising these questions now, without answering them, is to suggest that no account of our responses to individual moments can begin to be satisfactory unless it faces these larger problems – and faces them in a specific context (unlike this one) where some widespread agreement exists about the impact of the character, or the differences between audience and reader responses to the given character or speech or scene or play.

If we can agree that the assassination scene is, in Shakespeare's play, Caesar's noblest moment, we can then see why Jonson objected so vehemently to the absurdity of 'Caesar doth not wrong, but with just cause' – and why subsequent editors and critics, while vilifying Jonson for attributing the line to Shakespeare, have usually implicitly or explicitly accepted Jonson's criticism of it. Shakespeare has finally, in this scene, given us something like the Caesar we expect; this is satisfying in itself, and even more satisfying (for reasons I shall try to define more clearly in the next chapter) in what we know to be the character's final appearance. The line in question comes dangerously close to upsetting this happy consummation, by again reducing the historical superman to pompous absurdity.

Jonson's singling out of this line has at least one other critical implication: the fact that Jonson was struck by it, and remembered it, testifies that the line was found both striking and memorable by at least one contemporary spectator or reader. One could easily make a list of other lines in this scene which fulfil these two conditions. Besides this one I think most people would agree on these others.

The Ides of March are come. – Ay, Caesar, but not gone.

What touches us ourself will be last served.

And turn pre-eminence and first decree
Into the law of children.

For I am constant as the Northern star.

Let me a little show it, even in this.

Speak hands for me!

Et tu, Brute?

Most of these I have already discussed. The second acquires most of its power from the fact that it explains Caesar's death (which we know is coming) by explaining his rejection of Artemidorus's warning (which we also knew was coming), and does so through a selflessness of motive which directly contradicts the assumptions of those gathered to assassinate him. The next three all come, as does the line that struck Jonson, in the middle portion of this movement, where the action slows to a virtual stop, the tension steadily mounting, attention concentrating almost wholly on the irony, intellectual content, and character of Caesar's speeches. All are sententiae. One depends for its effect on a striking image ('the law of children'),[25] and also perhaps, though less obviously, upon the linking of *pre*-eminence and *first* decree, both suggesting predestination, primordial or unalterable law, while playing upon the identity of *first* as prior in time and *first* as most important. Another depends upon hyperbole and irony ('I am constant as the Northern star'); another on paradox and ambiguity ('Caesar doth not wrong, but with just cause'). It is rather more difficult to explain the impact of 'Let me a little show it, even in this': perhaps its memorability derives in part from its easy applicability to the minutiae of our own lives, so that, unlike some of these other grand pronouncements, it produces an immediate spark of recognition. In another way the statement confirms our expectation that the actions chosen for dramatic representation should be those which reveal a character's essence, an expectation finally being satisfied in this scene. All four of these memorable lines from the middle of the scene are directly relevant to the obvious and central concerns of the whole play.

My assertion that these are the most immediately striking and memorable lines in the first seventy-seven lines of III.i is based on my own reactions, on limited inquiries among students and colleagues, on consultation of books of famous quotations, and on an unsystematic check of the lines most often quoted in critical discussions of the play. Most spectators and readers agree on the most striking, most memorable, most 'important' utterances in this scene. This has obvious implications for interpretation.

I have dwelt on this single line at such length because it illustrates so many of the themes and techniques of my own aesthetic: the use of evidence of early responses, where we can get it; the use of critical and theatrical (and even editorial) history as evidence of the responses of generations of readers and audiences; the potential value of comparing different attempts to solve a similar technical problem; the need to relate our responses to one moment to a whole complex of others; the unavoidable connection between our responses to a given moment and our perception of character generally; the importance of expectations, whether exact or diffuse; the inherent selectivity of a spectator's memory, and the influence of that selectivity upon perception and audience response; the possibility of a central difference between spectators and readers in their responses to particular verbal styles; the distinction between manipulation of an audience by the text itself, and manipulation required by the text but delegated to the performer. No inquiry into audience response can afford to ignore any of these considerations.

The scene suffers from being torn from its context. This limitation is inherent in the study of moments (unless we confine our attention to opening scenes), and I am quite willing to concede that this is a serious limitation, involving as it does an inevitable distortion of the work of art. But equally inevitable, and to my mind more serious, distortions are perpetrated by talking about whole plays without analysing in depth the fractions of which those wholes are composed; yet analysing whole plays (or a whole corpus, or genre, or age) is the dominant mode of contemporary critical discourse. Sometimes the limitations of that mode are explicitly recognized, sometimes not; sometimes the results are stimulating, sometimes not. A concentration upon moments is certainly no *more* distorting than the standard alternative, and it at least has the advantage of remaining closer to the artistic experience; moreover, the widespread and detailed analysis of moments would eventually lay much securer foundations for the analysis of wholes.

Two further limitations may seem rather more surprising, given my insistence upon minutiae of pleasure: I have said relatively little about the scene's actual intellectual content (rather than its moments of intellectual *attention*) or its poetry. A good deal of a spectator's or a reader's pleasure in encountering this scene, or this play, or Shakespeare's plays generally, is intellectual pleasure, the delight springing from individual moments of intellectual perception or intellectual challenge; even more obviously, much of our pleasure is verbal, and directly related to potency and felicity of style. But Shakespeare's intellectual and verbal acuity have been expounded by many able critics; these are aspects of momentary pleasure which have for the most part been well canvassed, and which it is convenient for me to scant, rather than repeat what has been better said elsewhere.[26] But this excuse, though genuine, is only partial. For one thing, the intellectual content of the scene and the issues it raises are, in one sense at least, self-evident: to say that the scene makes us think about the morality of assassination by dramatising an assassination is hardly very illuminating. In another sense, the intellectual and ethical issue here is one element of the scene most likely to depend upon a spectator's or reader's perception of the full context, the whole play.

There is, however, also another and more basic reason for the limitations of the foregoing analysis. Our responses to the scene are responses to the actions and speeches of a number of individual 'characters'. We cannot hope to analyse those responses satisfactorily until we have some hypothesis about the nature of dramatic characters, and of our responses to them. Our intellectual perceptions and our delight in verbal fitness are both integrally related to this larger problem. It is thus to character that I must now turn.

3   Who is Viola? What is She?

In asking how or by what means a fiction approximates fact, it
is necessary to define the real. The art critic, confronting a
painting, can bring to bear a number of facts about the nature
of the visual world: the law of perspective, the known structure of the human anatomy, the refraction of light through
water. In the case of a portrait or a landscape, he may even be
able to compare the painting with the place, or with a photograph of the sitter. By such means he can analyse how the
image of the painter reflects or distorts known features of the
physical world. The literary critic lacks such guidelines. To
compare Shakespeare's Caesar with the Caesar of his sources,
or the Caesar of modern historians, does not tell us whether or
why the character is dramatically convincing (though it may
tell us something about Shakespeare's interpretation of him).
But, even if such comparisons were useful with historical
figures, with fictions such as Viola even they are denied us.
Where the art critic refers to anatomy, the literary critic,
attempting an anatomy of mind, can refer only to the sciences
of psychology; however, attempts to make use of psychological models usually, for a variety of reasons, fail. To begin
with, psychological 'models' are formally distinct from characters in plays in a way that a painter's or a sculptor's 'model'
is not distinct from a painting or a sculpture. In the visual arts
both the 'model' and the masterpiece are visual objects, which
can to that extent be readily compared. By contrast, a psychological model consists of an intellectual construct, described
in discursive prose, whereas a character in a play exists by
virtue of a series of actions performed by a single persona.
(Speeches are, of course, actions.) This disparity exists
whether the psychological 'model' the dramatist employs is
drawn from Freud or Holinshed or a novel; in each case, the

critic must juxtapose narrative descriptions of a character's essence with a dramatic presentation of that character's actions. Of course, that presentation has been designed to lead an audience to infer an essence generating the actions, but the formal problem of 'creating' a character nevertheless, and self-evidently, differs from the problem of describing one. Psychology cannot even give the literary critic a law of exclusions. If we could say, with the authority of an anatomist, 'A and B cannot coexist in the human frame', we could then definitively establish whether and why Hamlet or Cleopatra or Bertram is an organic unity, or a hodge-podge. Any critique of the unity of Shakespeare's characters founders on this, the absence of a law of exclusions. Thus, Schücking objects that Cleopatra the whore is incompatible with Cleopatra the noble and transcendent suicide;[1] to which I can only reply that I believe that these incompatibles can and often do coexist. Unfortunately, my assertion is hardly less subjective than Schücking's own. Neither does much to explain the plausibility of Shakespeare's characters.

Fortunately, Viola does not stir such perplexities, because she does not yoke polarities as Cleopatra does, being limited to a small range of tones. No one has doubted the reality and unity of her character.[2] But in fact theorists such as Schücking radically misstate the problem of character. In the theatre, as in life, the reality and (for the most part) the unity of a character can be and are presumed; they do not need to be proven. As an actress is manifestly real, for the theatre the problem is not to convince us Judi Dench is real, but to convince us Judi Dench is Viola, or that Viola is Judi Dench (a problem greatly complicated, of course, if the audience knows actress or text beforehand). The reader must construct a character from speeches and actions alone, and a reader may complain it doesn't come to life, it doesn't crystallize. But in the theatre the evident physical reality and unity of the actor all but banish such doubts. For this reason, on the television, in the cinema, at the theatre we are convinced by the flimsiest of characters; for this reason, before judging the excellence of a characterisation, we turn from the theatre to the printed text, thus (so to speak) subtracting the actor.

Unity or consistency is, we are told, an aspect of real persons. Certainly, a reader, trying to infer a character from a

set of disconnected speeches, will seek for a unity in those
speeches, as a means of deciding whether the character is
'real'. But a spectator, who sees a living, breathing, moving
real person there upon the stage, will deduce that, like other
persons, this one must have unity or consistency. Both reader
and spectator will try to understand the character, to relate all
his words and actions to a central conception of his nature,
but their activities are importantly different: for the reader,
that consistency will often be a precondition of his assent,
while for the spectator the search for unity will be the consequence of an assent already given. A spectator's trust can of
course be insulted, in which case he will recoil into disbelief;
or, after the play, deprived of the actor's physical assertion of
reality, dependent now merely upon his memory of disconnected acts and speeches, he may well decide that the
character was not after all very convincing. But the distinction
between the two modes of perception remains generally valid.

Our assent to the reality of a character is the precondition
for other responses, emotional and intellectual. I have spoken
of Brutus and Caesar as though they were real, for that essentially is how we respond to them. But we are also aware they
are only acting, that John Gielgud is not really Julius Caesar.
In my own experience these two ideas (that he *is* Caesar, and
isn't) do not actually coexist, but alternate – like the rabbit
and duck of the ambiguous figure. The illusion is thus never
complete. But this ambivalence in fact give us pleasure. For,
after all, there would be nothing amazing about me behaving
like me: our pleasure in mimicry depends upon our sensing
dissimilarity overcome. We are delighted by the *process* of
illusion, not the product. The pleasure of an Impressionist
painting, or a Gainsborough, comes in moving back from the
canvas, until one passes the magic threshold where suddenly
the blobs of paint or the sketchy lines leap into the image of a
face, or a pond of waterlilies.[3] One moves back and forth,
delighted and intrigued by this transformation – just as we are
delighted and intrigued by the transformation from Olivier to
Othello and Othello to Olivier. With the famous or familiar
actor this alternation will occur, whatever the role; but Shakespeare's characters, on an illusionless stage with frankly
theatrical conventions, encourage that alternation, whatever
the actor; indeed the text occasionally enforces an awareness

of the illusion. We are delighted not by the state but by the process of illusion; so too with unity. There is nothing amazing about people behaving consistently. We have all suffered from the consistency of a bore. If for the reader unity is merely a precondition of assent, if for the spectator unity is merely an assumed property of the reality before him, what active pleasure can either take from the perception of unity alone? We take pleasure not from the maintenance of unity or consistency, but from its creation, from the discovery of relation, from the perception of similarity where there seemed none. Because these discoveries occur at particular moments, the analysis of even the unity of Shakespeare's characters must be an analysis of the pleasure of such moments.

The most glaring disjunction between art and life – the fact that the role of Viola was originally created by and intended for a male actor – confirms this emphasis upon the process rather than the achievement of illusion. To see a woman pretending to be a woman hardly in itself excites much interest; or, rather, it may excite an interest in the object represented, but hardly any in the process of representation itself, as a representation of femaleness. Female impersonation, on the other hand, depends upon our consciousness that the 'woman' is a male; as a consequence each detail of the illusion becomes an achievement, the spectator's delight springing from his very awareness of the distance between actor and role. In a theatre where all female parts are played by males, each one becomes an actual or potential *tour de force*, eliciting the same kind of attention to and appreciation of its technique as did Frances de la Tour's 1979 Hamlet.[4] This may be why the use of boy actors did not bother Shakespeare's audiences; if anything, they may have gained from what seems to us the inadequacy of the representation.

But I am talking about a very particular kind of inadequacy, what might be distinguished as a deficiency of materials rather than of workmanship. A change of mask to indicate that a character has blinded himself; a woman played by a boy; the amputation of the limbs of an outsized and unlifelike dummy – an audience will respond emotionally to these representations, as though they were real (approximately).[5] So long as the detail of the representation is convincing, its premiss need not be. Indeed, make its premiss too convincing – show a real human being whose leg is apparently being amputated on stage – and the detail almost certainly will not be. As we are all aware, the more realistic the stage gore, the less we actively believe in it, the more distracted we become by wondering 'How did they do that?' And this incredulous curiosity seems to me quite different from our delight in the process of impersonation: in the former we want to discover 'the trick' (which, once discovered, ceases to interest us), whereas in the latter everything is up front, above board, happening before our eyes, so that – unless we are actors ourselves, or students of histrionic technique – we do not stop to puzzle out how the pretence has been manufactured. The realistic stage gore is a product which attempts to conceal the antecedent process (blood bags, etc.); the impersonation of a female by a male makes the process itself the object of our attention.

There is nothing startlingly original about any of these observations. They can be summarized by saying that any convention will do, so long as it is sufficiently implausible; execution is everything. Conventions which come too close to reality remove a discrepancy which we take pleasure in seeing overcome, a visible gap which the playwright must himself actively and vigorously strive to make invisible. Naturalism, by making it so easy to create vaguely plausible characters, makes it correspondingly difficult to create startlingly real ones. And this applies not only to physical fictions such as the pretence that a man is a woman, but to implausibilities of plot and diction as well. It is the irreality of the premiss which makes possible moments of triumphant reality.

'The real' may be imagined as a sphere: that is, a polygon of an infinite number of sides. (Of course, as the concept of infinity is itself a mathematical fiction, I am here defining reality in terms of fiction.) From among this multiplicity of aspects, each artist selects a few, which and how many according to his talents and his times. All art is synecdoche. Naturalist playwrights have elevated into law a handful of the more mechanical aspects of the real. Theirs is a realism by contagion: a figure sitting in a real chair smoking real cigarettes must himself be real. The naturalists reinforce the reality of the actor's presence with the reality of his stage environment. But the set merely persists; after its initial assertion, it fades from our attention, it becomes truly redundant (in the pejorative sense). This is the bombast of naturalism, its inflated insistence upon a reality spectators are only too willing to concede – up to a point. Beyond that point the rhetoric of chairs and cigarettes cannot persuade us to go; it cannot prevent our remembering it's only a play; it cannot forestall our seeing the rabbit as well as the duck. Art is not life. The painter's materials are only two-dimensional; the sculptor's materials cannot move; the play cannot last a lifetime, and yet, for so long as it does last, it must secure the attention of its audience. The artist compensates as he can for the limits of his material, foreshortening lines, polishing stone flesh, contorting time. Shakespeare creates by the marshalling of combinations in time, so that at any moment the brilliance of one quality obscures the absence of another. Naturalists therefore find it wonderfully easy and gratifying to reveal contradictions, silly conventions, artifice of motive and timing and language. They find it less easy to explain why Shakespeare's fictions convince, more than their own.

The other characters describe Viola for us. They allude thirty-two times to her youth. Less frequently but more emphatically, Orsino and Olivia and Sebastian praise her for physical beauty. They mention also, though in passing and only half a dozen times, her wit, her eloquence, her intelligence – but, as they do not so finely demarcate the boundaries between these qualities, we might as well lump them all under Wit (which was, in any case, a more comprehensive term in Shakespeare's day than it is in ours). The Captain calls her a lady, or 'madam', and thereafter in disguise she is a gentleman, insistently and to all. No one says any more than this. This is a Viola pretty, witty and well-off, but little else. Of these attributes, we would call only her wit a character trait, and even that we see for ourselves, which makes description redundant. The others – age, looks, status – would besides be obvious to an audience at a glance. Why then burden the play with vague and useless adjectives?

Since for most of the play Viola dresses and acts as a servant, we must be reminded that her true nobility makes her a fit match for the Duke, and that her subservience to him reflects choice, not birth or social need. For most of the play too she is a man, therefore we must be told how beautiful she is. Youth must be stressed because her disguise depends on it; because some characters who do not know her name must speak of her; because the word's sexual neutrality lets us think of her as female when they address her as a male; because youth belongs to the Petrarchan ensemble of beauty, wit, virtue and money. All these traits, so cheerfully shallow, are simple panegyric, and, like the immediate and deep affection she inspires in the Captain, Orsino, Olivia and Sebastian, they prejudice us in her favour, they ensure our emotional allegiance.[6]

But there are men and women, members of audiences, who cannot forgive others money or eloquence or innocence or a fortunate face. Malvolio and Olivia call Viola's wit rude, Toby calls her a coward, Antonio an ingrate, and the final scene heaps calumny on her. These opinions are variously discredited. Malvolio's distaste for her follows his diatribe against Feste, which earned him Olivia's rebuke; wit is usually thought rude by its victims; Viola only does what Orsino ordered, even repeating his metaphor. Olivia, who first dislikes the messenger for the master's sake, soon more than compensates by falling in love with him (her). The later accusations are all misunderstandings. When alone with Fabian, Toby praises her, so that his criticisms afterward belong to the gulling of Aguecheek. Viola's generosity and gratitude the play dramatizes repeatedly and early, as though expressly to anticipate Antonio's intense but mistaken charge. Besides, Viola does give him half she has. Even if the accusations of cowardice were justified, cowardice was and probably still is judged forgivable in a woman, especially a young one. The Viola they call coward faces death at Orsino's hands 'most jocund, apt, and willingly'. Shakespeare thus broaches Viola's faults only in contexts which discredit criticism, reserving the bulk of it for her last scenes, by which time our allegiance is secure. But he does broach faults. In bodying an ideal (as Viola is), decoys must be planted for cynicism, so that it wastes itself on trifles; otherwise it wells up against the whole. Viola is an inkblot, which various minds on stage interpret variously. We read them by how they read her. And the flux of their opinions looks likelier than massed choruses of unchanging praise and suspect unanimity.

These are qualities peripheral and narrative. Critics have put such stress on commentary of this kind, on the testimony of other characters, only because it seems a way to simplify the task of interpretation. But we do not take Viola on hearsay: we see her ourselves, before anyone has a chance to talk of her, or tell us what to think. We experience her ourselves, mostly through her own words. But of Viola's many sins against realism, we in this century are perhaps most sensitive to her unnatural mouth.

> Mine own escape unfoldeth to my hope,
> Whereto thy speech serves for authority,
> The like of him.

No one talks like that. Shakespeare nevertheless was and is admired for capturing the form of speech and the particulars of a voice, and I do not think it rash to assume there is some reason for the praise.

Viola begins in the fourth line of her first scene a digression, a parenthesis seventeen lines long, about her brother.

> And what should I do in Illyria?
> My brother he is in Elysium.
> Perchance he is not drowned. What think you, sailors?

The digression begins almost imperceptibly, suggested by association of sound and situation, and the contrast between herself arriving on this shore and her brother arriving on another and stranger shore. But a digression it remains, as can be seen by cutting lines 3–23 of the scene.

> What country, friends, is this?
>
> Know'st thou this country?
>
> Who governs here?
>
> What is his name?

He was a bachelor then.

What's she?

A real Viola might in fact ask uninterrupted just such a string of questions. But to an audience, if 'the tenour of the dialogue' seems too governed by a goal, that goal can easily look like the playwright's not the character's, because the audience knows the playwright must get through his exposition, and because conversation as commonly practised is seldom linear or directed: each party to the dialogue steers a different course, while even within a single mind cross purposes compete for mastery and expression. Speakers are interrupted, or interrupt themselves. The tacks conversation takes thus serve the revelation of mind, the contrasts of purpose between and within minds. Viola begins, detours, begins again, putting parentheses within parentheses: from Illyria to Elysium, to the thought that perhaps her brother is not drowned after all, to asking the sailors for their opinion, to the Captain's cautious reply, to Viola's exclamation 'O my poor brother!', which responds to the Captain's caution by assuming the worst, before she reverts to the comfort of 'perchance', making the best of the Captain's reply. Indeed, up to the mention of Orsino, the entire dialogue is structurally parenthetic, as it exists without relation to what goes before. It thus seems unattached and free, and, though eventually it submits to its place in the plot, that cannot diminish the freedom we feel meanwhile.

These and other digressions overlapping and in concert obscure an otherwise naked exposition. The scene must tell what did and what will happen, and without Viola's false start it breaks in two: the past in one package, the future in another. Arthur Miller called 'how to dramatize what has gone before' 'the biggest single dramatic problem'.[7] Shakespeare did not think so: he gives almost nothing of the past (which partly explains the frustrations of psychoanalytic criticism). We are informed of Viola's immediate past incidentally, through the Captain's narration of Sebastian's. Shakespeare does not bother over Viola's name, or where she came from, or her motives for coming or for disguising herself, or the other helps John Kemble was happy to supply:[8]

> Thou shalt present me as a page unto him,
> Of gentle breeding, and my name Cesario: –
> This trunk, the reliques of my sea-drown'd brother,
> Will furnish man's apparel to my need.

Here Shakespeare does not (as he did in the first scene of *The Comedy of Errors*) spoonfeed us facts. Instead, just when other playwrights are scrambling to piece together a plot, he drops morsels of a time distant and gratuitous, unelaborated, obviously not summoned up for the plot's sake, but again intimating discreetly life outside the play's limits. And these particulars are not only delightful or intriguing in themselves, but positively distract us from a consciousness of the exposition.

> Ay madam, well, for I was bred and born
> Not three hours' travel from this very place.
>
> Orsino! I have heard my father name him.
> He was a bachelor then.

This last line cues, naturally enough, the Captain's mention of Olivia. Orsino is not named till now, and, though we may suspect he is the Duke in question, until they link him to Olivia we cannot be sure. But Olivia is a dead end. The talk of her comes to nothing, as much talk does. Afterwards begins another parenthesis, this one with no immediate relation whatever to the preceding dialogue.

> There is a fair behaviour in thee, Captain,
> And though that nature with a beauteous wall
> Doth oft close in pollution, yet of thee
> I will believe thou hast a mind that suits
> With this thy fair and outward character.

Only as she continues does the relevance of this panegyric become apparent.

> I prithee – and I'll pay thee bounteously –
> Conceal me what I am, and be my aid.

The talk of Olivia turns out not to have been wasted after all, and, since Viola must convince the Captain to act for her, exposition of her plans seems here necessary and natural. Her praise of the Captain is thus motivated in retrospect.

In her next scene, she and Orsino discuss Olivia without once naming her, referring to her simply by pronouns, leaving the identification to our intelligence. Viola and Olivia in their first encounter answer questions with questions, speak at cross purposes, Olivia testing hypotheses about the intruder; Maria interrupts them; Olivia interrupts Viola; the message is never delivered.

> *Olivia.* If I do not usurp myself, I am.
> *Viola.* Most certain, if you are she, you do usurp yourself,
>   for what is yours to bestow is not yours to reserve.

The nature of wit is to digress, to pounce upon peripherals and explode them into prominence.

> *Olivia.* Were you sent hither to praise me?
> *Viola.* I see you what you are: you are too proud.
>   But if you were the devil, you are fair.
>   My lord and master loves you. O, such love
>   Could be but recompens'd, though you were crown'd
>   The nonpareil of beauty!

Viola does not answer Olivia's question, but judges it, as an expression of pride (the devil's own sin). But Olivia is beautiful, and so has cause for pride – except that beauty, however great, could never deserve more than the kind of love which Orsino offers.

The technique is everywhere much the same, employing a variation or postponement of the expected sequence. The pattern and quantity of such digression varies according to the number and complexity of the participants. But the discontinuities never become obtrusive, as they do in the mannerist dialogue of Pinter and Mamet:[9] the quantity or incongruity of the diversions does not lead an audience to generalize that the eccentricities of individual consciousness forbid any possibility of communication. Instead, the norm of directed and interacting conversation highlights occasional changes of course, which seem as a result to reveal the particular internal pressures of an individual personality. Moreover, the impression of natural speech derives not only from the deployment

of sentences in a natural haphazard, but from the sentences
themselves.

Know'st thou this country?

Who governs here?

What is his name?

Orsino! I have heard my father name him.

He was a bachelor then.

What's she?

I'll serve this duke.

I thank thee. Lead me on.

I thank you. Here comes the count.

Say I do speak to her, my lord, what then?

I'll do my best to woo your lady.

Good madam, let me see your face.

I left no ring with her.

She loves me, sure.

None of my lord's ring? Why, he sent her none.

How will this fadge?

What will become of this?

But if she cannot love you, sir?

(Save you, gentleman.) – And you, sir.

I pity you.

(Gentleman, God save thee.) – And you, sir.

I am no fighter.

Pray you, sir, do you know of this matter?

I beseech you, what manner of man is he?

Pray sir, put your sword up, if you please.

What money, sir?

He nam'd Sebastian.

Why do you speak to me? I never hurt you.

Of Messaline: Sebastian was my father.

My father had a mole upon his brow.

These are natural enough. But my singling out of these does not imply that elsewhere Viola's every word proclaims itself poetry and made not born. The proportion of art to nature varies from line to line.

> Say that some lady, as perhaps there is,
> Hath for your love as great a pang of heart
> As you have for Olivia; you cannot love her;
> You tell her so. Must she not then be answer'd?

Here only 'pang of heart' and the displacement of the preposition 'for your love', between the verb and its object, seem literary. To modern ears 'hath' sounds archaic and 'poetic', but though 'has' was displacing it even in Shakespeare's lifetime, its literary flavour must have been much weaker than now. 'Then' would probably seem more natural at the beginning or end of the question, although this might be challenged – especially because, as its position is right metrically, any slight syntactical dislocation tends to be erased. Meter and syntax give us two competing definitions of 'rightness', which can in such marginal cases be used interchangeably. For instance, in 'What country, friends, is this?', only the displacement of the vocative suggests the written not the spoken word, and meter tends to obscure this – as does our own familiarity with the line. (Familiarity is as important as changes in linguistic usage in obscuring for us the exact feel of much of Shakespeare's dialogue.)

The lilt of speech can be found in varying amounts everywhere in the poetry. But again, this balancing and map of words is perpetual, and so to analyse its relation to character we must isolate Viola's wholly natural and unadulterate lines from the rest. The list is small, but its items are surprisingly prominent: 'Good madam, let me see your face' (because it is a *non sequitur*, because Viola here changes from a passive to an active role in the dialogue of I.v, because we know what motivates the change); 'I left no ring with her' (her first bewildered response, alone after Malvolio's exit in II.ii, to the second major irony of the plot); 'I pity you' (her only reply to Olivia's tortuous long confession in III.i); 'Pray sir, put your sword up, if you please' (her small voice after the hubbub between Antonio, Sir Toby, and Fabian in III.iv – the more remarkable for its contrast with Antonio's 'Put up your sword!'); 'What money, sir?' (her first words to Antonio after his repeated requests, in the play's first mistaking of brother and sister); 'Of Messaline: Sebastian was my father' (her first words to Sebastian after his string of vocatives, tantalizing us with the expectation of 'Sebastian was my brother', in the moment of recognition to which the whole play leads, and which lends its power to her next lone sentence too); 'My father had a mole upon his brow'.

These examples owe their emphasis to their contexts, contexts in which stylized or poetic language would be as or almost as emphatic, but elsewhere Viola's plainness stands out simply because it's plain.

> *For saying so, there's gold.*
> Mine own escape unfoldeth to my hope,
> Whereto thy speech serves for authority,
> The like of him. *Know'st thou this country?*

> Most radiant, exquisite and unmatchable
> beauty – *I pray you tell me if this be the*
> *lady of the house.*

> *Orsino.* Tell her my love, more noble than the world,
>   Prizes not quantity of dirty lands;
>   The parts that fortune hath bestow'd upon her,
>   Tell her I hold as giddily as fortune;
>   But 'tis that miracle and queen of gems
>   That nature pranks her in, attracts my soul.
> *Viola. But if she cannot love you, sir?*

Such collisions of style advertise each. Unrelieved naturalism is inconspicuous because constant; Shakespeare's is strategic realism.

In achieving for Viola this impression of artless speech, Shakespeare employs sentences with no great complexity of syntax or rhetoric or vocabulary. But he also employs little or no slang, or interjection, or commonplace, or imagery of everyday life, nothing bathetic or trite, no repetition of unmeaning social formulae (though Olivia so interprets Viola's claim to be her 'servant'). Judged by this progress of negatives, Viola may well seem less real than Sir Toby – which is only to say his reality is the more easily explained.[10] In fact, Toby's easy coexistence with Viola itself lends her life: the differences between them thus seem less the gap between natural and manufactured than the variety and distinction of two reals. The means used to enliven each fiction will themselves individuate it. What they are proves that they are. We know Viola partly by what she's not, by all the kinds of language she does not use. The vocabulary she does use is unphysical (notoriously chaste), often latinate and polysyllabic, often abstract, with a preference for verbal nouns ('my having is not much'), substantives and personifications, and for a balanced syntax making analytical distinctions ('what is yours to bestow is not yours to reserve'). What imagery she has tends to the conventional and consciously poetic ('Elysium'), to comparisons so familiar they need only be implied.

> 'Tis beauty truly blent, whose red and white
> Nature's own sweet and cunning hand laid on.

Such sunken imagery suggests an unassertive elegance.

Character is repetition: repetitions of speech, as we have seen, but also repetitions of action. Viola expresses her gratitude to the Captain, to Valentine, to Fabian and then Antonio, to Antonio again in the last scene. 'I hate ingratitude more in a man / Than lying, vainness, babbling drunkenness.' She offers money to the Captain twice, to Feste twice; she gives Antonio half she has. She often has occasion for gratitude and generosity, because she depends often on others: the Captain, Valentine, Olivia, Feste, Fabian, Toby, Antonio. Though she knows more than any other character on stage, she is forever in the position of having to ask others questions. Helpless herself, she trusts to time. Repeatedly and at length she praises others, especially Olivia, Feste and the Captain. She feels for her brother, for Olivia, Antonio and Orsino; typically, even her love she expresses as sympathy for someone else, either Orsino or a 'sister'. She does describe Malvolio as a 'churlish messenger' (II.ii), and does wish Olivia ill luck in love (I.v) – this is the most malice she can muster, and she soon regrets cursing Olivia. Despite (or because of) her own social rank, respect and courtesy – 'my lord', 'my lady', 'sir' – are always on her lips. Unlike Petrarchan women, she honours and obeys her husband *before* marriage, serving him in the most selfless manner imaginable, and is literally his servant when metaphorically he should be hers. She doubts her own abilities, a modesty which extends to things sexual: of all Shakespeare's comic heroines, Viola has the most chaste mouth and mind. But, like them all, she is practical and persistent. Circumstance does not permit her the luxuries of grief for her brother; she understands better than Orsino how futile his romance diplomacy is; she will not let Malvolio's excuses or Olivia's questions or Maria's interruption deflect her from her business; she does not let despair canker her love. She shows her wit off stage with Malvolio, on stage with Olivia, Maria, Feste and Toby; she shows her intelligence in deducing Olivia's love and Antonio's mistake.

What this list brings together the play disperses, so that we are seldom conscious of repetition. Viola's redistribution of wealth – of all her repetitions the one most physical, and thus most prone to look mechanical – is carefully varied. She first gives, then only promises, the Captain money (I.ii); Feste wittily begs for what she gave the Captain unasked (III.i); Antonio passionately demands money, she only offers him

half, he refuses it (III.iv); Viola herself refuses a fee from Olivia
(I.v). Others remark upon her wit, and that she hates ingratitude she says herself, but the other repetitions pass without
comment, and are so subtly interfused I do them violence by
disentangling them. Generosity is financial gratitude; praise
turns to gratitude, sympathy turns to praise. That sympathy
itself blends into her own sorrows for her brother's death and
her unanswered love. Her sorrow is reticent and practical; her
wit persistent; her reticence patient; her love sorrowing. Her
self-doubts naturally spring from helplessness and naturally
contribute to her reticence and passivity.

We need never conceptualize her aspects in this way;
Shakespeare himself need not have. But this interrelation of
traits is what allows the character to assimilate new material.
For instance, in the duel with Aguecheek, if Viola is petrified
with fear, her cowardice will seem in character, because related to her helplessness, reticence and passivity. We have
already had occasion to laugh, when her disguise entangles
her in absurd difficulties, and we will laugh now at her helpless perplexity. But, equally, if Viola soundly thrashes
Aguecheek – as some actresses have done – that too will seem
in character, by analogy with her practicality, her persistence,
her repeatedly demonstrated ability to better her opponents
(of whom Aguecheek is no doubt the least daunting). If she
decides the fight cannot be avoided, then she must do her best,
and she will no doubt be surprised and delighted by her own
success.

Viola then is a system of repetitions – descriptions repeated,
patterns of speech and action repeated – repetitions varied
and intertwined, authenticated by natural speech, authenticated too by the presence of other characters defined by different patterns of repetition. It has long been recognized that, in
M. C. Bradbrook's words, 'Romeo and Juliet without the
Nurse and Mercutio, Navarre and his lords without Armado,
Costard, Moth and the worthies, Richard without Bolingbroke, York, Gaunt and the Queen, would in effect cease to
exist with the dramatic depth and significance which makes
them what they are.'[11] Richard and Bolingbroke define each
other dialectically, as do Creon and Antigone. But such oppo-
sitions, though they have naturally attracted critical attention,
are not the only, or even the normal, method of distinguishing
and relating character. Olivia and Viola are not alike, and to

that extent each defines the other by opposition, but they are
never offered as dialectical alternatives, and in fact Olivia
might easily seem too like Viola, both being highborn women,
both in love, both unrequited, both mourning a brother. The
individuality of the two impresses us partly because (as with
Jane Austen's six clergymen) in outline they are so similar.

Olivia commands; Viola entreats and obeys. Olivia in her
first scene criticises Feste, Malvolio, Sir Toby and Viola; she
gives sermons and expresses curt moral disapproval. Viola
praises. Olivia shows Orsino no sympathy; Viola sympathizes
even with Olivia, her rival. Olivia is proud, and told so; her
anticipation of praise is all the more striking after Viola's
silence during Orsino's praise, in the preceding scene. And,
though Olivia has on the whole a ladylike vocabulary, she
does not have Viola's latinity, and is occasionally capable of
'bird-bolts', 'rudesby', 'fat and fulsome howling', 'inventor-
ies', 'utensils', 'lids for pans', of 'What ho!', 'Fie on him!' and
'Go to'. She mocks conventional imagery. She describes her
own love violently:

> Even so quickly may one catch the plague!

> Have you not set mine honour at the stake,
> And baited it with all th'unmuzzled thoughts
> That tyrannous heart can think?

> A murd'rous guilt shows not itself more soon
> Than love that would be hid.

> A fiend like thee might bear my soul to hell.

Viola in love waits and is silent; Olivia acts, and openly, con-
fessing her love, persisting, calling Cesario back, hurrying
Sebastian to a priest. Viola first communicates her feelings in
an unelaborated aside, Olivia in a long soliloquy, full of exclamations, repetitions, headstrong images. And, unlike Viola,
she does not mourn her brother long, or feelingly. Admittedly,
Sebastian can be resurrected at play's end (as Olivia's brother
cannot), and Viola may in the meantime intensely communi-
cate her loss without unbalancing the comedy. Viola's grief
directly contributes to the joy of the denouement, as Olivia's
could not. Admittedly also, Viola does not recall her own grief

in Olivia's company, and no one speaks of Olivia's brother after Act I, which is to say Shakespeare does not focus moral disapproval, or demand comparison, as he easily could. Stressing Olivia's broken vow, when she falls in love and gives up mourning, would make a situation already complex and painful even more so. But, still, Olivia must either cease to wear black early in the play, and so physically announce an end to grief, or by continuing in black invite a contrast between her clothes and her thoughts, which are by now oblivious to her brother. Viola's grief impresses us as central; Olivia's never does. Her vow is instead a typical expression of her will, and a (conscious or unconscious) defence against Orsino.

Olivia also abhors yellow. No one need extrapolate conclusions from such differences; no one need notice them; but imperceptibly the impressions accumulate, and being imperceptible they seem the more real, they seem like life, and unlike characters demarcated by their opinions on this and that. We know Viola is not Olivia, but do not know quite why or how we know – though, if asked, we could begin to formulate and conceptualize distinctions. Our experience of human beings leads us to expect variety and individuality. If one actress stands before us on the stage, her reality is proven by her presence; but if another enters we shall expect not only reality but also distinction. Of course, they may share many traits, but, as the actresses must now convince us they represent two different persons, their own vitality is no longer sufficient for the illusion. But, though we require differentiation, the differences need not *mean* anything, any more than the difference between apples and pears means anything, though we might expect a still-life to distinguish them. Such variety becomes a condition for our assent. But the variety itself gives us pleasure, too, by perpetually supplying fresh sources of interest, new claims on our attention.

Other characters invite other contrasts. Orsino's language is intense, inventive, polysyllabic, self-conscious, complex and metaphorical, without Viola's lucidity or simplicity, and as if to emphasize this contrast Viola is at her most reticent in his company: in their first scene together (I.v), she speaks seven lines to his twenty-four. He speaks of his love loudly and at large, and seems to relish his pain as a proof of sincerity.

> There is no woman's sides
> Can bide the beating of so strong a passion
> As love doth give my heart; no woman's heart
> So big, to hold so much. They lack retention.
> Alas, their love may be called appetite:
> No motion of the liver, but the palate,
> That suffer surfeit, cloyment, and revolt.
> But mine is all as hungry as the sea
> And can digest as much. Make no compare
> Between that love a woman can bear me
> And that I owe Olivia.

If his sorrows do not touch us as Viola's do, that is perhaps because he pities himself enough for us all, and because the very beauty of his poetry impersonalizes it, distracting our attention from the man to the phrase.

Sebastian grows rapidly exasperated then angry at the very misunderstandings Viola suffers comically; when brother and sister meet, he expresses wonder and plain-faced astonishment, she quietly and surely reveals herself, savouring and drawing out their reunion:

> *Sebastian.* Do I stand there? I never had a brother,
>   Nor can there be that deity in my nature
>   Of here and everywhere. I had a sister,
>   Whom the blind waves and surges have devour'd.
>   Of charity, what kin are you to me?
>   What countryman? What name? What parentage?
> *Viola.* Of Messaline; Sebastian was my father.
>   Such a Sebastian was my brother, too;
>   So went he suited to his watery tomb.
>   If spirits can assume both form and suit,
>   You come to fright us.

When he turns to Olivia and offers her himself, Viola does not speak, but waits for Orsino.

Unlike Malvolio, Viola does not misinterpret Orsino's actions according to her own vanity, or deceive herself into confidence. Malvolio is an aspirant lord; Viola willingly and without complaint humbles herself to service. Malvolio is an unnecessarily churlish messenger; Viola, having excellent reasons to misdeliver the message, speaks it as passionately as she can.

To Viola's characterization Aguecheek, Toby, Fabian, Maria and Feste all contribute one contrast, an attitude to money, sex, food, drink, fighting, singing, manners, life – a contrast which also defines Olivia and Orsino, though to varying degrees. It is perhaps most easily defined as a class contrast, though it disregards class boundaries. Feste sings for Toby and Aguecheek in II.iii, then for Orsino and Viola in the next scene, thus juxtaposing the leisure amusements of the two sets; Maria and Toby plot the discomfiting of Malvolio just after Viola in soliloquy decides, after Malvolio leaves, to continue her disguise, in sympathy for all and at some cost to herself. Feste's perpetual begging and the financial tie of Toby and Aguecheek illuminate Viola's generosity; duelling as a practical joke shows up her peaceable nature. She crushes Aguecheek's pretensions to culture and Toby's to eloquence. But she does not morally condemn them. She will pun with Feste, bawdily too, without objecting to his indecencies, and she does not blame anyone for wanting money, though she does not want it herself and feels insulted by mercenary treatment. She praises Feste's singing and fooling just as Toby and Aguecheek do. Though in the duel Aguecheek and she may both be dupes, he has contributed to his own confounding, while she is pure victim; though she may be as cowardly as he, she had no pretensions to valour, and her sex will excuse her.

The Captain, the priest, the officers, Valentine, Curio, even Fabian and Maria and Antonio, are the kind of characters E. M. Forster called flat.[12] Not that we judge them the less real on that account, any more than a background seems, because less detailed, less real than the foreground. We know Viola well; these others are acquaintances only, a society of potentials, alive enough without distracting. Occasionally what we thought background isn't. In *Julius Caesar*, Antony long seems a cameo part, like Cicero; Marullus and Flavius begin importantly, but aren't. This fact helps to create the illusion, within individual plays and across the canon, that any part of the background has its own foreground, which might become our foreground at any time. It suggests that all of the characters, even the flattest, have an unexpressed but expressible potency.

These minor characters not only enhance Viola's scale, or

highlight certain of her features. She also responds appropriately to each. She gives Valentine prose and Orsino verse.
She pounces upon Maria in a tone and idiom foreign to her
conversations with Olivia. After the comic prose of the duel
she honours Antonio with intense and thoughtful verse. Witty
and at ease with Olivia, she has a marked reticence and
seriousness with the Duke. Viola has like us all a social
malleability, which occasionally stimulates from her reactions
which elsewhere have no opportunity for expression. With
Feste in III.i, she accepts and even briefly contributes to his
puns and sexual innuendoes; Aguecheek's French prompts
French from her; Maria's and Toby's nautical metaphors
make her speak sailor. These qualities, unsuspected until
glimpsed, of course detail her character, but they do so not
just by an arithmetic accumulation of one detail plus another,
but suggestingly and as though geometrically. Viola knew
French all along, but the fact had no occasion to surface.
These and how many other attributes sleep in her awaiting
expression, until a particular encounter and stimulus call
them out. Viola need no more know French than her father
need have had a mole upon his brow: like the Captain's birth
'not three hours' travel from this very place', these are gratuitous particulars. They are not used but leak unconcernedly,
an overflow of unfathomed possibility. Shakespeare establishes the uniformity of a voice by repetition, through habits
of language, among them the tendency to sparse and elegant
imagery, so that concentrations of imagery – particularly
those that smack of jargon, or the colloquial – stand out
emphatically from their context.

> I would be loath to cast away my speech, for besides that
> it is excellently well penned, I have taken great pains to
> con it. . . . I can say little more than I have studied, and
> that question's out of my part. . . . I am not that I play.

Maria. Will you hoist sail, sir? Here lies your way.
Viola. No, good swabber, I am to hull here a little longer.

Sir Toby. Will you encounter the house? My niece is very
  desirous you should enter, if your trade be to her.
Viola. I am bound to your niece, sir – I mean, she is the
  list of my voyage.

Her reactions to Maria and Toby may be mockery, may be the
pretence of hearty masculinity.[13] It is in any case a language
put on for the occasion, just as her romantic diction is put on,
when she plays ambassador. Likewise, in a context of relatively unimaged speech, concentrations of intense and developing
imagery convey climax and emphasis.

> Make me a willow cabin at your gate,
> And call upon my soul within the house;
> Write loyal cantons of contemned love,
> And sing them loud even in the dead of night;
> Halloo your name to the reverberate hills,
> And make the babbling gossip of the air
> Cry out 'Olivia!' O, you should not rest
> Between the elements of air and earth,
> But you should pity me.

> A blank, my lord. She never told her love,
> But let concealment like a worm i'th' bud
> Feed on her damask cheek; she pin'd in thought,
> And with a green and yellow melancholy
> She sat like Patience on a monument,
> Smiling at grief. Was not this love indeed?
> We men may say more, swear more, but indeed
> Our shows are more than will: for still we prove
> Much in our vows, but little in our love.

Admittedly, our knowledge of Viola's secret alerts us to her
feelings here, but nothing immediately stimulates either
release of poetry, and against Viola's norm these two famous
speeches do seem a release, which we naturally and automatically interpret as the expression of emotions otherwise contained or suppressed. The second speech contradicts not only
her usual style, but also her usual pronounced reticence in
Orsino's company. If these images or those other masculine
ones came unannounced, unprompted, not in clusters but
here and there at random, they would be wasted and unseen.
They would only confuse not complicate the character. Only
the security of the norm alerts us to the significance of variation; as in an experiment, Shakespeare varies only one factor
at a time, keeping the others constant. Moreover, in each
instance he provides an immediately apprehensible stimulus

or motive for the variation, whether it be Toby's ludicrous metaphor or Viola's secret, so that, again as in an experiment, by isolating the variable, Shakespeare illuminates the relation of cause to effect.

Thus to put side by side such moods and tones intimates layers and strata of personality, ever-present if only occasionally displayed. This trick of juxtaposition begins in Viola's first 'parenthesis', where grief and a practical curiosity coexist. Moods or motifs once sounded may later be summoned and combined by the briefest allusion, as in

> I am all the daughters of my father's house,
> And all the brothers too – and yet I know not.
> Sir, shall I to this lady?

After the concealed longing of her talk with Orsino, the mention of her brother wakens another and unrelated longing, until the next line as abruptly returns us to the practical issue, Olivia, unmentioned now for almost forty lines. Again:

> *Viola.* I pity you.
> *Olivia.*   That's a degree to love.
> *Viola.* No, not a grize: for 'tis a vulgar proof
>   That very oft we pity enemies.

Viola's two versions of Olivia (as rival and fellow sufferer) here are yoked in all their unannealed disparity, as they were, less emphatically, when her sympathy for 'poor Olivia' followed the success of her own curse. Moreover, this serious and simple 'I pity you' itself stands out against Viola's light-heartedness in this scene, which began with Feste and, after this interruption, continues until she answers Olivia vow for vow.

If, as I. A. Richards said, metaphor is 'the interanimation of contexts', or Dr Johnson's 'unexpected copulation of ideas', such juxtapositions are metaphors:[14] they force our imaginations to leap distinction and discover relation where there seems none. Metaphors implicate us; they make us act the text rather than receive it. Literalists dislike any fleshing out of the airy nothing of a dramatic fiction, but Shakespeare in constructing life advertises vacuums which demand filling, which imagination duly fills. This happens even in what

Schücking and Stoll would dismiss as 'popular entertainment'. In *City Lights*, Charlie Chaplin fights a boxing-match
to win money for a blind girl. Between rounds, he hallucinates
that she is sponging his face. In the next and final round, he is
losing badly and evidently exhausted, when suddenly and
without explanation, in a burst of energy, he fights brilliantly
and passionately, until finally he collapses. One cannot but
notice the disjunction; one is *asked* to account for it. And the
context provides an obvious explanation, that he suddenly
remembers the purpose of the fight, and makes a last heroic
effort. And, just as this technique can be found in 'popular'
drama, so it can be found in ancient drama, proving that there
is nothing anachronistically 'modern' about this notion of
subtext. In Sophocles's *Antigone*, Creon's son Haemon never
mentions his own love for Antigone, in the course of his long
argument with his father (though it has been mentioned,
earlier in the play, by Ismene); after that scene, the Chorus
sings a stasimon to *"Ερως*,'Love', a hymn which 'has little to
do with the main issue of the play'.[15] In the next scene
Antigone, on her way to her death, laments her misfortunes,
in particular regretting (three times: 813–16, 867, 876) that
her early death robs her of the fulfilments of marriage. Yet,
just as Haemon never mentions her, so she never mentions
Haemon. Like Viola, Sophocles's lovers impress us partly by
their emotional restraint. An audience cannot help but sense
powerful emotions operating beneath the surface.

Chaplin, Sophocles and Shakespeare create a vacuum, and
supply us with the means to fill it, so that, without ever impos-
ing an explicit statement of motive, they make the unspoken
chain of thought immediately apprehensible. Linking Viola's
grief for Sebastian to her longing for Orsino suggests a predisposition and a pattern of mind, where we saw before only
isolated, wholly independent reactions to circumstance. Her
abrupt turn to the practical, by echoing the striking movement of her first scene, reinforces this pattern; further, it
implies a repeated effort to suppress pain through action, an
effort not entirely successful, since we see memories of
Sebastian well up without warning, and since we understand
her sublimated confessions to Orsino. Again, proximity of
pity and enmity invites an explanation, for instance that her
harshness means immediately to discourage Olivia's hopeless
passion – just as, because we know Viola knows Olivia loves,

we may interpret her witty deflections and interruptions
earlier in this scene as a deliberate attempt to forestall un-
pleasantness. Viola's confession

> yet, a barful strife!
> Whoe'er I woo, myself would be his wife

likewise catalyses an alchemy of context, in that her reluctance to negotiate with Olivia – which we first take at face
value, as characteristic self-doubt – seems now motivated in
part or whole by private interests. The very forcing of the
paradox into a couplet asks us how such feelings can accompany such actions. So by a metaphor of motive Shakespeare
lures us into swamps of interpretation. In a Cleopatra or a
Hamlet, these contradictions and contractions, huddled more
frequently and violently together, continually tease us out of
the text into exploration and connection. But the artistic principle (which we have seen in the small parentheses and digressions of unlinear dialogue, in the clash of styles, in the
juxtaposition of opposed moods) is simple: an abrupt change
of direction compels us to seek an explanation, on the
evidence of what we already know about the character or the
context, and that explanation in turn compels us to revise our
picture of the character.

I have spoken of layers of mind; the actor speaks of subtext;
the psychologist, of the subconscious. These spatial metaphors all attempt to describe the relationship between a
surface of behaviour, which is palpable but unexplained, and
its underlying causes or motives, which are real and necessary,
but unseen. Viola's disguise creates a similar structure. We are
aware in listening to her words both and at once of their
surface and of their ulterior. We perceive her both inwardly
(as in life we do only ourselves), and obscurely and outwardly
(as the others do, and as in life we do others). We are not only
informed of her motives: we see them moment by moment
influencing her actions. Viola's is a physical disguise; Hamlet,
Macbeth, Iago disguise their minds. As early as 1915 V. O.
Freeburg discussed the contributions of disguise to characterization; in 1960, Bertrand Evans wrote usefully of 'discrepant

awareness' as an organizing principle in the comedies.[16] As
Evans describes it, grades of ignorance among characters –
such as those created by Viola's disguise – allow a rich and
varied laughter, or a balancing of emotional tones, at no cost
to clarity. Simply the number of perspectives conceals Shakespeare's technique, by letting him interrupt one with another,
so that characters in their various ignorances seem perpetually and anarchically intruding. Viola, atop this pyramid of
perception, acquires the look of intelligence, an impression
reinforced here and there in the play but largely undeserved,
were it not for her privileged position in the plot. Discrepancies also differentiate, and, though I would hesitate to claim
we are in a complicated scene so precisely conscious of the
hierarchies of awareness as Evans implies, certainly that hierarchy does distinguish Jack from Jill, and certainly we can be
made conscious at will of any particular imperception. Our
awareness of awareness concentrates into moments of intense
pleasure, rather than diffusing over entire scenes.

But Viola's disguise does not simply or neatly divide real
from false, for, while obviously by birth Viola need not wear
livery, by nature she inclines to service, so that her role fits her
self, as Hamlet's antic disposition fits his. This coincidence of
Self and Seeming blurs the nice distinction in Evans's 'know
or not know'. But Shakespeare does profit greatly from the
distinction, and from the relationship between Viola and
Cesario. We are Viola's confidant, and no one else consistently understands or judges her fairly – indeed, the Captain disappears from the play to ensure that the audience is Viola's
only confidant. This is the source of Viola's isolation and
intimacy. We share in her soliloquies; they speak to and for
us. (By contrast we *watch* Olivia's, almost as if it were dialogue.) But Viola wants to reveal her secret, which in itself
distinguishes her from virtually all Shakespeare's characters.
When our relation to her fluctuates, as in the duel with
Aguecheek, Viola has not changed, but our perspective has,
so that in two hours we not only see and hear how various she
is, but also experience her variously. This is a distinction of
some importance, as it is possible to respond quite simply to a
complex fact, and complexly to simple ones. Shaw paints
Caesar with a variety of traits, a multiplicity of detail Shakespeare's Caesar cannot equal; yet Shaw to all this detail invites
essentially one response. Shakespeare presents instead a few

basic but ambivalent qualities in contexts where they produce radically opposed responses. Viola's helplessness can draw from us sympathy or laughter, depending on the circumstance.

Once such layers of mind have been suggested, the difficulty is to know which layer is functioning at any given moment. When Viola begins her oratory of love, then stops in mid sentence, does she perpetrate or suffer the incongruity? She has after all outwitted Malvolio in the immediately preceding scene; but, then again, she sounds at times almost like Bottom's mechanicals. 'Alas', she says, 'I took great pains to study it, and 'tis poetical' – who can say if this is an 'Alas' serious or satiric? As Keats said, 'Writing has this disadvantage of speaking, one cannot write a wink, or a nod, or a grin, or a purse of the lips, or a *smile – O law!* One cannot put one's finger to one's nose, or yerk ye in the ribs, or lay hold of your button in writing.'[17] So, when Viola says,

> I am all the daughters of my father's house,
> And all the brothers too, and yet I know not

she may mean either that she does not know whether the fictive sister died, or that she does not know whether Sebastian lives. J. R. Brown has called attention to the theatrical impact and ambiguity of Viola's silent response to Orsino's last words, and her exit at play's end.[18] At play's start, the words, 'He was a bachelor then', we may make innocent or meaningful at will.

In both cases the text tells nothing: we must deduce the detail from our vision of the whole, a vision itself constructed from evidence dubious and conflicting. Ambiguity results from Shakespeare's providing at once too much and too little evidence. In the first of Viola's scenes, lamentation takes its place in a dialogue otherwise spright and lively, so that our first impression of the woman depends largely upon how the actress manages or the reader imagines the combination of those moods. Viola's 'willow cabin' speech contains in almost equal proportion images boisterous and still; her soliloquy in Act II offers scope for reflection and feeling or for clowning and a Launce-like confusion. Then, too, even within the play there are conflicting descriptions of her. Perhaps Malvolio sees for what they are both Feste and Viola; perhaps Viola's is a mere pretence of aristocratic generosity, which Antonio shatters; perhaps she *is* a snivelling coward and a dissembling cub; perhaps the concentration of denunciation in Act V should suggest that these last scenes explode the seeming virtues of the first. In Viola's case these perhapses have seldom surfaced; come Cleopatra, they are legion.

This is no licence for fantasy: certain interpretations remain richer, more probable, truer to the whole. The task of criticism is to unsettle complacencies, to define the bounds of ambiguity, to localize indefinition (as the artist does). For different types of ambiguity create different problems for interpretation. Viola must leave the stage in one way, or in another; she cannot leave both ways; the actress must choose. Here we can only recognize the necessity for choice, and the consequent variety of theatrical interpretation. But, when Lady Macbeth faints, unless the actress 'winks at the pit',[19] a performance can do little to resolve the ambiguity, for the ambiguity is of motive, not action: we ask, not how to perform the scene, but how to interpret it. Shakespeare constructs a vacuum, and forces each spectator to choose one of two ways to fill it. Here we can only recognize the freedom of choice, and the consequent variety of response. But, when Cleopatra runs from Actium, though her desertion determines the course of the battle and the play, Shakespeare does not explain her motives, or even offer alternative explanations. He offers no explanation at all. He thus compels the spectator to construct one, but leaves him free to choose whichever he likes. Here we can only recognize the necessity for choice, and the fated impotence of interpretation.

Shakespeare has not specified Cleopatra's motives at Actium precisely *because* of the overwhelming importance of her act, and our consequent intense curiosity about its causes. For that curiosity ensures that we shall raise the question of motive, and actively seek to answer it. Shakespeare's is strategic indefinition. (Compare Rembrandt, deliberately leaving the eyes, the feature most important for interpretation of a portrait, in shadow.[20]) No one has ever thought Cleopatra's desertion 'out of character' or 'inexplicable', and this is worth remembering, for the dramatist needn't explain why his characters behave as they do; he must only convince us they would or could have behaved that way. Cleopatra is like Viola a system of repetitions, and we can immediately sense that her desertion fits into that system, without knowing where or why it fits. We can only understand this her central act by compre-hending the whole of her character, so that to define Cleopatra becomes a prime activity and interest for every spectator. Only the very greatest characters stimulate this conscious pursuit of definition; Viola for instance never does. The search for definition, for meaning, derives from a biological impulse to organize our experience; that impulse will only be activated when there is a perceived disequilibrium in the environment, the presence of something that shouldn't be there, the absence of something that should. Shakespeare stimulates this impulse by creating such disequilibria in his major characters, leaving things out when we expect them, putting the unexpected in. The incompetent dramatist either pre-empts the search for meaning, by offering stereotypes, or satisfies it, by explaining his characters; Shakespeare does neither.

Why then are we not simply frustrated and bewildered? All critics would agree that, in her final moments, Cleopatra speaks and behaves in a new manner. The change is of course ambiguous: as Dean Frye says, either 'we believe the char-acter has changed, or we believe that we have simply learned more about' her.[21] Either Cleopatra has changed her tune, or we are finally seeing the true nature of her relationship with Antony. But, in either case, an audience will likely feel, at that moment, that it has learned the truth about her, that it has been shown her essence; for, even if Cleopatra has changed, we are disposed to assume that 'the essence of a thing can be defined ... in terms of its *fulfilment* or *fruition*'.[22] (This, incidentally, helps explain our satisfaction that Caesar is most Caesarian on his last appearance.) Consequently, however they interpret Cleopatra, audiences will probably feel that their desire for definition has been satisfied by the end of the play, and this feeling will be reinforced by the very fact that death puts an end to the flow of new impressions, of new data. Cleopatra's infinite variety has been by death made finite.

We leave the theatre satisfied. But by the time we arrive home that satisfaction may already begin to look illusory, as the ambiguity reasserts itself. As the play recedes in time, the moment of Cleopatra's death will lose the exaggerated empha-sis position gives it; her death will come to seem only one moment among many, all equal, all requiring explanation, all to be assimilated into our definition. What is more, we may come to feel that the moment of death is of all moments the least useful for interpretation, for we can only understand her motives then if we have understood the whole of her character, when it reaches that final moment; we may decide, as some have done with Cleopatra and Othello, that the final change of manner is false, is bombast. Thus the pursuit of meaning begins all over again. The satisfaction at play's end is no more and no less real, no more and no less legitimate, than the subsequent dissatisfaction. Both are part of the total response the play stimulates; neither is right or wrong. Here we can only recognize the inevitable progress of our responses, and its causes. For instance, we can recognize that in the final speeches of Cleopatra and Othello either the author or the character is trying to manipulate our responses, and that we have no way to determine which. We can also recognize that, though our first encounter with the play stimulates the second, that second experience is a directed and motivated encounter, liable to distortion for that very reason.

Viola is less difficult to interpret, and she also illustrates the kind of satisfaction Shakespeare grants us, even while avoiding final definition. The exposed layering of her personality lets us appreciate most of her motives instantaneously. Because we know Viola's interior, we know at once, and without reflection, why she speaks as she does to Olivia or Orsino, and therefore we feel that Shakespeare motivates his people continually and in depth. Insights into human cause and effect concentrate themselves into single sentences. Viola's 'Whoe'er I woo, myself would be his wife', like Brutus's 'Portia is dead', releases in an instant all the pleasures of perception, vistas of meaning in retrospect, which lesser playwrights dilute and draw out over whole scenes.

But, though Shakespeare has always been recognized as a master of characterization, the very issue of motivation has, oddly enough, proved a recurrent stumbling-block for academic critics. 'In no department of Shakespeare's art do we find such irregularity as in his dealing with the motives for action.'[23] In the examination of motives, certain simple rules of logic can be brought to bear; these rules seem to offer us a law (like the law of perspective) which can be used to measure the artist's adherence to or violation of the nature of the real. The application of these logical rules has therefore been a popular, though seldom fruitful, approach to character. It has been seldom fruitful, because Shakespeare's characters remain convincing, despite these undeniable logical inconsistencies, and so we can only deduce that audiences do not notice them. (This is another reason for the failure of psychoanalysis in interpretation: it depends upon locating and explaining contradictions which audiences in fact never even see.)

Microscopically examined, Viola's motives are more often than not specious. Why Viola disguises herself Shakespeare never explains.[24] Barnabe Riche, in Shakespeare's source, did give an explanation; Shakespeare omits it. No motive can alter the absurdity of the postulate of disguise, therefore any motive would be inadequate, and call attention to its own inadequacy; since the motive lies outside the play proper anyway, it will (as Aristotle saw) be forgotten or forgiven. Shakespeare 'study'd more to work up great and moving Circumstances to place his chief Characters in, so as to affect our Passions strongly; he applied himself more to this than he did to the Means or Methods whereby he brought his Character into those Circumstances'.[25] Shakespeare does not want any creaking of plot in I.ii, Viola's first scene, or want to begin his story before the shipwreck and so turn it into the rambling *Cymbeline*-thing Riche made of it. Viola in male company (sailors, no less) can hardly say, as Julia does, 'I would prevent / The loose encounters of lascivious men'. Besides, if Viola has too good a reason for disguising herself, she perpetrates a practical joke on all Illyria, thus becoming a female Toby and not the helpless victim of circumstance Shakespeare intends.

For these and perhaps other reasons Shakespeare does not supply Viola with a credible motive. But he must convince us that he has supplied one.

> O that I serv'd that lady,
> And might not be deliver'd to the world
> Till I had made mine own occasion mellow
> What my estate is.

Indeed, serving Olivia would make more sense than becoming a man to serve the Duke, and, since this talk of Olivia soon comes to nothing, we do not scrutinize too closely her motives here. When ten lines later she without warning announces, 'I'll serve this Duke', we automatically apply this earlier explanation, as though Olivia and Orsino were interchangeable. The mere fact she would have preferred Olivia makes her choice seem only a last resort. But even that earlier speech, of course, explains precious little, beyond 'I have a reason'. But this vague affirmation suffices, because the Captain presumably knows what she means. This makes her allusiveness seem only natural – more natural than a long explanation, for our sakes, of what he knows already (an absurdity all too familiar to audiences). Viola implies that her reasons will be gone into in detail later, and, though as it happens no clarification ever comes, its promise sates for the moment our curiosity, which will soon be too engrossed elsewhere to mind Shakespeare's default on this promise. And we shall also not notice – for reasons I shall try to explain in the next chapter – that Viola, who here asks the Captain to present her 'as an eunuch' to Orsino, is evidently *not* a eunuch by the end of Act I, when Olivia falls in love with 'him'. It is more immediately plausible for a woman to disguise herself as a eunuch than as a man; but later the eunuch notion, having served its immediate purpose, becomes an inconvenience, and so simply disappears.

Viola next agrees, though already in love with Orsino herself, to go woo Olivia for him. Were her motives elaborated, she would look stupid or culpable, and the postulate of the plot nonsense. Julia in similar circumstances in *The Two Gentlemen of Verona* does soliloquize her motives at length; she and the play suffer for it. Viola instead agrees to Orsino's request before we have any inkling she loves him; we are thus unconscious of the absurdity when it occurs, and, when Viola does reveal her feelings, the perception of past motives and the delicious irony and the promise of entertainment flood over us at once, drowning doubt. Then, before reason can recover, she leaves, and remains off stage until she arrives in Olivia's presence. By then the decision has been made *de facto*; it recedes into a necessary given, though neither audience nor character has had an opportunity to debate the choices. The promise of entertainment so brilliantly fulfilled in the scene with Olivia short-circuits further thought. Shakespeare does not prove that Viola's love was strong enough to motivate such sacrifice; instead, her willingness to woo for Orsino itself implies the magnitude of her devotion and obedience. Instead of the motive justifying the act, the act proves the motive.

Upon the evidence of a ring churlishly delivered, Viola concludes that Olivia loves her. When Malvolio, on much better evidence, leaps to such conclusions, we laugh at him. Viola's deduction here seems unexceptionable and even admirable only because we know it's true, as we know Malvolio's deductions are false. 'The poet quite naïvely exchanges the point of view of the speaker for that of the audience.'[26] The assertion of naïveté is entirely unjustified, and blatantly prejudicial; worse, Schücking regards as a fault what should be considered a virtue. For the dramatist, like the painter, must create the illusion of reality through an inherently artificial medium. Schücking rebukes Shakespeare for the limitations of the medium, instead of praising the ingenuity which surmounts them.

In the same soliloquy Viola decides to continue her disguise, though by discarding it she could both spare Olivia pain and make herself eligible for Orsino's love. Shakespeare obscures the absurdity of this decision by denying it's a decision at all. Viola says 'How will this fadge?' and 'What will become of this?', but never 'What shall I do?' The form of the questions implies the eventual answer: waiting, rather than action. Meanwhile, she says nothing of her original motives for the disguise, thereby preventing an audience from questioning whether her new reasons for discarding it outweigh her old ones for assuming it.

> How will this fadge? My master loves her dearly,
> And I, poor monster, fond as much on him,
> And she, mistaken, seems to dote on me.
> What will become of this? As I am man,
> My state is desperate for my master's love;
> As I am woman (now alas the day!),
> What thriftless sighs shall poor Olivia breathe?

The contrast between 'As I am man' and 'As I am woman' creates a false dilemma, making both alternatives seem equally disastrous and equally a matter of choice. In fact she *is* a woman, not a man; in fact her love for Orsino must outweigh her sympathy for Olivia; in fact Olivia would be best served by being told the truth. But the parallel clauses hopelessly complicate and bewilder anything so simple as a fact.

My last and most complex example concerns an inconsistency of motive discussed at length by Bertrand Evans. Viola in Act III guesses that Antonio has mistaken her for Sebastian, but when in Act V we next see her she does not 'disabuse the tormented fellow' Antonio, or extricate herself by explaining that all Illyria has mistaken her for her brother. For Evans, to say that Shakespeare would 'sacrifice plausibility in order to . . . achieve a spectacular denouement' is 'a damning answer',[27] and he prefers to deduce motives for Viola's silence. To all of this T. M. Craik rightly replies that plausibility need not require consistency, and that in the theatre no one notices.[28] But audiences do not deposit their brains in the cloakroom; they notice readily enough absurdities in other plays, and so, if Shakespeare seems despite these inconsistencies not only plausible but uniquely and intensely real, that plausibility has been achieved, not handed him free when he stepped into the Globe. The inconsistencies have been called carelessness; they seem to me the products of great care, for each solves a serious dramatic problem, and each has been painstakingly concealed.

The contradiction exists. Why?

The contradiction goes unnoticed. Why?

Shakespeare does not want Viola to seem to know about Sebastian in Act V because, if she knows and tells, she deflates a joke five acts in the making, but, if she knows and doesn't tell, she seems intentionally cruel. But Shakespeare could have prevented her from guessing the secret earlier: Antonio in Act III needn't have named Sebastian, or been so explicit. *The Comedy of Errors* fills five acts with mistaken identities, and no one catches on until the end; our sensibilities would not be unduly shocked if the very first such encounter in *Twelfth Night* caused only blank amazement. But one need only cut Viola's soliloquy, to see how much the play would lose by its absence.

Methinks his words do from such passion fly
That he believes himself; so do not I.
Prove true, imagination, O prove true,
That I, dear brother, be now ta'en for you!

He nam'd Sebastian. I my brother know
Yet living in my glass: even such and so
In favour was my brother, and he went
Still in this fashion, colour, ornament,
For him I imitate. O if it prove,
Tempests are kind, and salt waves fresh in love!

The soliloquy strongly confirms Viola's intuition and intelligence. She will be absent for all of Act IV, and this provides her with a powerful and memorable exit. It sounds again the brother theme, which her first appearance had given a full sustained chord, but which we have since heard only briefly (if at all) in her scene with Orsino. This is her only chance before the reunion to express love and longing for Sebastian, and Viola's wonder in the recognition here anticipates a major emotional chord. Many of Sebastian's speeches in Act IV will echo and elaborate this emotion, until in the final scene these feelings join and reverberate in a moment intense and convincing partly because so intensely and convincingly prepared. Viola's anticipation also allows her an advantage over Sebastian when they do meet, so that they may react differently to the recognition.

Viola's speech is essential to the emotional structure of the play. As for the logical contradiction it creates in Act V, Evans himself says that Viola cannot know 'of one fact', Olivia's marriage, and that this ignorance explains her initial caution. But Viola seems more ignorant than such a summary suggests. She does not know any of what we saw in Act IV; she does not know Antonio is Orsino's enemy; she cannot know whether Aguecheek's accusations are true, or only another trick. On her last appearance she was thoroughly duped (for the first and only time) by Toby, and bewildered by Antonio. More, Orsino has now decided to see Olivia himself; he disregards Viola's pleas for Antonio; he soon accuses her of being 'the instrument / That screws me from my true place' in Olivia's favour. Since Orsino has been her chief friend and chief goal, Viola must now seem more helpless and dependent

than ever. Logically she still knows all she needs to unravel
the play, but beset by such confusions she will seem hopelessly misinformed and vulnerable. The repeated interruption of
one incident by another reinforces this impression of uncontrollable concatenations of event. As in her soliloquy in Act
II, confusion seem motive enough for inaction, especially
since Viola has by now a habit of helplessness, a pattern of
passivity. Her speech in Act III hardly commands the forefront of our conscious thought anyway, since she has been off
stage for 246 lines, silent another forty-seven, and in that
interval hardly mentioned. When Sebastian does arrive, she at
once understands, reveals and answers while he questions,
wonders, gapes and exclaims, so that, at the one moment
when her earlier speech most comes to mind, she does not
contradict it.

I have avoided a possible and popular reply to Evans, that
in conventional comic conclusions we will swallow even
elephantine absurdities. I have avoided it because we notice
those absurdities before we swallow them, and in Viola's case
we do not even notice. If we did, the contradiction would be a
fault, because Shakespeare does not exploit it, and conventional comic conclusions succeed by calling loud attention to
their own absurdity. Conventions may like all else be clumsily
or adroitly used. For instance, the standard theatrical jokes
about a boy become a girl become a boy find no place in
Twelfth Night, whose heroine is too modest and chaste to
entertain or survive such reflections. Her asides don't mock or
undermine others, as comic asides conventionally do. She has
three soliloquies (which contribute to her intimacy with the
audience and isolation from the cast, especially since they are
in essence long asides, in which she openly talks things over
with us), but she has no soliloquy expressing her love for
Orsino (which would relieve the impression of restrained feeling central to her part). Shakespeare applies conventions dis-
criminatingly.

Some earlier critics objected to the conventions themselves,
regardless of their application. If we no longer believe that
soliloquies and asides 'shatter the illusion', it is because we
consider the illusion a rather more flexible, fluctuating,
evanescent thing. But we could also reply that the conventions
themselves are not necessarily or entirely artificial. There
are, in the real world, asides, spoken or unspoken, so that,

when Viola speaks an aside to the audience, she creates a relationship with us, which we have experienced in other contexts, and so find natural. After all, we are real and palpable people, that woman on stage is a real and palpable person, so that, when she is left alone with us, why shouldn't she turn and tell us what she thinks of the man who's just left? After Malvolio has delivered the ring, why shouldn't she do what we may have done, when overcome by confusions: stop, try to organize, to think through, to disentangle, the complications? Of course, we should probably do so silently – though, when really confused, most people resort to thinking out loud, decorum permitting. But let us grant, for the moment, that it would be more realistic if Viola thought silently, in this case. In the context of her relationship with the audience, that would in fact seem unnatural. She's alone with us, we're friends, we understand her difficulties – why isn't she talking to us? Or let us suppose she spoke out loud, but pretended the audience wasn't there. That would seem even more artificial, because, deprived of the justification of a relationship, it becomes apparent that her words are simply a dramatic convenience, to tell us what she's thinking. A character's relation with the audience is like any other relationship in a play: it both enlivens the character, and places limits on the range of his or her behaviour, in any given situation.

Of Viola's recourses to convention, only one might be thought uncharacteristic: her soliloquy on Feste – indeed, her whole dialogue with him – where she transparently expresses Shakespeare's theme or plays straight man to Feste's vaudeville clown. Here presumably we have an example of the tendency Schücking descried, for characters to lose their unity for a scene or part of one.[29] In performance or undirected reading, I enjoyed this scene; when first I examined it with an eye to character, I was inclined to fault it; if it occurred early in the play I might fault it still, as Champion faults Helena's first encounter with Parolles.[30] But in its place the scene adds rather than subtracts, because the play has already established Viola's wit; because her soliloquy and aside draw upon and cement her special relation with the audience; because the scene throws together, for comparison and contrast, two characters who are both in a sense outsiders, and both sympathetic; because Viola here praises Feste as she has praised others; and because, by making her the mouthpiece of authorial wisdom, Shakespeare here draws upon and reinforces our sense of her intelligence and sensitivity. For the rest, her behaviour is not so much uncharacteristic as acharacteristic. But late in a play material otherwise neutral may take colour from its surroundings; late in a play we will accept, as just another part of a complex and unfolding whole, actions which earlier would only have disoriented us.

The importance of a scene's position in the play is obvious enough to be often overlooked. Toward the end, Viola's self overcomes her disguise, and she speaks uncomplicatedly in the first person, or deals in rather straightforward ironies. In her scenes with Olivia in Act III, especially the second, the differences between role and self grow unsubtle and broad, seldom reflecting intensities of personality, until in the duel with Aguecheek her womanhood is food for laughs, no more. The discrepancies on the level of plot between Viola and Cesario broaden rapidly, while the layering of mind collapses into a simpler unity, until in Act V there are two Violas, one the calumniated public image as far as possible from fact, the other private and whole and true. Deliberately Shakespeare weans us from character; he must. Viola's great moments with Orsino and Olivia are duets, which enforce attention to personalities, but for the last scene variety which has been temporal must become spatial, the multiplicities of four acts must be fitted into one scene, into an ensemble, where any one figure or event competes for interest with a mélange of others. Consequently character becomes impressionistic, personality must funnel itself into spotlighted moments of speech or business, which steal attention briefly but emphatically. How we interpret or perform these last lightning flashes of character will much alter our understanding of the play, but at just these moments ambiguity grows most insistent, for to their interpretation we bring as never before too much and too little evidence: too little, for the competing claims of until-now discrete interests forbid the elaboration and reinforcement clarity would require; too much, because the whole play now is evidence. All play long we look forward; at play's end comes an about-face. What we see there will depend increasingly on what we thought important earlier, and each memory will come differently equipped. The playwright can and must control emphases, but the better the play the fiercer the competition between interests, and the more depends upon the final scene. In *The Two Gentlemen of Verona* Shakespeare notoriously did not solve these problems; in *Twelfth Night*, as in *Hamlet*, he famously did.

On top of the difficulties of all endings the plot of this play must now pay for its absurdity. Jonson said that he had never adapted Plautus's *Amphitrio* because he could not find actors who were identical twins.[31] But most audiences are willing, for two hours of pleasure, to wink at an absurd minute. Shakespeare like all great poets elects the implausible. What's plausible's inconspicuous. The implausible *means*, it allows contrast and emphasis, it challenges belief; by a confessed absurdity, the author can acknowledge the fragility of his illusion, and he can do so at a moment of *his* choosing, so that the admission itself delights us, and is never turned into reason's weapon, to bludgeon the poor poet.

At that implausible moment of recognition, Shakespeare provides a styled and formal wonder, which is among other things a means of concealing the obvious – for the reader, who does not see the physical contradiction, will take the words for truth, and the audience which does see responds communally, and so may be the more profoundly swept up in wonder than any cool and solitary reader. Our inevitable twinkle of disbelief is simply absorbed in the mood of the moment – for the characters too are incredulous. Only the Malvolios in the audience will cavil at the inescapable inadequacy of performance: Jonson might as well complain that he never wrote tragedies, because he could never find enough actors who would actually kill themselves on stage.

Few readers and fewer audiences have objected to the contradictions noted by Evans and Jonson, but many, myself among them, have been disturbed by Orsino's offer of marriage, coming as it does so indecently upon the heels of his offer of murder. This discomfort is a fact; nothing I have yet said can deny it. Though the acceleration of the plot does tend to slight complexities of character, it actually increases interest in Orsino, because we know he must here change – and change radically. His prominence and Viola's virtual disappearance from the beginning of Act V confirm and encourage this interest. His threats disturb us because even as he speaks them we know he must in a moment marry Viola, and so the contradiction strikes us not only later when he does change, but now, when we know he must, and see the distance to be travelled. Postponing his proposal till after Malvolio's exit thus would not solve the problem. Such postponement, though more probable in life, would in the play be less convincing, as what probability the change has depends upon proximity to wonder. (Placing the Malvolio sequence after the reconciliation has, besides, two great advantages: it juxtaposes Malvolio with a stage full of happy and united characters, and it separates the realignments from the end of the play, so that we do not leave the theatre with an implausibility in mind – as we do in *All's Well that Ends Well*.)

Orsino differs from Viola in being a character who must change his mind in order for the expected denouement to be achieved: he illustrates a problem in development, not depth. Orsino, Demetrius in *A Midsummer Night's Dream*, Prince Hal, Shylock, Bertram, Claudio, Posthumus, Iachimo, Cymbeline: the audience realizes during the play that each must change, willingly or under pressure, before play's end, and surely it is not coincidence that of these characters so many have so often been called failures. Each attracts particular attention, a directed interest in how the required change will be brought about. Thus each presented Shakespeare with a similar technical problem, which he solved, or failed to solve, in a variety of ways. With Demetrius, Shakespeare achieved the only change in character actually required by his plot in the midst of so many others which were not required, and through the agency of a supernatural machinery so vastly disproportionate to its function that the change in Demetrius seems merely one among many instances of the universal law of inconstancy – and Demetrius is, of all these characters, the one whose change of heart has not been faulted. This might seem odd, because in his case the only explanation given by the plot is a supernatural one (magic potion), which we are unlikely to credit. But, as in Greek tragedy, the supernatural gloss is only a diagnosis of actions actually observable in human behaviour, so that, even when we do not accept the diagnosis, we can grant the credibility of the behaviour itself.[32] With Prince Hal, Shakespeare by anticipating the change does make it credible, but in doing so opens the character to charges (intended, or not?) of insincerity and coldness. With

Shylock, Shakespeare motivates the change by putting so much pressure on the man that his yielding immediately convinces us – but at the same time the very magnitude of that pressure elicits our sympathy, and if that sympathy becomes excessive it will invariably produce a backlash of antipathy for Shylock's 'persecutors', the hero and heroine. Even if the reaction does not go so far, in the process of making Shylock credible Shakespeare has made him more interesting, perhaps, than the beautiful platitudes of Belmont. Because Shylock is forced to change, though he alters his actions one need not believe he alters his nature. But in cases of love the audience must believe that the character has indeed altered his nature, an alteration far more difficult to make convincing; hence Claudio and Bertram, both supreme examples of Shakespeare's structural cunning – for, if he convinces us of the change of heart, he will have succeeded, and, if he doesn't convince us, he will also have succeeded, showing us how hollow these conversions (and these men) are.

Orsino's alteration is far more convincing than either of theirs, and indeed it must be. Earlier in the play, Shakespeare undermines the substantiality of Orsino's love for Olivia, and establishes a 'drift' toward Viola. But this creates two problems, which only the final scene can solve: the drift must be accelerated, and Orsino must be forced to abandon his hollow public posture (in which he has invested so much pride), by acknowledging the change which has already taken place inside him. But, because Shakespeare's illusion of plausibility is achieved, as we have seen, through the subtle manipulation of details, it is in some danger of being obscured by misinterpretation or misperformance of trifles, especially in the last scene, where such impressions or misimpressions matter so much.

Orsino and Olivia do not until this scene meet face to face. When they do, Orsino's own reaction is surprisingly perfunctory:[33]

Here comes the Countess: now Heaven walks on earth.
– But for thee, fellow: fellow, thy words are madness . . .

Orsino has, after all, been waiting for this moment since the first lines of the play, yet when it comes he seems almost embarrassed by it; certainly, his mind quickly turns away from it. Olivia's attitude toward him exacerbates this real but initially unobtrusive confusion. She first ignores him for his servant's sake, then says,

> If it be aught to the old tune, my lord,
> It is as fat and fulsome to mine ear
> As howling after music.

This cannot be excused or explained as a misunderstanding, as can most of the nastiness in this scene. She treats Orsino more harshly than she did her own servant Feste: she is curt, vulgar, brutal and rude. To Olivia's other denials Orsino has responded confidently, but here for the first time he shows intense pain (more than a 'sweet pang').

> *Orsino*. Still so cruel?
> *Olivia*. Still so constant, lord.
> *Orsino*. What, to perverseness? You uncivil lady,
>   To whose ingrate and unauspicious altars
>   My soul the faithfull'st off'rings have breathed out
>   That e'er devotion tendered – what shall I do?

But the asyndeton of despair in 'what shall I do?' elicits from Olivia only a flippant 'Even what it please my lord, that shall become him' (i.e., do whatever you like).

If Olivia's rudeness and Orsino's astonishment are played only for laughs – as they easily can be – Orsino's bewilderment and pain will not be noticed, and the consequences of this omission will be particularly serious because editors and time have conspired to obscure the agony and bluster of Orsino's central speech, immediately after.

> Why should I not, had I the heart to do it,
> Like to th'Egyptian thief, at point of death
> Kill what I love? A savage jealousy,
> That sometime savours nobly. But hear me this:
> Since you to non-regardance cast my faith,
> And that I partly know the instrument
> That screws me from my true place in your favour,
> Live you the marble-breasted tyrant still –
> But this your minion, whom I know you love,
> And whom, by heaven I swear, I tender dearly,

Him will I tear out of that cruel eye
Where he sits crowned in his master's spite.
Come, boy, with me. My thoughts are ripe in mischief.
I'll sacrifice the lamb that I do love,
To spite a raven's heart within a dove.

The bluster, which sounds first in 'Had I the heart to do it',
recurs in the allusion to Thamyris, and in what I have
always considered an allusion to Abraham and Isaac ('I'll
sacrifice the lamb that I do love', 'Come boy with me',
'And whom, by heaven I swear, I tender dearly'). Helio-
dorus was not only popular reading but a major source of
Elizabethan dramatic plots, which makes it likely that a
significant minority of Shakespeare's audience would have
realized that the Egyptian thief – who is meaningless to
modern audiences – did *not* kill his love. Neither did
Abraham (another allusion a modern audience is much
less likely to catch than an Elizabethan one). Our ignorance of or inattention to these allusions has also obscured
their equation of feeling. Orsino contemplates whether to
kill what he loves, then resolves to kill – Viola, calling her
'the lamb that I do love' 'whom, by heaven I swear, I
tender dearly'.[34] Orsino's agony has also fallen victim to
the itch to repunctuate the Folio, from 'Like to th'Egyptian thief, at point of death / Kill what I love' to 'Like to
th'Egyptian thief at point of death, / Kill what I love'. It
makes some difference whether Orsino or the Egyptian
intends to die. Likewise, to change the Folio's 'And
whom, by heaven I swear, I tender dearly' into 'And
whom, by heaven, I swear I tender dearly', diminishes a
conscious oath into something close to common interjection.
Viola replies to Orsino with two speeches.

And I must jocund, apt, and willingly,
To do you rest, a thousand deaths would die.

After him I love
More than I love these eyes, more than my life,
More by all mores, than e'er I shall love wife.
If I do feign, you witnesses above
Punish my life, for tainting of my love.

Orsino in the theatre must react to these her most transparent and passionate confessions of her love. Even to ignore her is to react. I find it hard to believe that these speeches should leave him wholly unmoved, or that he does not understand them. His first words after hearing them are 'Come, away'. Editors have disguised the neutrality of this line by interpolating an exclamation, or a stage direction *'To Viola'*. But whether he speaks only to Viola or to his whole train, and his tone of voice in doing so, will fundamentally alter his meaning, and our interpretation of his character. The words themselves may express either his determination to kill her, or a weary and confused collapse of will. How ambiguous the phrase is Olivia tells us.

> *Orsino.* Come, away.
> *Olivia.* Whither, my lord?

In the theatre Olivia's is a potentially laughable question, but it does I think confirm the ambiguity of Orsino's words, for the audience and for the on-stage characters.

If we interpret the scene in this way, Orsino's threat becomes not a contradiction but a barometer of his feeling for Viola, and his own pain excuses him from any excess.[35] Orsino then contributes to the same pattern as Antonio, Olivia, Viola, Toby and Aguecheek, for the beginning of Act V seethes with bitterness, the sense of betrayal being a measure of the intensity of love and commitment. Wonder requires the energies of pain.

Orsino's characterization may legitimately be judged by how well Shakespeare handles the development required by his plot; one measures the achievement against the function. But such a standard will not serve Viola. She maintains her status among Shakespeare's women not for any development, but for her constancy, and chiefly for two scenes, one with Olivia (I.v), the other with Orsino (II.iv). Any full account of the power and pleasure of either scene would take a chapter in itself, for that power and pleasure involve much more than Viola, my immediate subject; but *some* account of these scenes is essential. We remember characters not for their aver-

age but for their best, and Shakespeare makes their best triumphant. Every device I have yet mentioned for animating
character Shakespeare employs in these scenes, though elsewhere Viola (or any character) must subsist on a few. Both are
duets, duets between characters carefully established in
advance, whom we expect to see together. But nothing
happens, really, in either scene; nothing is allowed to distract
from the dance of personality. Drama approaches lyric.
Characters of course speak verse often in this play, but usually
an elegant verse without pressure of feeling or thought, where
rhythm may please but does not enchant. These two scenes
are easily the most musical, emotionally and intellectually the
most abstract, in the play. The first is about falling in love, the
second about staying there.

Viola and Olivia meet – a thing normally banal, but potentially profound. There are in Shakespeare many reunions and
recognitions, but few meetings, and no other scene which so
telescopes into one encounter this deepening and persistent
exploration of one another.

The honourable lady of the house, which is she?

Your will?

Whence came you, sir?

Are you a comedian?

Are you the lady of the house?

What are you? What would you?

Have you no more to say?

Good madam, let me see your face.

Have you any commission from your lord to negotiate with
my face?

Were you sent hither to praise me?

Why, what would you?

What is your parentage?

They seek privacy, they undress their minds, they begin spontaneously to put off their social selves, to reveal their heart of
hearts. They discuss what they enact, love and what makes
love: beauty, pity, procreation, chaste and ideal communion,
causeless inclination. Viola comes to put Olivia in love with
Orsino, so we watch the stages of Olivia's behaviour intently.
Even so, the full meaning and pattern of the scene probably
only strike us when she's alone, when they strike her. Then
the pattern of events we had sensed imperfectly before rises
into consciousness, as in order to retrieve Cesario Olivia sends
the same messenger she had before sent to dismiss him.[36]
Olivia falls in love before our eyes; Viola has fallen in love
already, off stage, in the interim between scenes ii and iv. But,
because we know so little about Viola's love, because her
couplet aside told us only enough to intrigue us, we watch her
in this scene as closely as we watch Olivia, for expressions of
the growth and nature of her feelings. All that she says in
Orsino's behalf we interpret as evidence of her love, not his.
This in turn helps explain Olivia's own reaction: for she too
responds to the messenger, not the message.

Harold Jenkins has observed that this scene subverts old
romantic forms – letter, portrait, ring – transforming them
into symbols less stylized and newly individual: Viola does
not deliver but enacts the message; Olivia's portrait is her face;
she returns a ring never delivered.[37] Each of these transformations mocks the convention, and through such literary criticism of artifice Shakespeare authenticates the natural spontaneity of his own scene (as the Mousetrap authenticates
Hamlet). Thus, in unveiling her own face Olivia calls conscious attention to, and mocks, the portrait convention, and at
scene's end she uses the rejected ring to communicate the very
opposite of its conventional meaning. Whether or not we are
so conscious of Viola as a living letter, the scene does allow
Olivia to have a dialogue with a love-letter, to mock the
artifice of its language and of its whole function as intermediary in a transaction which permits none.

But though in one sense Shakespeare mocks these romantic
conventions, in another, by a kind of etymological demonstra-

tion, he resurrects the meaning fossilized in them. Olivia uses the ring because she cannot bring herself to articulate her feelings more openly. Orsino sends a messenger as a rehearsed, perfected image of himself – but one capable of a certain necessary rudeness, which he would not permit himself; though the premeditation of this projected image of himself may be condemned as insincere, it is itself a gesture of respect and love, expressing a desire to please, to make himself worthy, and Olivia is rude to mock that effort. In *The Two Gentlemen of Verona*, Proteus, denied Sylvia's 'substance', asks for her 'shadow', a picture (IV.ii). By speaking of her own face as a portrait, Olivia reminds us that it too is just a shadow of her inner self, that many women's faces are as 'painted' and artificial as a portrait, that for all its beauty 'this present' is transitory and will fade, never to be recaptured, unless by art. But the dialogue also reminds us that poets first spoke of their mistresses as paintings because they could only express such beauty in terms of a work of art, the artist God. And Olivia's reference to the convention is, like her use of the ring, an attempt to shelter her boldness under the forms of decorum: for the point is that she shows Cesario not the shadow (a portrait), but the actual and precious substance (her face). In doing so she breaks her vow, and gives the servant more than she would grant the master.

Just as the scene deflates and then reanimates these romantic conventions, so too it mocks, then powerfully and freshly reasserts, the conventions of love's poetry. To Olivia goes most of the mockery; it is Viola who defends the imagery of romantic love.

> Make me a willow cabin at your gate,
> And call upon my soul within the house;
> Write loyal cantons of contemned love,
> And sing them loud even in the dead of night;
> Halloo your name to the reverberate hills,
> And make the babbling gossip of the air
> Cry out, 'Olivia!' O, you should not rest
> Between the elements of earth and air,
> But you should pity me.

This speech is the formal summit of the scene, just as Viola's other great speech climaxes the other great scene, as her love-in-an-aside ends the first dialogue with Orsino, and as in Act III, when she and Olivia trade vows, Viola's comes last. Her soliloquy caps and abstracts the dialogue with Feste; her realizing that Antonio took her for Sebastian is the formal and emotional resolution of the long duel scene. Sebastian at the end questions, she replies, she finalizes the recognition; Sebastian turns to Olivia before the Duke turns to Viola, so that of the four lovers she has pride of place; the play's last spoken words Orsino speaks to her. So simply does Shakespeare magnify a character who speaks only 325 lines – as simply, indeed, as he magnified Brutus in the assassination scene – while, even as he does so, her place so often at the end of things makes her seem always to respond not initiate.

How Shakespeare focuses our attention upon one character rather than another is a question any satisfactory model of his plays must eventually answer. If we all agree that Viola is 'more interesting' and 'more important' than Sebastian, and that consequently we pay her more attention than him, then we have the beginnings of a hierarchy of attentions, and we can study how such hierarchies are constructed. Most questions of interpretation boil down to questions of attention, depending as they do on what we are watching at any given moment; and the variety of theatrical enactments depends upon a subtle (or not-so-subtle) reordering of this structure of attention, in ways sometimes legitimate and sometimes not. Likewise, Shakespeare's success in concealing contradictions depends upon his ability, like the magician, to distract our attention at the crucial moment (as he did in the transition from street to Capital, in the assassination scene).

Of these two great scenes of poetry and character, only Viola appears in both. After we know she loves him and before he knows, only once do we see Viola with Orsino, and of this scene they speak only half (sixty-six lines) to each other: a fleeting stillness boisterously preceded by Toby and company, then interrupted by Feste. During the first half, we know Feste will soon come, and Feste when he comes can hardly be made to leave. He looses upon Orsino our irritation, which Viola cannot express but which the scene must somehow relieve without disturbing their intimacy. Their second colloquy begins inevitably with Olivia, and will end with Olivia.

We know by now Orsino has no chance with her; we know

Sebastian waits in the wings, Olivia's happy ending person-
ified, when once the characters fall into their proper order,
like digits in a slot machine. We therefore know Orsino by
play's end must love Viola. She told Olivia she would 'Make
me a willow cabin at your gate', and call and sing and write
and halloo and cry out, were she in love; but she does not.
Though we naturally apply Feste's song to Viola's feelings,
she does not express those feelings, and never fully does
express them, even to us.[38] Viola will not speak, Orsino cannot see. The gap between what she knows and what he knows
seems, as in Chekhov, to express the unrelieved and necessary
isolation of each individual. Seeing the breach between
them, wanting it healed, we are unnaturally sensitive to the
least movement toward a communion of soul, and in this
sensitivity we are like Viola herself, like every lover in that
suspense of feeling where he desperately seeks evidence of a
mutuality of emotion, himself knowing that he may (as
Malvolio does) see what is not there, see only what he wants to
see, so that he cannot trust even his own eyes, for fear self-
interest has corrupted them. We can never be sure quite how
much or just where in this scene Orsino's feelings begin to
shift. Characteristically, Viola never tells us that she sounds or
searches Orsino, but, because Shakespeare manipulates us
into doing so, we unthinkingly attribute our feelings and our
thoughts to her, as we unthinkingly apply Feste's song. Again
the structure of the scene asserts her modesty and self-distrust.
At scene's end, when she cuts off the conversation, we may
assume she does so because she sees no sign of reciprocity –
though we by then surely do.

Any adequate theory of characterization must be able to
account for and describe failure as well as success: those who
praise everything cheapen the value of their praise. Therefore,
because I may seem to have dismissed the validity of the usual
criticisms of Shakespeare's characters, let me now briefly turn
my attention to some characters whose construction we may
legitimately and usefully fault.

Such a character as Julia, in *The Two Gentlemen of Verona*,
can be criticized chiefly for the absence or underdevelopment

of certain enlivening qualities we have seen in Viola's characterization: it is not that there is anything positively or blatantly *wrong*, but that from moment to moment there is less fullness, less specific life.[39] Most dramatic characters fail to
achieve greatness for this reason and this reason alone.

John Ford's *The Lovers* (or *Lovers'*, or *Lover's*) *Melancholy*,
written in 1627–8, offers a particularly instructive example of
such failure. Like Viola, the character Eroclea in Ford's play
spends most of her time in disguise as a young man, 'Parthenophil'; like Viola, she secretly loves the ruler of the country,
but cannot reveal her feelings; like Viola, she has the misfor-
tune to attract the instant amatory devotions of another
woman (Thamasta), a 'proud' young lady who spurns the love
of Eroclea's master (Menaphon), for whom Eroclea has been
sent to plead; like Viola, as a result of these unwanted attentions she eventually finds herself being denounced by her
master, as an ingrateful rival. Yet from these very similar
materials Ford creates a wholly uninteresting, unmemorable,
unconvincing character.

Parthenophil/Eroclea's introduction consists of an unbe-
lievable long narrative of his/her (secretly observed) musical
competition, off stage, with a nightingale; this contest ends
with the nightingale dying from shame, after 'Parthenophil'
defeats her: 'for grief down dropped she on his lute, / And
broke her heart', after which 'It was the greatest sadness / To
see the conqueror [Parthenophil] upon her hearse / To weep a
funeral elegy of tears.' Thamasta then falls in love with this
youth upon their first meeting – which also takes place off
stage. Parthenophil/Eroclea thus speaks his/her first words on
stage late in scene iii: 'Not any, lady' (in answer to whether
s/he has seen in his travels anything better than the off-stage
garden s/he has just visited). During the remainder of the
scene s/he speaks twice (each time, again, in answer to
Thamasta):

> Great princess, I am well. To see a league
> Between an humble love, such as my friend's is,
> And a commanding virtue, such as yours is,
> Are sure restoratives.

> You're all composed of fairness and true beauty.

The dramatic dullness of these utterances rivals their verbal vapidity: the character makes no impression by what s/he says or does, or how s/he interacts with the others on stage. This unimpressive presence undermines all the discursive praise of the character we have already heard, and disappoints all the expectations those praises roused. Moreover, Ford has as yet given the audience no hint that the young man 'Parthenophil' is in fact a young woman, Eroclea, and the Jacobean convention by which boys played women's parts would have given the audience no physical clue to the character's true gender; consequently, Ford has made no use of the disparity between appearance and reality, though at the end of Act I his plot has reached a point almost identical to Shakespeare's at the end of his Act I. In particular, because we do not see Eroclea before she puts on her male disguise, we are not conscious of her nervously assuming maleness: Ford's plot does not encourage us to attend to Eroclea/Parthenophil's performance, as we do attend to Viola's.

At the beginning of Act II another narrative, by Rhetias, presumably alerts most members of the audience to the strong presumption that 'Parthenophil' is in fact a woman. This creates considerable interest in the character's first encounter with Palador (Eroclea's eventual Orsino); but this encounter, like his/her first appearance, occurs on a stage crowded with other characters, and s/he speaks only once:

> All the powers
> That sentinel just thrones double their guards
> About your sacred excellence!

Ford instead focuses attention on Palador's distraction. 'Parthenophil' speaks more in the remainder of the scene, when she is kept behind by Thamasta's lady-in-waiting (Kala). She briefly answers three questions, then – on hearing an ambiguous proposal – she tries to excuse herself politely. These few speeches are immediately intelligible in themselves, and an audience which has guessed 'Parthenophil's' secret will sense a deeper motive in what a performer could easily convey as distracted impatience ('Yet, pray, be brief'), and in her 'unsettled thoughts' when trying to excuse herself, after the proposal. However, when Thamasta unexpectedly

re-enters, 'Parthenophil', not only unexpectedly but unnecessarily, tells her,

> If ever I desire to thrive
> In woman's favour, Kala is the first
> Whom my ambition shall bend to.

An audience may well appreciate the irony of this echo of
Rosalind's avowals to Phebe, and it has the dramatic effect of
making Thamasta jealous, and hence in turn of prompting
Kala to pursue 'Parthenophil' for herself. Ford in this brief
scene thus creates a complex set of interlocking 'discrepancies
of awareness', like those which Bertrand Evans praises in
Shakespeare: most of the audience aware (as Thamasta and
Kala are not) that 'Parthenophil' is a woman, Kala and
'Parthenophil' aware of the innocence of a conversation
which Thamasta misinterprets, Thamasta and Kala aware of
Thamasta's love for the ignorant 'Parthenophil', the audience
at the end aware that Thamasta's jealousy has in fact created a
rival by suspecting one. Yet these overlapping ironies make
Parthenophil/Eroclea less real, not more so. Attention focuses
on Thamasta's jealousy, just as earlier in the scene it had
focused on Palador's distraction: Eroclea stimulates dramatic
reactions in others, without ever becoming a centre of emotional reactions, or dramatic consciousness, herself. Since
Thamasta's jealousy manifests itself immediately upon her
entrance, an audience is aware of the effect of Eroclea's ironic
avowal even as it is spoken; the effect of the words eclipses
their motive, and this in turn makes one suspect that the effect
is indeed the (dramatist's) sole motive. If Eroclea had made
the same avowal to Kala before Thamasta's entrance, we
could appreciate its effect on Thamasta without doubting its
dramatic authenticity as an expression of Eroclea's nature;
but, instead, before Thamasta's entrance Eroclea seems intent
only on begging herself out of an embarrassing situation. Perhaps we are to imagine that Eroclea makes the avowal only in
order to please Thamasta, for her servant's sake, but if so the
dramatist does little to assist such an inference, nor does he
remind us of Eroclea's earlier (off-stage) efforts to plead
Menaphon's case, or attempt to use that relationship as a
means of explaining Eroclea's desire to please Thamasta.

What, in any event, are we to make of Eroclea's announcement? Phebe, after all, deserves to be misled, and (we are clearly assured) will profit from having been so; but, when Eroclea similarly misleads Kala, Kala has done nothing to merit the deception, and as a result of it only further entangles herself in an impossible situation. Eroclea remains, apparently, completely unconscious of these complications, just as she remains blind to Thamasta's feelings. The contrast with Viola could not be more acute: we perceive Viola so strongly as a character partly because she so evidently perceives and responds to the world about her.

One might justify Ford's procedure by claiming that he does not intend to create an intelligent, sensitive, alert character like Viola, but one impervious to much that goes on around her. This in fact seems unlikely, given the drift of Ford's plot, the importance of Eroclea, and the admiration and affection accorded her by all the other characters. Even if it were Ford's intention, however, one could legitimately complain that his dramatic strategy elsewhere *requires* an audience to assume that Eroclea responds sensitively and deeply to other people, even though she barely speaks, and displays hardly any emotion. This was true, for instance, of her encounter with Palador earlier in the same scene, and it is true again of her next appearance (II.ii), when she is 'introduced' to her mad father, and the sister who cares for him. Again, she enters in a group, and speaks only twice in the central section of the scene: 'You much honour me' and 'This sight is full of horror.' Afterwards, attention is drawn to her being 'moved', and she says, 'All is not well within me, sir.' Ford relies entirely upon the performer's ability to convey suppressed feeling; he does nothing to structure, particularize, or intensify our response to the performer's contribution. Furthermore, as in her encounter with Palador, this meeting with Meleander does not provoke anything *but* suppressed feeling; it issues in no action, no development; it has no discernible motive, either, beyond Menaphon paying his respects, and bringing 'Parthenophil' along in tow; the whole thing seems, therefore, simply a contrived occasion for generalized histrionic display. The fact that Eroclea's sibling does not even recognize her (unlike Viola's) intensifies this sense of contrivance.

Eroclea's next scene is her most sustained appearance, but

again the reactions of other characters monopolize an audience's attention. The scene begins with Kala offering herself to 'Parthenophil'; 'Parthenophil' first says that he 'dare not wrong' Kala's honour; then flatly announces that 'you never can be mine, / Must not, and – pardon though I say – you shall not'; and finally assures her that he will 'Never, I vow' prate about her offer. In short, 'Parthenophil' extricates himself from this embarrassment of his own creating as abruptly and honourably as possible. Kala speaks three times as many lines, among them two asides; afterwards she remains on stage for a brief soliloquy, leading into a plot to discredit 'Parthenophil' with his master Menaphon. Once Menaphon has been placed where, unseen by the characters, he can see but not hear their dialogue, 'Parthenophil' re-enters with Thamasta, who proceeds to woo him herself. We know, of course, that this wooing cannot succeed; 'Parthenophil', the apparent object of these suasions, therefore receives little of our attention, since no change in 'his' feelings can possibly occur. The real psychological interest of the scene centres wholly upon the deceived Thamasta and the deceived Menaphon (the latter possibly visible to the audience, on the upper stage). 'Parthenophil' must simply proffer a series of excuses, and advance a collection of reasonable arguments, in an effort to dissuade Thamasta; these are, predictably, parried, so that – predictably – 'Parthenophil' must eventually play 'his' unanswerable trump, by revealing that he has 'no weapon', i.e. is 'a maid, a virgin'. The risibility of this moment spends itself on Thamasta: she first asks, 'Are you not mankind, then?' and then 'Pray, conceal / The errors of my passion.' But Parthenophil throughout behaves in an honourable monotone. Viola, by contrast, pities Olivia, but is also her rival; 'very oft we pity enemies' alerts us to the complexity of her position. Moreover, although Viola never explicitly condescends to Olivia, or judges her, one is conscious of the fact that Olivia in effect throws herself upon the 'man' she loves, soon after Viola has poignantly not done so. No such complexities ever complicate the wholly decent character of Eroclea. Eroclea, in fact, never offers anything but 'grounds of reason'; Ford's scene offers none of the pretended and/or real harshness of Viola's similar scene with Olivia. And of course Viola does not disabuse Olivia by revealing her sexual identity. As I have said, her alleged reasons for maintaining her disguise are in fact specious, but they have nevertheless been managed in such a way that they seem dramatically more real than Eroclea's. Because Viola has not revealed herself to Orsino, despite the strongest of motives for doing so, I don't think an audience expects her to let Olivia in on the secret; the scene does not, as a result, seem organized toward any such climax, and if it does seem so then the absence of such an easy solution makes us take the involuted emotions of the protagonists more seriously, as the intractable stuff of life rather than the manageable and stage-managed stuffings of melodrama.

Menaphon's deceived jealousy only provokes from 'Parthenophil' two sputters of protest ('Sir, noble sir – ' and 'I do protest – '); then the character disappears for three and a half long scenes. S/he returns undisguised, as Eroclea, presenting herself to Palador. He at first does not believe it can be her; we of course know it is, and since he already avowedly loves her the revelation and acceptance of her identity resolves the plot. Her nature is not at issue, only her name. Neither character develops, as Orsino must in the final scene of *Twelfth Night*; once she reveals herself, Eroclea's only complexity – the secret of her sex – vanishes, leaving her with nothing like the range of emotions and responses evident in Viola in the scene of her unmasking. Moreover, Rhetias has carefully stage-managed her appearance, and her interview, alone, with Palador: the whole scene is, literally, contrived.

Similarly, her mere appearance in the final scene 'cures' Meleander of his madness. This scene as a whole obviously owes its structure and much of its detail to Lear's reunion with Cordelia. After her entrance, and before her father regains his sanity, Eroclea speaks just four times:

> *(kneeling)* Dear sir, you know me?

>   The best of my well-being
> Consists in yours.

>   I have not words
> That can express my joys.

> Heaven has at last been gracious.

Ford here strives for the affecting simplicity of 'And so I am, I am' and 'No cause, no cause' – strives, but falls badly short. In addition, the scene lacks the emotional complexity of the reunion in *Lear*: without guilt, without anxiety, without the threat of anger, without the unpredictability and uncertainty of Lear's recovery, without the still-disguised Kent. It has also been, like so much else in the play, contrived: Eroclea enters as the climax of a series of 'messengers', each bringing Meleander something he had lost when he lost his daughter and his reason. The restoration of his daughter, as the final ingredient, of course predictably restores his reason. This whole playlet has, like the reunion with Palador, been arranged in advance. Whether we compare this with *Lear*, or with the series of entrances in the final scene of *Twelfth Night*, we cannot help but discern how much Ford's play (and his character) lose by their own contrivance.

Eroclea is, artistically, stillborn. Much more interesting critically are characters who are full enough, but full of the wrong things, or full in the wrong way. Casca, for instance, does quicken into life – though perhaps we should say, '*do* quicken', for Casca is probably best regarded as a plural noun. Only thirty lines separate his second from his first appearance, and in both he narrates and describes a scene. The contradictions between the two appearances are not so much of logic, like those of Viola – arguably a real Casca might contain such diversity, whereas a real Viola could not both know and not know Sebastian was alive in Illyria – as of impression. The first Casca's first speeches convey the essential matter, so that thereafter we may attend to his manner, a brilliant and a memorable manner. Throughout his narrative he not only uses the same words but also narrates the same sequence, qualifying only to deflate. But he who first denigrated must in his second scene ennoble; he whom Cassius and Brutus had to prod and prod must now volunteer elaborations while Cicero stands by unconcerned. Gross hyperbole replaces understatement; a hundred ghastly women replace three or four wenches. Where before Casca's whole method was to dissociate action from its meaning – so that, mute, it grows ridiculous (most famously when he reports that Cicero spoke, but as for what he spoke, ''twas Greek to me') – he now insists emphatically upon the meaning of the portents. The first

Casca is a 'Why' and an 'Ay' (and another and another), whose vocabulary includes 'chopt', 'sweaty', 'stinking', 'clap', 'hiss', 'foamed at mouth'. The second Casca never uses either of the interjections before so forcibly stamped on our imaginations; his adjectives are unphysical and latinate; he practises not wilful repetition but elegant variation and the multiplying of descriptions. The second Casca:

> I have seen tempests, when the scolding winds
> Have rived the knotty oaks, and I have seen
> Th'ambitious ocean swell and rage and foam,
> To be exalted with the threat'ning clouds;
> But never till tonight, never till now,
> Did I go through a tempest dropping fire.
> Either there is a civil strife in heaven
> Or else the world, too saucy with the gods,
> Incenses them to send destruction.

The first Casca:

> Nay, an I tell you that, I'll ne'er look you i'th' face again.
> But those that understood him smiled at one another, and
> shook their heads; but for mine own part, it was Greek to
> me. I could tell you more news too: Marullus and Flavius,
> for pulling scarfs off Caesar's images, are put to silence.
> Fare you well. There was more foolery yet, if I could
> remember it.

The ragtag organization of this second paragraph – unrelated topics bundled together, the farewell in the middle – typifies a style of mind. When Brutus asks, 'What said he *when he came unto himself*?', Casca answers (yet 'tis not an answer neither, 'tis one of these replies), 'before he fell down' – and so on for six lines before arriving at the business: '*When he came to himself* again'. One might suppose from this organization that the before somehow illuminates the after, but Casca's left hand (or lobe) is contentedly ignorant of his right. Three times at the end of a speech he gratuitously characterizes the mob, his mockery being purely disgressive, since he quite approves of their denying Caesar the crown. But the second Casca builds rhetorical periods: each of his two long speeches ends on a point, an emphatic conclusion.

In life, how do we get to know a person? We form an initial hypothesis, which we modify or revise or supplement repeatedly, to fit new data. Occasionally, something happens which is radically incompatible with our existing interpretation of a person, so forcing us to entirely abandon the old hypothesis. But in such cases we cannot simply start with a new hypothesis, which fits the new data; we must also, retrospectively, reinterpret the old data, in the search for a pattern which can incorporate both old and new. Something of this kind happens with Casca. But, though the disjunction is fundamental and unmistakable, we are in the theatre given neither time nor the evidence to explain it. Nor, for that matter, do we have the inclination to try, because Casca does not seem important enough to make the effort worthwhile. On the other hand, unlike the Duke's conversion at the end of *As You Like It*, Casca's transformation is not self-consciously or unashamedly artificial; we cannot dismiss it as a formal convenience, because Shakespeare apparently asks us to take it seriously. So we simply note the disparity, and then ignore it, taking the new Casca at face value, without any attempt to reconcile him with the old. Nevertheless, we cannot help comparing him with the original Casca, and that comparison is inevitably disappointing. Decius Brutus, however flat, never disappoints us; Casca does. We may not in the theatre be able to explain why he does, we may not be articulately conscious of the contradiction in his manner; but a character who makes a memorable first impression, and whose second appearance therefore raises expectations, does not satisfy those expectations. Casca is an artistic blemish in that he arouses expectations which he does not fulfil. And that failure in turn weakens a pivotal moment in the assassination scene. 'Speak hands for me!' has an exact and telling aptness in the mouth of the first Casca; but because, in the interim between I.ii and III.i, the character has lost his initial sharpness and clarity of definition, the line too loses some of its potential resonance.

Casca first strikes Caesar. Therefore, as an important conspirator, he must be kept prominently on stage; but, as, unfortunately, the story leaves him little to do, he turns into a mere messenger. As Caesar's assassin, his initial comic tendencies may have been deliberately suppressed, and his second scene does put him squarely among the serious, where he will thereafter remain. Shakespeare may also have felt that having the sceptical Casca confirm and believe the portents would encourage us to believe them, as the sceptical Horatio authenticates Hamlet's Ghost. But Shakespeare's possible intentions – or Dover Wilson's face-saving speculation that the prompt-book unauthoritatively conflated two distinct characters – does nothing to justify the actual results. The play keeps Casca on stage and serious, but only at the cost of making him less real; the marriage of scepticism and credulity discredits both the portents and the speaker. As Edward Gordon Craig said, if in a play things supernatural are to convince us, they must be exactingly prepared;[40] here we leap (or trip) from arrangements for dinner to 'Men, all in fire, walk up and down the streets'. For this very reason, producers have felt compelled to turn the scene into a Gothic extravaganza (when they have played it at all) . J. P. Kemble 'suppressed all the lines in that scene describing supernatural horrors, yet by darkening the scene ("Lamps down and turned off") and by a generous display of thunder and lightning, he created a proper mood of darkness and danger'.[41] This theatrical tradition continues right up to the 1977 National Theatre production: darkness, lightning flashes, loudspeaker thunder, backstage wind, even clouds. It solves the problem of Casca by diverting our attention from language and character to spectacle.

It could be argued that the apparent failure of Casca is an unperceived success, that incoherence is indeed the 'point' of the characterization. After all, Antony and Brutus and Caesar also possess 'double' selves, which are perhaps never adequately reconciled. But, if this was Shakespeare's intention (and such a defence shifts the issue from character to theme, when in fact Shakespeare usually expresses theme through character), then comparison of Casca with the other three 'double' personalities demonstrates how imperfectly that intention was realized.[42] The moral complexity of Brutus's nature organizes the play: an audience is in no danger of mistaking it for inadvertence, or ignoring it, or being disappointed by it. In fact, audiences are actively interested in exploring the complications of his nature (as are other characters). No such intrinsic importance or developed interest encourages an audience to contemplate or extrapolate from

the fissures in Casca. Likewise, Caesar's assassination inter-
venes between the early hedonist Antony and the brutal,
astute politician of Acts III–V. Spectators easily accept the
assassination as sufficient motivation for Antony's change of
course. Indeed, for an audience familiar, from the beginning
of the play, with Antony's legendary greatness, the conspirators' ready assumption that he is *no more* than a reveller must
seem, even then, a colossal blunder. Moreover, Antony's political cynicism does not seem inappropriate to the immoralist
of the play's first half; nor does his success in courting popular
favour seem incompatible with the vulgarity of his previous
pursuits. What changes is not Antony's style of speech or
mind (as with Casca), but his commitment to serious political
action – a commitment directly attributable to the serious
political act committed by the conspirators.

Caesar too, unlike Casca, is on the surface entirely satisfactory: from the beginning he combines political authority with
human weakness. There are no sudden jolts, and the contrast
of public role and private self is in any case so common a
feature of human experience that few spectators could ever
have been bewildered by it. But, although, at this level, the
strategy of Caesar's characterization works well enough (and
so cannot be used as a parallel or excuse for Casca's), at
another level Caesar himself illustrates a different failure of
characterization, one rather more important than the problem with Casca. Shakespeare has tried to solve the problem of
excessive expectation partly by emphasizing the frailty and
ordinariness of the titanic historical figure: his inability to
beget an heir, his epileptic fit, his partial deafness, his occasional pomposity. If we see character as a system of interlocking repetitions, we clearly have such a system here, one which
naturally combines with the stereotypical image of Caesar as a
balding figure crowned with laurel. Balding, impotent, deaf,
incontinent, pompous. It is difficult not to relate all these
features to the character-type of the *senex*, the comic old man,
a type which Polonius magnificently embodies. But *Hamlet* is
a play about parents and children; *Julius Caesar* is not.
Consequently, we are left at something of a loss exactly how to
respond to Caesar's infirmities, how to relate them to the political and personal issues of the play, how to combine them
with the other side of his characterization. One can see ways

in which Caesar's age might be made relevant: Caesar as the venerable embodiment of the old order, like Duncan; Caesar as the decrepit embodiment of a decaying order; Caesar as an old man on the brink of dying, who therefore represents no real threat to democracy, if the conspirators would just let him pass away in peace; Caesar as a surrogate father killed by Brutus; Caesar as a great man who has outlived his greatness. Caesar's infirmity could have been developed in any (or all) of these ways; but Shakespeare in fact develops none of them, with the result that the details never coalesce into a meaningful pattern, one which by illuminating and contributing to individual moments would make them individually more satisfying and significant.

Viola, compellingly and compactly realized, seldom victim to controversy, is for those reasons useful as an example, and for those reasons suspect. Hamlet and Lear and Falstaff and Cleopatra are greater and more complex creations than any I have here examined. But only when we have understood the norm can we begin to attempt an explanation of the masterpiece. And before we can tackle any of these greater and more complex characters, we must face a problem not much in evidence with Viola, but crucial to many of Shakespeare's other characters: the disparity between the play in performance and the play as read.

4   Readers and Seers:
Henry V

Many critics intensely dislike *Henry V*. The play and the protagonist now often arouse a pitch of opprobrium like that
which Coleridge once reserved for *Measure for Measure*. But
both the play and the protagonist have been applauded by
centuries of audiences; indeed, critics have often clapped in
the stalls before going home to hiss. Those who have defended
the play and the character have done so in terms of the
theatre, or – more recently – have defended the play at the
expense of its hero (assuming or asserting that Shakespeare
found him as distasteful as they do), or defended the character
at the expense of the play (assuming or asserting that Shakespeare meant to make a hero but didn't know how, and
bungled it). The play and the character are still sometimes
openly branded artistic failures; more subtly, and more commonly, ironic interpretations of the play all depend, one way
or another, upon accusations of aesthetic failure: a failure of
Henry's rhetoric to convince, a failure of the subplot to be
very funny, contradictions of detail or direction.

This disparity between the pleasure of spectators and the
displeasure of readers will be the focus of this chapter. To
analyse the pleasures of spectators, I have studied the
responses of audiences to one important and popular production, that by the Royal Shakespeare company in 1975, directed by Terry Hands, which toured Europe and America in
1976 and was revived in England in 1977. My own views on
the play as a whole have been expressed in my recent Oxford
Shakespeare edition (1982); here I shall make no attempt to
analyse or interpret the entire play, or even the entire RSC
production.[1] For instance, I shall say almost nothing about
Henry himself, who has monopolized critical attention, or
about Alan Howard's performance of the role, which mono-

polized reviews. I have avoided Henry partly because that monopoly does a disservice to the play, but primarily because, in the absence of a consensus, any adequate account of our responses to Henry would require a comprehensive account of our responses to the entire play. If one weakness more than any other has disabled previous studies of audience response, it is the ambition to treat of whole plays. As the preceding chapters show, to analyse our responses to even a part of one play requires the most exacting attention to the complexities of each moment, so that, within the limits of one book, to treat of several plays in their entirety compels the critic to summarize, and by summarizing either to distort, or to leave unanalysed portions of the play fundamental to his argument. And, because the analysis of Henry, or of the great tragic protagonists, would require an analysis of our developing responses to the whole play, until we have faced or overcome certain obstacles to a comprehensive analysis of the whole, it would serve little purpose to follow the chapter on Viola with one on a more difficult and significant character, such as Henry or Hamlet. Consequently, in what follows I shall discuss only a succession of moments culled from one production, moments selected for their relevance to a central methodological problem, the difference between our reactions to the written text and to any single performance of that text – which is of course a problem for all critics of Shakespeare, but one fundamental to any study of audience response.

It is a commonplace that every audience to a production responds differently. Indeed, Barrie Rutter (who played MacMorris) has given an excellent example, in his description of the audience's uncomfortable reaction at the Gala performance.[2] Obviously, French and German audiences would respond differently from English ones; so (though this may seem less obvious) would American audiences. I did not attend performances in Berlin or Paris or New York, but one would expect such differences, and the actors confirmed this expectation. But, when critics discuss the varying responses of audiences, they are not talking about French and German reactions to an English-language production of *Henry V*. We also generally discount the differences in the responses of audiences which are produced by accidents – as on the night the wall failed to rise for the breach scene, or the night the Archbishop forgot his lines in the middle of the Salic Law speech, or the night Henry forgot his during the ultimatum to Harfleur. We can discount such accidents because the audience on such nights responded differently only because it was presented with a different stimulus, a different play: a play in which the English army did not pour over the wall in retreat, a play in which Henry did not stand on that wall to address his soldiers, a play in which Catherine did not appear, magically, from behind that wall, after the surrender of Harfleur.

When critics speak of the differences between audiences, they mean that audiences respond *differently* to the *same* stimulus. But, the more familiar one is with a production, the more apparent it becomes that most differences between audiences are the consequence of differences in the performance itself. For instance, the night the Archbishop bungled the Salic Law speech, the audience did not laugh (as audiences usually did) at the line, 'So that, as clear as is the summer's sun' (I.ii.86). The first part of the speech (down to 'the Salic Law / Was not devisèd for the realm of France') was normally spoken slowly, clearly, emphatically, so that it was quite easy to follow. The next eight and a half lines (56–64) were cut. The second part of the speech, containing genealogical precedents from the French monarchy, was then spoken much more quickly, and, being a more tortuous argument to begin with, this rapidity made it virtually impossible to follow. As a result, when afterwards the Archbishop – returning abruptly to a slow and clear delivery – called this legal chaos 'as clear as is the summer's sun', the incongruity between the Archbishop's assertion and its own befuddlement was so obvious that the audience laughed, suddenly realizing, with relief, that it was not *expected* to make sense of the speech. The effort of mental concentration demanded by the preceding lines was no longer necessary, and was released in laughter.[3] However, on the night in question the Archbishop lost his way at the beginning of the second section, so there was no quickening of the pace, but instead a marked deceleration, with several long pauses. The audience thus had no difficulty in following his words, and no difficulty in perceiving the actor's unfortunate condition, either; there was no contrast of rhythm, and no antecedent bewilderment, to emphasize the incongruity of 'as clear as is the summer's sun'.

The failure of the line to produce laughter was thus a consequence of two alterations in the Archbishop's performance. But this failure itself had consequences beyond the Archbishop's speech. When the Archbishop did not get a laugh, neither did Henry's rejoinder ('May I with right and conscience make this claim?'), though Alan Howard spoke it as he had always done. Henry would only get a laugh if the Archbishop set the appropriate mood. Specifically, 'as clear as is the summer's sun' had to assure the audience that the Archbishop's arguments were not meant to be understood, or understandable; the laughter of the other spectators confirmed, for each individual, that he was not the only one bewildered. In these circumstances, when Henry asked, 'May I with right and conscience make this claim?', he created a complicity with the audience: *he* thought the Archbishop was talking nonsense, too. If Henry did not get a laugh on this line, the mood of the entire scene was appreciably altered, and the audience was much slower to respond to the humour in Howard's response to the French ambassador. It hesitated to laugh because, without the two laughs earlier, it was less sure that laughter was appropriate, less sure it was *supposed* to laugh. So the fact that the audience did not laugh later in the scene was a consequence of the Archbishop's blunder.

But there were also occasions (infrequent, but undeniable) when the audience did not laugh at the Archbishop, even though he played his part without flaw. This was no doubt partly because the actor and director 'never quite made up' their minds about whether a comic denouement was appropriate,[4] and because Paul Imbusch, who played the Archbishop in 1977, did not consciously work for a laugh, and said he was surprised when he got it. Since the incongruity of the line depends on precision of timing, such uncertainties are bound to affect an actor's performance, and consequently an audience's response. But there is, I think, another reason for the occasional failure to get a laugh. An audience will only laugh if (a) it does not understand the speech, and then (b) realizes it was not meant to understand it. But when a modern audience attends a play by Shakespeare, it *expects* not to understand chunks of the dialogue, simply because of the differences in the language, and the complexity of the poetry. When confronted by nonsense, such spectators will simply assume that it makes sense, or made sense 400 years ago. Such spectators did not laugh because they did not see that they were supposed to laugh.

I have dwelt on this example at such length partly because of the importance of this speech to all interpretations of the play, but primarily because critics assume that differences between the responses of one audience and those of another result from valid differences in interpretation. But most differences in response arise from simple differences in perception. When the Archbishop forgot his lines, the audience perceived something different from what the audience the night before had perceived. When Spectator A thought the Archbishop's speech obscure only because it was Elizabethan, he perceived it differently from me. It was not that I thought Henry had a weak claim to the French throne, while Spectator A thought he had a strong one, but rather that I saw a difficult speech, where he saw a clear speech accidentally obscured by changes of usage. In an experiment, subjects are shown a pack of cards, half the normal size, ten feet away, and asked to estimate its distance; some, assuming that the pack is full size, will correct their perspective accordingly, and say it is twenty feet away.[5] Spectator A automatically corrected his own initial response, because he assumed the speech made sense, and that its apparent obscurity must therefore be an illusion. Of course, this could also be called a difference in interpretation, in so far as all perception involves judgement – but when the critic speaks of interpretation this is not quite what he means. After all, the pack of cards is only ten feet away, and can be proved to be only ten feet away, whatever Spectator A claims.

Such simple differences in perception often produce complex differences in response. Probably half an audience on any given night, because of their distance from the stage, could not see Alan Howard weep after the surrender of Harfleur (III.iii.131ff.); they could see the physical relaxation, the exhaustion, but not the tears of relief. How much difference this makes to the interpretation of Henry can be seen from reading the reviews, for all the reviewers had good seats, and they were all eloquent in their praise of this piece of characterization.[6] Again, when Henry ordered the killing of the French prisoners (IV.vi.37), where you sat in the theatre virtually determined which prisoner you saw killed. I did not even notice Le Fer till my third or fourth performance. Even afterwards, when aware that both he and the Constable were being killed, because of the staging and timing of the executions I never succeeded in seeing both events in any one performance, but only one or the other. (This has been confirmed by other spectators.) This means that, although two prisoners were killed, almost all spectators saw only one – and which they saw would make some difference in their response to the whole scene. The Constable was killed far upstage, lying prone in his armour, so that it was impossible even to tell who he was, unless one happened to notice him (and follow his movements) in the confusion of the simultaneous French exit and English entrance between scenes v and vi of Act IV. Le Fer, on the contrary, fresh from a memorable and endearing comic scene with Pistol, had his throat cut centre-stage; and, because he had his helmet off, we could see his face when Henry gave the order.

Simple differences in physical perspective thus produce complex differences in emotional response. Because plays do not control the focus of an audience, in the way films can, such differences are inevitable. I do not mean to conceal these differences; indeed, part of my purpose is to isolate, describe and explain them. But, on the whole, every spectator I met responded to the play in much the same fashion.[7]

The distance between reader and spectator is perhaps at its greatest in Catherine's English lesson (III.iv). If we are to explain the inevitable joy this scene produced in RSC audiences – indeed, if we are to explain the reactions of any audience to any scene from any production – we must analyse the naked text, the text as altered by the nature of theatrical representation, and the text as altered by the nature of this particular theatrical representation. Thus, a reader could perceive the importance of this scene's juxtaposition with the surrender of Harfleur. Readers might not infer (what any production will immediately convey) the fact, or the importance of the fact, that Catherine will enter in the habiliments of a princess, and that Catherine will be beautiful. No reader or spectator unfamiliar with the Hands production would be likely to imagine that Alice does not enter with Catherine, but only afterwards, when called, so that Catherine's beauty and the elegance of her dress are for a moment the sole objects of our interest; or that Catherine's entrance and Henry's exit overlap, so that 'the presence of both characters on stage at this moment lends weight to her desire to learn English';[8] or that Catherine does not actually enter, but appears as the wall upstage declines, so that she seems 'like a Venus, rising from the waves';[9] or that in combination these details produce a moment of absolute stillness and beauty, of yearning, which accentuates and embodies the qualities of the text itself, and secures at once the affection of an audience for Catherine. But, though any comprehensive account of a spectator's delight must incorporate all three elements, in practice the pleasure of the 1975 RSC production was, in many cases, no different from the pleasure of any competent theatrical representation, while at other times it illuminated qualities which *could* have been derived from a study of the text alone – although in fact no reader or critic had so derived them, so that in a sense no one saw them till the RSC pointed them out. My analyses will thus sometimes dwell on one of these three approaches to the virtual exclusion of the others. But in Catherine's English lesson, some attention must be given to all three.

First, the naked text. This language lesson, domestic and apolitical, fills a lull after the English victory at Harfleur and before the French reaction to that victory, which will culminate at Agincourt. The French nobles will make clear the causal relation between the campaigns, but dramatically they are framed and demarcated, so that we experience them as independent and patterned wholes. By its omission of things political, the scene characterizes Alice and Catherine, whom, alone of the French, we experience solely as private persons. Indeed, the text does not even name Catherine, does not hint her specific political identity: it offers only Alice and 'madam', two women, a princess and her lady-in-waiting. After the crowds of men, two women: a sudden access of femininity. In the following scene, when the French nobles complain, 'our madams mock at us', the political implications of Catherine's interest in English will be underscored, and the

RSC, by slightly overlapping the men's entrance with the women's exit, stressed the juxtaposition. But initially Catherine's interest in English was personal, motivated by her vision of Henry – and, though the scene could be played differently, and 'Il faut que j'apprenne à parler' interpreted differently, still, even if Catherine's lesson is the consequence of a political decision off stage, the actual content of the scene is personal, and thus distinct from the activities of the French (and English) nobles. Recent critics, in their anxiety to defend the scene against earlier charges of irrelevance, have heavily stressed Catherine's inferred motives, at the expense of the actual business of the scene. But in fact the impression of irrelevance is a major source of the pleasure and relief this scene affords. If Catherine's wordplay seems irrelevant, it is meant to seem so, because Catherine is peace, a peace not consummated until the final scene. Here, between battles, her private comedy seems an intrusion and a promise from another world.

We could also perceive, from the text alone, most of Catherine's character, although in fact few critics have done so. The naming of parts of the body, the increasing eroticism, the four-times-repeated mispronunciation 'sin',[10] her indignant then embarrassed repetition of the final obscenities, even the interest in dress and food, all make sensuous her innocence. She is not a naïf, later abused by gross sexist Henry; instead, like most (fictive) Elizabethan women, she has a healthy and unashamed sexual appetite of her own. Anyone who doubts the fullness of Catherine's characterization should examine this scene in the 1600 Quarto, which by omission and simplification produces a Catherine denied the leisure of long sentences, denied the courtesies of polite society ('excusez-moi', 'sauf votre honneur'), denied her familiarity and occasional irritation with Alice, denied her balance of modesty and self-congratulation, denied all ceremony, elegance, reticence: a Catherine left with only scraps of questions and mismouthed English. In the Quarto, everything not obviously related to the French–English wordplay disappears, and the Quarto is thus a compelling demonstration of how much more than wordplay the scene contains.

Though he probably never saw it performed,[11] Dr Johnson attributed the scene's success in the theatre to 'the grimaces of two French women, and the odd accent with which they

uttered the English'.[12] There can be no denying the odd
accent, but at least in the 1975 RSC production the scene was
grimaceless, and rightly so, for facial pantomime is hardly
consonant with the elegance of Princess Catherine. In a 1976
BBC radio broadcast of the play, Catherine so laboured over
her every syllable that all gaiety succumbed to constipation.
By no means did she 'gagné deux mots d'Anglais vitement';
she seemed instead only pitiably stupid.[13] But the RSC
Catherine was rapid and confident. This blithe desecration of
English of course made her funnier. But Catherine's ease is
also structurally necessary, in contrast to (and as a relief from)
the physical and imaginative labour, the strain and difficulty
of achievement, which the rest of the play is at pains to
impress on us. If unsuspected, Catherine's comic entangle-
ments with language resemble Jamy's, MacMorris's,
Fluellen's. As their verbal idiosyncrasies elicit a bemused
affection, so do hers. All commit their blunders in the total
confidence of total innocence. As Johnson observed, 'Alice
compliments the princess upon her knowledge of four words
and tells her that she pronounces like the English themselves.
The princess suspects no deficiency in her instructress, nor
the instructress in herself.' Unfortunately, from such magnificence Johnson descends to a moral lecture upon 'French
servility and French vanity'. The adjective would have been
better omitted than repeated. In tutoring prospective
monarchs, of whatever nationality, the imputation of servility
can seldom be forestalled, though the tutor's dilemma calls
perhaps for more amusement than indignation. Certainly, no
discernible indignation was vented on these women by any
audience I saw.

As Catherine's ease is communicated partly by her pace,
and as a reader tends to read all scenes at the same speed, a
reader is somewhat less likely to appreciate her facility: a
reader will, if anything, read this scene more slowly than
usual, because it is French. But the more important difference
between reader and spectator in this scene is in the way each
responds to the 'odd accents' and the final puns. Audiences
find them funny, readers do not. Even M. M. Mahood calls it
meaningless and dismal humour.[14] The mispronunciations
raise issues relevant to many other comic scenes in this play;
but the final obscene puns belong to a different category of

joke. Though scholarship has of late busied itself unearthing and defending Shakespeare's puns, they remain an oral rather than a literary virtue; though now learnedly excused for their contribution to characterization or complexity of meaning, rare is the editor who finds them funny, or will say so. More than most dialogue, puns depend on the illusion of spontaneity, an illusion the printed word inevitably belies. Puns are the easiest jokes to make – which largely accounts for their disparagement by critics.[15] But the relative ease with which puns are created is for the dramatist an advantage, in that his characters can credibly pun without all being uniquely witty people. Puns let the author make the audience laugh, without forcing him to make his characters indistinguishably ingenious. Finally, puns are social: in company, even the occasional awful pun has its uses, for it unites audience and actor. If unanimous, a groan is as good as a laugh: witness Menenius's exclamation, 'I would not have been so fidiussed for all the chests in Corioles' (*Coriolanus*, II.i.130), which must rank among Shakespeare's worst puns, yet serves a purpose by its very badness. I do not think the wordplay in Catherine's scene of this kind, for audiences do laugh (not groan), but Menenius's pun is an extreme example of a tendency inherent in the genre, which readers are unlikely to appreciate.

Catherine asks Alice the English for 'les pieds et la robe'; Alice means to answer, 'the foot and the gown', but she herself mispronounces 'gown' as 'cown'.[16] 'Foot' and 'cown', Alice's translation of 'les pieds et la robe', sound like the French words for 'fuck' and 'cunt' (*foutre* and *con*), and Catherine is suitably shocked (Plate 2). The joke was not original,[17] and its technique is elementary. These two facts are prime sources of a reader's (particularly a scholar's) dissatisfaction: Mahood, for instance, in a book devoted to the techniques of wordplay, is predictably harsh on this scene. But Freud pointed out long ago that obscene jokes, though immensely funny, and probably the source of more laughter than any other category of joke, are almost invariably wretched in terms of technique.[18] We must therefore distinguish between the source of a laugh (which here, as often elsewhere, is quite simple) and its function (which here, as usually in Shakespeare, is rather complex). 'Foot' and 'gown' are, in English, innocent sounds;

mispronounced in French, they are not. If we think of these as puns, as Mahood does, they are poor ones, for the similarity of sound does not reveal a similarity of significance: one does not suddenly 'see' an unsuspected relation between 'foot' and 'fuck'. But in fact the joke is not properly, or not mainly, a pun at all. Instead, the two languages are an ideal image of displacement, the psychological mechanism whereby one can both think a prohibited thought, and not think it, commit the prohibited act, and yet remain innocent.[19] Displacement is a basic technique in jokes. The discovery, through a homonym, of such an avenue of displacement results in a liberation of psychical energy, through laughter. Catherine herself takes pleasure in the discovery – after her third repetition of the word, she and Alice both laughed – and so does an audience.

Some critics have seen this as a play about Babel, misunderstanding, the difficulties of communication in a world where everyone speaks a different language. But in fact misunderstanding is in this play a recurrent source of pleasure, not pain. Catherine has, so far, been the butt of her own mispronunciations; she now becomes their master, through them discovering for herself and for us a secret source of pleasure. This creates in the audience a sense of complicity, or even admiration, as we might be said to admire someone, or to be grateful to them, for telling us a good joke. But Catherine's 'puns' do even more than this: they characterize her as well, and in doing so provide yet another source of pleasure for an audience. By saying 'fuck' or 'cunt', one summons up in the mind of the listener an image of the thing the word stands for. For a man to do this, in a woman's presence, is sexually aggressive and provocative; for a woman to do so, in a man's presence, is an act of passive exhibitionism.[20] (In some modern social contexts, of course, these words have degenerated into expletives, and thereby lost their provocative character, by losing their ability to enforce a mental image.) Catherine's obscenities are the opposite of Mistress Quickly's. For Quickly, in trying to say something sexless, accidentally summons up a sexual image, but Catherine, in three times repeating 'foot' and 'cown', deliberately summons up in her own mind a sexual image, when in fact the English words are innocent of such content. It is as though someone had cut a large and revealing hole in the back of Quickly's dress, without her knowing it, so that we may look at her, though she never shows herself. (That is why Quickly is almost always played as a physically unattractive, neuter creature: if she were young and alluring, we should suspect she had cut the hole herself, and was deliberately being obscene. And this pronounced absence of femininity explains why, when Catherine and Alice enter, one feels they are the first women to appear in the play.) But, unlike Quickly, Catherine keeps lifting her skirts when the men's backs are turned, so that in speaking English, by saying 'foot' and 'cown', she shows herself without being seen. The audience on stage and the audience in the theatre stand in a similar relationship to Quickly, but Catherine thinks no one but Alice can see or hear her; so the theatre audience sees Catherine as more willing, sexually, than she would appear to be, and thus takes pleasure not only in the displacement joke but also in the voyeur's spectacle of an alluring woman displaying herself, by saying words which encourage us to imagine parts of her body. It is probably easier for a man to enjoy this joke than for a woman to do so. In Shakespeare's theatre, Catherine would have been played by a boy, so that a male actor in the guise of a woman would be encouraging us all to envisage the female anatomy; this makes the joke even more aggressively male. But in another way using a boy softens the joke, by making it less 'real', by making it a self-confessed male fantasy about women, rather than a dramatic assertion of what women objectively are. So the boy actor may have made less difference than we might think, for these two tendencies almost cancel each other out.

For some people, no doubt, the foregoing analysis has made the joke seem even more distasteful than it seemed before. The very vocabulary and structure of psychoanalysis emphasize the hidden sexual content of the joke at the expense of its overt innocence, when in fact our pleasure is in the combination and simultaneity of the two incompatibles: the joke gives us a Catherine both sexually knowing, and innocent. An audience need not have read Freud to appreciate this: if you compare Desdemona, who cannot bear to say 'whore', with Catherine, who three times voluntarily says what sounds to her like 'fuck' and 'cunt', the degree of Catherine's complicity is evident. It is as though, mildly and subtly, Catherine were flirting with the audience. That certainly is how the RSC played the scene, and it seems to me the proper way. If Catherine is entirely innocent, then the joke becomes only and brutally voyeuristic; if she does not collaborate, it becomes symbolic rape.

Of course, there were a great many people in every audience who did not understand this joke at all, for it cannot now be understood without some knowledge of French, and of a kind of French seldom taught in schools. (For Shakespeare's audience, the slang use of 'cony' would probably have made the joke apparent, even to the Frenchless.) The joke got less laughter than the other mispronunciations, and less than 'vous prononcez les mots aussi bien que les natifs d'Angleterre', which also requires some knowledge of French, but is easier to decipher, simply on the basis of cognates ('prononcez', 'natifs', 'Angleterre'). Moreover, the laughter was noticeably slower to develop. Like all delayed-reaction jokes, this one depends on a moment of consternation, followed by the joy of discovery and relief.

To summarize: a reader, and more specifically a critic, is unlikely to enjoy the joke because on the page puns lose their spontaneity and social context; because a critic will tend to judge the joke by its technique rather than its effect, or the function of that effect; because the critic knows the joke was not original to Shakespeare (as few audiences would know, or care); because the undertone of flirting depends in part on Catherine's physical presence, and her performance of the lines; because a delayed-reaction joke will lose much of its pleasure for a critic rereading the text who thus knows the solution in advance, or for a reader who consults a footnote rather than discovers the solution himself; and, finally, because many spectators will not understand the joke at all, while the critic has a professional obligation to ensure he understands it, and by understanding it is the more likely to be repelled by it, since it represents a species of sexual humour no longer socially acceptable (until quite recently) or intellectually respectable (still).

But the failure to appreciate Catherine's scene, and Catherine's joke, will seriously distort the structure of the play. For this scene, and the relaxed sexual innuendoes of the French before Agincourt, prepare audiences for the final scene. The language lesson does more than that: it makes audiences *desire* that wooing-scene, *will* Catherine's return, as the stoicism of Brutus and the repeated yielding of Cassius make audiences desire the quarrel scene. If the reader does not enjoy the English lesson, he will not desire or anticipate the final scene, and is thus likely to consider it an irrelevance – as did eighteenth-century critics especially, having cut the language lesson entirely.

In that final scene the RSC again brilliantly exploited comic opportunities. 'I cannot speak your England' (V.ii.102–3) was a speech obviously prepared in advance, and proudly pronounced, which Catherine only flubbed on the last syllable, quite without realizing it. (This detail was lost in 1977.) Henry answered with a dismayed 'O'. Henry's 'when I come to woo ladies I fright them', Catherine answered with laughter; his 'la plus belle demoiselle du monde', a rehearsed rush of syllables, provoked excited tittering and consultation; and, breaking off a kiss, he intoned, 'Here comes your father' with a sufficiently colloquial and adolescent air.[21] Catherine's 'Is it possible dat I sould love de enemy of France?' was taken seriously, by Catherine and Henry and the audience, and throughout the wooing the play of advance and retreat was visualized in a choreography by turns comic and tender, approaching the condition of dance. But, although one is grateful for such touches, the exhilaration which suffused this scene, and has in the theatre so often suffused it, has deeper sources. Shakespeare permits us only a taste of Catherine until the final scene, so that the romantic and personal issues focus there. By contrast, Aaron Hill's 1723 adaptation replaced the comic subplot with a romantic one, which reached its climax before Agincourt – thereby sacrificing the sense of release and achievement in Shakespeare's fifth act, and at the same time diluting our interest in the wooing by spreading it over the whole play, so that it becomes merely an irritating interruption of the main business.[22] In Shakespeare, the war won, we and Henry are permitted the comedy of peace. But not the comedy of repartee between matched wits. We watch the courtship of Beatrice and Benedick from outside, committed to neither but to both; we watch this courtship from one side, Henry's. Of course the self-conscious feminist recoils indignant from this male fantasy, but it need be no more partial, or distasteful, than the female fantasy of *As You Like It*, where Rosalind rules the dream. Catherine's innocence of English gives Henry the freedom disguise gives Rosalind – gives him, as disguise gives Rosalind, such superiority he can play. (He began by working at wooing, in verse, in Petrarchan diction, by asking her to tell him how to speak.) The true king becomes, momentarily, Lord of Misrule, enemy to tyrant inhibition, able to speak the unspeakable to his lady's face ('that I shall die, is true; but for thy love . . . by the Lord, no – yet I love thee too'), to flout the proprieties of time ('Give my your answer; i'faith, do; and so clap hands and a bargain'), to mock logic, like Shakespeare's clowns ('when France is mine and I am yours, then yours is France and you are mine'), and finally to overturn 'nice custom' and kiss 'Kate'.

Petruchio also christens his Katherine Kate, but in *The Taming of the Shrew* the change of name is disputed, and thereby its significance made lengthily explicit; in *Henry V* the implications speak themselves, because a princess is so nicknamed, because by such means French Catherine becomes English Kate. Like Petruchio, by renaming her Henry asserts his power to remake her – asserts, more generally, fantasy's triumph over the mundane real. This confidant buoyancy characterizes all Henry's wooing, from his repeated affirmations ('I know you love me') to his jovial self-deprecations and the ease which lets him, like Rosalind, mock what he most craves ('which I am sure will hang upon my tongue like a new-married wife about her husband's neck, hardly to be shook off'). We laugh with Henry *and at him*, partly because he laughs at himself, but also for the patent inadequacy of his logic and his French, for his belittling himself, for the spectacle of his undignified volubility, when forced to carry on a dialogue single-handed. We relish in this scene precisely what neoclassicists condemned, its mix of public and private.[23] And Shakespeare frames this holiday with ceremony and social form, combining thereby order and joy.

Both Catherine's scenes owe much of their stage life to wordplay and 'odd accents', as do scenes with MacMorris and Jamy and Le Fer, and of course Fluellen. Trevor Peacock's brilliant Fluellen (as Fleullens have often been) was brilliant because he was always Welsh, and always more than Welsh. Unlike his counterparts in the Olivier film or the 1976 BBC broadcast or the 1977 open-air production in Regents Park, he insulted MacMorris quite unintentionally, his 'there is not many of your nation' (III.iii.62) being an interrupted sentence as the syntax suggests, rather than a deliberate provocation followed by a long pause to let the point sink in. During the fist fight with Williams, Henry's jovial and colloquial 'What's the matter?' (IV.viii.25), which broke up the general mêlée, created a comic atmosphere in which Fluellen's refrain ('Let his neck answer for it ... if there is any martial law in the world') was so out of key as to be ludicrous. The RSC arrangement of the battle also relieved Fluellen of the traditionally tearful delivery, with the Boy's body in his arms, of 'Kill the poys and the luggage!' (IV.vii.1). It is hard to wring pathos from 'poys', hard to weep for murdered luggage; harder still, when the elegy includes Fluellen's catchphrase (a kind of trip-wire for laughs), ''tis expressly against the law of arms'; impossible, when the next speech requires 'Alexander the pig'. The usual tears only damp the hilarity of what follows. The pity of the thing can be left to itself, and the verbal incongruities exist to discourage the actor's temptation to sentimentality. (The same is true of Quickly's speech on the death of Falstaff, and sentimental renderings can be immediately recognized by their suppression of the obscenity in 'and so up'ard and up'ard, and all was as cold as any stone'.)

The reader or actor who misses such details is prone to reduce Fluellen to 'p'-for-'b'. But, again, even a sympathetic critic may find Fluellen dull reading. As Hilda Hulme observed in another connection,[24] though we adjust easily to unusual pronunciation,

> it is far more difficult to adjust to the unexpected form when we meet it in written or printed language: for the present-day reader the identity of the printed word is rigidly established. ... When we are confronted with some passage of ordinary modern English on which an unusual ... spelling has been consistently imposed, we have to read much more slowly and perhaps even to read aloud.

This applies as well to MacMorris and Jamy, to the mispronounced English in Catherine's scene, and the mispronounced French in Le Fer's. The mental concentration required by such phonetic spelling itself seriously impairs our

ability to laugh.[25] More important, it undermines the innocence of such characters, and their innocence is the precondition for our laughter. In the theatre Fluellen is a born Welshman; on the page we are perpetually reminded of Shakespeare
making him Welsh. On the page he loses the illusion of an
effortless unconscious spontaneity.

But the rhythm and structure of this play depend upon our
affection for Fluellen, whom we can morally commend,
whose idiosyncracies are harmless (for the most part), and
who, though he does not begin as one of Henry's companions,
ends as one, thus reversing the progress of Falstaff. (After
Agincourt, in his panegyric on Henry's Welsh blood, Trevor
Peacock in his enthusiasm actually embraced Alan Howard.)
In Act V, defending Welsh tradition, he acts almost as a surrogate for Henry, as he does clearly in the glove episode. Since
Fluellen first beat Pistol back to the breach, steadily if unobtrusively the play has promised a showdown between them,
creating a desire for such a resolution just as the language
lesson created a desire for the wooing scene, so that the omission of the leek episode would leave the play feeling
unfinished.[26] Not only does the moral comedian triumph over
the immoral, and Pistol suffer the deflation which his verbal
balloon invites from the beginning: more important, Fluellen
against Pistol, Williams and the glove, Henry and Catherine,
all are comic celebrations after the victory at Agincourt.
Shakespeare equates victory with comedy; the contagion of
joy attaches itself, illogically but none the less, to Agincourt.
Shakespeare dramatizes the progress of emotions rather than
the logic of events, and therefore, though Act I contains
almost no comedy, Act V contains little but comedy. By such
sleight of hand Shakespeare persuades us to rejoice in the
slaughter of 10,000 French, by giving us other and more tangi-
ble cause for celebration and laughter.

Freud made a distinction between naïve and tendentious
jokes[27] which is of the greatest relevance to *Henry V*, and the
low esteem in which critics hold its comic scenes. Falstaff's
comedy is tendentious, overtly directed at ideas, institutions,
moral conventions. When we first encounter Falstaff, as readers or spectators, we laugh at his jokes. But, as with all jokes, it
is difficult to laugh at them the second time, and it becomes
progressively more difficult the more often we hear them. (In

1 *Julius Caesar*, III. i: (*left to right*) David Collings (Cassius), Sam Dastor (Casca) and Richard Pasco (Brutus) in the 1978 BBC production.

2 *Henry V*, III. iv: (*left*) Yvonne Coulette (Alice) and (*right*) Carolle Rousseau (Catherine) in the 1975 RSC production.

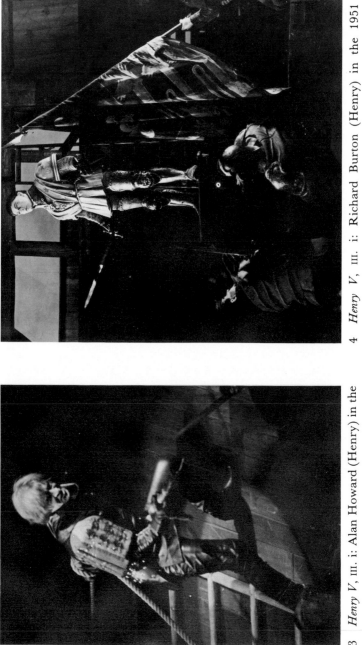

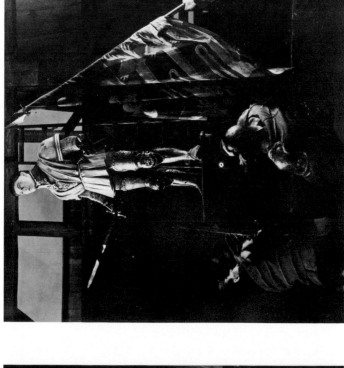

4 *Henry V*, III. i: Richard Burton (Henry) in the 1951 Stratford production.

3 *Henry V*, III. i: Alan Howard (Henry) in the 1975 RSC production.

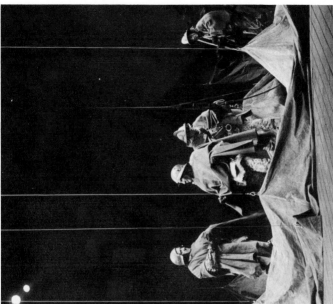

6 *Henry V*, III. vi: (*left to right*) Derek Smith (Gower), Trevor Peacock (Fluellen), Arthur Whybrow (Bates) and Richard Derrington (Court) in the 1975 RSC production.

5 *Henry V*, III. iii: Alan Howard (Henry) in the 1975 RSC production. (Compare Plate 7.)

7 *Henry V*, III. iii: Richard Burton (Henry) in the 1951 Stratford
production. (Compare Plate 5.)

8 *King Lear*, I. i: (*left to right*) Marilyn Taylerson (Cordelia), Judi
Dench (Regan), Barbara Leigh-Hunt (Goneril), John Woodvine
(Cornwall), Richard Durden (Albany), Donald Sinden (Lear) and
Bob Peck (Kent) in the 1976 RSC production.

the theatre, when we laugh at jokes we have heard before, it is either for the sake of something new in them – in the stage business, or the actor's delivery, or facial expression – or because the laughter of our fellow spectators lowers the threshold for our own receptiveness, so that even the diminished potency of an old joke is able in the theatre to generate new laughter.) But in Falstaff's case, when we can no longer laugh at the joke, we can still take pleasure in its idea, in its tendentiousness, and this is precisely what criticism has done. But Catherine's mispronunciations have no such overt tendentious content; they are, in that respect, and as Freud defined it, naïve. Consequently, although when we first hear them we laugh as hard as we first laughed at Falstaff, after we have heard or read them repeatedly we can no longer do so – but neither can we take new pleasure in their intellectual content, for they have none.

Moreover, tendentious jokes stand up to reading, as well as repetition; naïve jokes generally do not. Catherine and Fluellen and the rest do not realize they are funny; Falstaff does. In Falstaff's case, if we are aware of the joke as a creation, we attribute that creativity to Falstaff himself, and we admire him for his ability to be funny when he wishes so to be. But, since Fluellen takes himself quite seriously, and has no desire to amuse, we cannot admire *him* for making us laugh. But the written text, with its phonetic distortions of spelling, is perpetually reminding the reader of the creation of the joke, and since the characters have themselves no desire to be funny, we attribute that act of creation to the author. This intrusion of the author entirely spoils for readers the naïveté of the joke, which is its essence, and the reader instead becomes aware of the author holding up certain characters (who happen to be French, Welsh, Irish, Scottish) for ridicule. A joke which is for the spectator naïve becomes for the reader tendentious, the tendentiousness being entirely the author's, at the expense of his characters. And for the twentieth-century reader it is far more acceptable to ridicule people for their ideals than for their accents. Consequently, in becoming involuntarily tendentious, the comedy of *Henry V* or *The Merry Wives of Windsor* becomes for a modern reader positively repellent. As Freud saw, the very function of a joke is *to protect prohibited mental operations from criticism*.[28] (Freud meant moral criticism.) When the joke ceases to be funny – as it often does for a reader of this play – its mental content is suddenly exposed to hostile intellectual scrutiny, which duly pounces upon its apparent sexism, or its nationalistic and social prejudice.

The hostility of modern critics to jokes about Scots, Irishmen, Welshmen and Frenchmen is obviously influenced by anachronistic post-Freudian notions about the psychological functions of such jokes. I have myself used Freud's vocabulary to describe certain ostensibly permanent operations of the human mind, which existed before Freud discussed them. By contrast, the responses of the hostile critic are themselves influenced by his knowledge of Freud's theory, whether or not he actually refers to it; indeed, the theory has become so commonplace that he will probably *not* refer to Freud. Furthermore, Freud seems to me, on this particular point, mistaken or misleading. There can be little doubt that, originally, Scots were made the objects of English jokes as an expression of hostility or superiority. But such classifications can and often do outlive their social motives. I have personally laughed at 'Polack' jokes without knowing they were aimed at 'Poles'; to me, as an adolescent, a 'Polack' was the denizen of a wholly imaginary country. Moreover, Freud himself drew attention to an anomaly in the theory: certain peoples, like the Jews, have traditionally directed such jokes not at others but at themselves. The social and psychological role of this class of jokes can be explained, in a way that accounts for such exceptions, if we recall a factor to which Freud himself drew attention. Most jokes depend upon the listener's *knowing* they are jokes, and so knowing he is *expected* (and allowed) to laugh.[29] The classification 'Irish' or 'Polack' or 'Jewish' is a signal to the listener, that laughter is both intended and permitted. Any classification, real or imagined, will serve as such a signal, so long as it is widely recognized and accepted within a culture. Of course, such labels tend to be taken from minorities of low social standing, or from foreigners (including enemies) who are outside the culture, because it is safest to laugh at such groups; they can seldom do you harm, even if your laughter offends them. (Thus, for much of European history, it was not safe for Jews to laugh at anyone but themselves.) But the social identity of the joke signal is secondary and arbitrary. All that matters, from the standpoint of the laughter itself, is that the signal be immediately and widely recognized, and safe. For example, in America in the sixties, white hostility toward blacks undoubtedly increased, on the whole; blacks remained, socially and economically, heavily disadvantaged. But blacks ceased to be a safe joke signal, because a significant proportion of whites no longer accepted it, and because, if offended, blacks began to express their indignation openly and forcefully. In that social context, to tell jokes about 'niggers' became an unmistakable act of hostility, as in Freud's model. But that is a special case, not the norm: an innocent signal has been pathologically transformed.

National types also serve another technical function in jokes, which has nothing to do with their validity (real or imagined) as descriptions of actual human beings. One afternoon when I came home from work, in the course of an ordinary conversation my wife happened to mention that they'd 'had a Scot on the radio today; he'd just heard about decimalization'. It took me a moment to realize that this was a joke, its point being that the Scot had presumably not spent any money in the eight years since the currency was decimalized. This is a typical delayed-reaction joke, but the delay in reaction – that is, the whole point of the joke – depends upon the ambiguity of the generic noun 'Scot'. One need only substitute 'they had a miser on the radio today' to see that the joke would be ruined by the accurate generic noun. 'Scot' allows us to take it literally, when we first hear it, and then to 'solve' the apparent *non sequitur* which follows by redefining 'Scot' as a comic type. Again, such an ambiguity depends upon recognition of a type as a joke signal; in fact, it depends upon recognition that there is a *distinction* between the joke signal and the literal sense of the word. The example I have given might appear to restrict this technical function of the stereotype to narrative forms of joke; but something similar happens, I think, with dramatic stereotypes. Just as our knowledge of Viola's disguise, and of the real feelings which lurk beneath it, allows us to perceive immediately the motives for a particular speech or act, relating instantaneously the moment at hand to the larger structure of the character, so the Welshness of Fluellen lets us immediately recognize the appropriateness of individual remarks, and fit them at once into a larger pattern. Henry too is Welsh, as the play eventually reminds us; but his Welshness is literal, we are not encouraged to make it the key which will 'solve' the *non-sequiturs* in his behaviour. Fluellen, however, is a literal Welshman who also repeatedly behaves like a metaphorical Welshman: quite clearly an individual, but one whose eccentricities again and again are delightfully congruent with a well-known and recognizable pattern, associated with his literal nationality.

Johnson, in his remarks on *The Merry Wives*, isolates another source of dissatisfaction with this kind of comedy.

> Whether Shakespeare was the first [he was not] that produced upon the English stage the effect of language distorted and depraved by provincial or foreign pronunciations, I cannot certainly decide. This mode of forming ridiculous characters can confer praise only on him, who originally discovered it, for it requires not much of either wit or judgement: its success must be derived almost wholly from the player, but its power in a skilful mouth, even he that despises it, is unable to resist.[30]

We can see here two biases which should already be familiar to us, from the English lesson. First, the critic's demand for originality; second, the critic's evaluation of the joke on the basis of the ease with which it can be made. The credit for making us laugh must go to the actor, and this remark is closely related to the other two, for all three are concerned with judging the *author's* personal merits. But that standard of evaluation ill fits the theatre. If the play makes us laugh, as Johnson admits, then in the theatre we are not particularly concerned with whether the author or the actor should be praised, or whether the author learned the trick elsewhere, or whether the trick is easily done. (The trick may be easy for the author, but, to do it well, the actor requires considerable skill.) What matters in this case, in terms of critical evaluation, is not how the author makes us laugh, but the uses to which he puts that laughter.

This proliferation of barriers to a reader's pleasure explains why the comedy of *Henry V* and *The Merry Wives of Windsor*, though it has always been enthusiastically received in the theatre, has seldom been appreciated by critics, and this fail-

ure to appreciate the comedy probably explains the failure to
see its structural function. When the comedy is discussed at
all, it is interpreted as parody – that is, as tendentious commentary upon Henry. Certainly the beginning of the play
offers examples. The first and third scenes of Act II (Pistol's
rhetoric, Falstaff's death, the vulgar tawdriness of motive),
though they have other functions as well, do in part sully the
ardour of heroic aspiration, and at Stratford Bardolph and
Nim actually interrupted the Chorus and drove him from the
stage. Exit Bardolph–Pistol–Nim, enter Cambridge–Scrope–
Grey: two sets of triplets, each in its way an enemy to the
heroic aspirations of Henry and his court. Exit Bardolph,
Pistol, Nim and the boy; enter the French King, saying, 'Thus
comes the English with full power upon us' (II.iv.1). The
comic scenes and characters begin at the greatest possible
distance from Henry and the political plot, but as the play
proceeds the two coalesce, until the climax of the heroic at
Agincourt is inextricably laced with comedy, and Henry himself the prime comic agent. Before Act IV, Henry does not
appear in any comic scenes; thereafter he does so repeatedly,
and with increasing frequency. Catherine reinforces this
pattern, appearing first in complete isolation and then later as
the consummation of the enterprise. Henry begins isolated
from his court; he loses Scrope, then Falstaff; at Harfleur he is
entirely alone; afterwards he loses Bardolph. To an extent he
wills that isolation, by destroying Falstaff, by allowing
Bardolph to be executed, in the night scene by asking his
nobles to leave him alone. Henry must seem to conquer
Harfleur by the isolated strength of his will, imposed upon a
disparate and ragamuffin army only peripherally committed
to victory. But then, before Agincourt, Henry gains Erpingham, Pistol, Bates and Williams, Fluellen, Westmorland, his
entire army as a band of brothers – so that, while he alone
seemed to conquer Harfleur, at Agincourt he is not even
permitted the famous combat with Alençon. Harfleur is an
offensive victory, a general's victory, a demonstration of how
much and how little one man can compel history to submit to
his will; Agincourt a defensive victory, won by the army of a
chastened general who has learned to endure and embrace
whatever history gives him. Harfleur is Henry's victory;
Agincourt is England's.
     Out of diversity the play aspires to unity, the unity of the

band of brothers, of Henry and Catherine, of England and France, of politics and joy. The laughter at Fluellen and MacMorris and Catherine is an instrument to that harmony, for their confusions of the tongue are made sources of our pleasure, so that the objects of a prejudice become the donors of our joy, and difference becomes cause for delight not fear. The play advances dialectically: no sooner is a unity established, than we are made aware of what that unity excludes, until that too can be contained. After the divisions of the first two scenes, Henry and his court are by the end of Act I united in their common purpose – and immediately we are shown Eastcheap brawling. After Southampton, Henry can leave behind an undivided England – and we are reminded, through Falstaff, of an entire world Henry has excluded. So, scene by scene, the play proceeds, until, after the achievement of Agincourt, in the consummation of the dialectic, Burgundy insists that the harmony must include France as well as England.

I have as yet limited myself to analysing the sources, and structural consequences, of the pleasure audiences take in the play's comic scenes and characters. But any neat division of comic and serious itself distorts the play. In the second scene, when Henry's council urge him to war, they advance not one argument of policy or profit, though the sources supply such motives. Instead, this war England undertakes for pleasure. War is play. War is festive. War is a spectator sport.

> Whiles his most mighty father on a hill
> Stood smiling to behold his lion's whelp
> Forage in blood of French nobility.
> O noble English, that could entertain
> With half their forces the full pride of France,
> And let another half stand laughing by,
> All out of work, and cold for action.
>
> Others, like soldiers, armèd in their stings,
> Make boot upon the summer's velvet buds,
> Which pillage they with merry march bring home
> To the tent-royal of their emperor,
> Who, busied in his majesty, surveys
> The singing masons building roofs of gold.

When we have matched our rackets to these balls,
We will in France, by God's grace, play a set
Shall strike his father's crown into the hazard.
Tell him he hath made a match with such a wrangler
That all the courts of France will be disturbed
With chases.

These lines, and others like them – combined, in 1975, with
our laughter at 'as clear as is the summer's sun', and our
laughter at Henry's unimpressed reply to sixty-two lines of
legal fustian, and our laughter during his reply to the French
ambassador – all gave promise of a happy war.

Then, before Harfleur, war becomes the opportunity and
exercise of heroism. Then follows Bardolph's parody: 'On, on,
on, on, on! To the breach, to the breach!' (III.ii.1). But
Bardolph and the rest did not, in the Terry Hands production,
simply pop the heroic balloon; in a subtler way they sustained
it. Henry's speech, an unrelieved call to tension, immediately
gave way to total relaxation, comedy and song. From Exeter's
defiance of the French (II.iv) to the Chorus's 'imagined wing'
(III.o) to 'Once more unto the breach' (III.i), Shakespeare
escalates our exhilaration, then caps the build-up with
laughter. We need not pay for the excitements of heroism with
the consequent blood and pain, as such rhetorical stimulants
must in life be purchased. *Henry V* gives us exhilaration and
strain followed by immediate and joyful release: before the
breach, at the surrender of Harfleur, at Agincourt itself (where
the sustained development of expectation issues in Pistol and
Le Fer). Victory at Shrewsbury costs us the death of Hotspur,
the death of Blunt, the execution of a sympathetic Vernon.
The coronation costs us Falstaff. In each, we are as aware of
loss as triumph. At Agincourt even the boys die off stage (or
should, though the RSC could not resist the temptation to
sentimentality – few can). York and Suffolk die (off stage), but
as director Terry Hands complained, we have no previous
acquaintance with York and Suffolk.[31] Therefore we experience no loss when they die; we experience only an orgasm of
pity and admiration. Admittedly, the mawkish description of
their dying (IV.vi.7–32) embarrasses moderns. Perhaps Hands
was right to cut it; perhaps the Boy's death does for us what
Suffolk's did for Elizabethans. But the description, its leisurely

gentleness and distance, invites the luxuriating grief we associate with the late-eighteenth-century cult of sentiment, a grief
pleasant and quite self-conscious. The execution of the
French prisoners should shock, partly because Nim's and
Pistol's and MacMorris's jovial and exaggerated talk of throat-
cutting suddenly becomes literal. But the throats cut are
anonymous throats: most of the casualties at Agincourt are for
us only dead names.[32]

The interanimation of heroic and comic gives birth to the
characteristic exhilaration of this play. Emrys James as the
Chorus set exactly that tone, fusing high comedy and imaginative splendour:

> He makes little jokes – 'And thence to France shall we
> convey you safe', he says, and then adds, 'And bring you
> back again'. He reassures, teases the audience. And he's
> very disarming, very modest . . . 'Prologue-like', he says,
> mocking that whole convention.[33]

To these examples could be added a list of others from his
performance: searching for a word to describe the English
army, his discovery that the perfect word is French ('choice-
drawn *cavaliers*');[34] his dismissive image of an England
'guarded by grandsires, babies, and old women'; his vignette of
social satire, when the Mayor of London and his brethren are
imagined 'in best sort', to greet returning Henry. To this, his
personal illumination of the text, James added the imaginative ardour for which the Chorus is most famous, and which,
being appreciated by reader and spectator alike, needs no
illustration here.

The best description of the impact of the Chorus in the
theatre is Michael Goldman's:

> All but one of the half-dozen famous speeches of the play
> have in common a concern for encouraging their hearers to
> make some kind of demanding effort, whether of action,
> feeling, or imagination. . . like Henry, the Chorus is a man
> whose job it is to rouse his hearers to unusual effort.[35]

But, though Goldman is surely right to compare them,
Henry's great speeches – unlike the Chorus's – enjoy a reputa-

tion almost solely theatrical. 'Once more unto the breach' (III.i) convinces few readers. Its repetitions ('on! on!', 'wild and wasteful', 'mean and base') seem literally bombast to stuff out the line, the second word offering no appreciable or unexpected addition to the meaning. But doubling *is* meaning. Repetition conveys fullness, while the very redundance of content allows an ease which frees the mind to enjoy rhythm and acoustics and the skills of the actor. The repeated abstracting article ('*the* breach', '*the* wall', '*the* blood', '*the* action', '*the* tiger', '*the* blast', '*the* sinews') serves likewise to reduce the number of what Hilda Hulme calls 'full words'.[36] 'Imitate', 'action', 'tiger' are full words; 'the' and 'of' are form words, conveying syntactical relations only. Shakespeare quite deliberately forbids intellectual complication here. Henry's speech does not forcefully yoke adjectives or nouns; it offers no syntactical violence, no violence of thought, to gratify the leisured contemplations of a reader. Shakespeare gives Henry simile not metaphor, again because the more relaxed form of comparison diverts no energies of interpretation, requires less invention from the speaker: condensed metaphor forces the speaker and then the audience to supply the missing link between vehicle and tenor. In fact the similes resist attention: cannon-eyes and cliff-brows defy visualizing. Or rather, 'cannon-eyes' does encourage visualizing, by condensing the image into a single metaphorical compound, and forcing us to fill in the blank; but the looser form of comparison does not juxtapose the images so closely or so clearly or so elliptically. As in Homer, the initial pretext for comparison quickly surrenders to an elaboration of tone. Who can expostulate here upon the resonant aptness of particular words? 'Stiffen the sinews, [something] up the blood' (III.i.7): it makes small difference whether we read 'summon' with Rowe, 'conjure' with Walter, or 'commune' with Hilda Hulme and the Folio. The line demands an imperative, but which imperative hardly matters, so long as it makes no extraordinary demands on comprehension.

The proportion of such imperatives must strike any reader, though no one in itself be striking, for Shakespeare stresses them in ways wholly rhythmic and syntactic. Indeed, the opening line is a paradigm: 'Once more ... once more' dispenses with the verb altogether, leaving us to supply one, offering as it were a pure and departicular imperative. This happens again: 'On, on, you noblest English' and 'God for Harry, England, and St George!' But to a reader, these very imperatives reaching for you from the page seem clumsy and undramatic. In the theatre the army mediates between Henry's imperatives and the audience (though beyond that no one is allowed to pay it much attention). But for a reader the army does not exist at all. For a reader the empty space of the theatre itself does not exist, and that great volume is even more important than the army in mediating between us and Henry, for the emptiness must be filled by the actor, and by filling it with the swell of his voice he impresses upon us his power, his magnificence. Olivier's *Othello* most suffered, as a film, when the camera brought us too close to the great speeches, and some of the film's most effective moments occur when the camera withdraws to something approaching a spectator's perspective, so that we become aware of distance, and how the actors fill it, or fit into it. A man standing in a great hall, filling it with the resonances of his voice, commanding perfect silence and attention, is an image of magnificence; the same man speaking at the same volume to a single auditor across the table becomes ridiculous, excessive, shrill. The reader's intimacy destroys the distance which the speech must prove itself by overcoming.

The play builds toward such oratorical climaxes. After a heroic overture, the play proper begins with quiet talk about Henry's past, about the war's cost, begins with mixed motives and the political intricacies of Henry's claim, with strategic obstacles and a reluctant king who stresses the unavoidable sacrifice entailed. The play needs this slow start: that is the only justification for the length of the first scene, and the best justification of the RSC's controversial opening in rehearsal clothes. (Richard Burton's 1951 *Henry V* was faulted for beginning on too high a note, so that rather than structuring its climaxes it simply repeated them, until they became monotonous and disappointing.) Unlike those of the other histories, the nobles of Henry's council are unanimous and anonymous, and in the theatre the accumulation of their voices and bodies around Henry focused our entire attention on his anticipated reply. But Henry's decision to undertake the war is deliberately underplayed, in comparison to the structural preparation which precedes it; it was certainly underplayed by the RSC, which cut the speech (I.ii.222–33) by more than half. This deliberate anticlimax functions as does the anticlimax of Caesar's death, throwing the audience forward into the next section of the scene with a fund of unspent energy and unsatisfied desire. We are twice warned what to expect from the French embassy, but its entrance is postponed until scene's end, so that Henry's reply will climax Act I – just as, earlier in the scene, the Archbishop's bee-speech had climaxed the political debate. Henry speaks fifty of the last fifty-one lines; then enter Chorus to sustain the heroic pitch. At the end of Act II, in contrast to *The Famous Victories of Henry V*, and in contrast to history, an English-man conveys Henry's message to the French King. Exeter's defiance upstages all the French, who are allowed only brief and weak replies. Again Chorus follows, ending in a shot of ordnance, followed by 'Once more unto the breach'. Each of the play's great arias rests on such a structure of emphasis, and cannot be understood in isolation from that structure, from the needs which the structure creates and the speech satisfies.

This heroic lyricism the RSC expressed eloquently, visual-ly, physically: a great heraldic canopy aspiring as if in echo of Henry and the Chorus, then sagging into mud; the wall at Harfleur rising into perpendicular defiance, then sinking as Catherine rose. When the English soldiers exploded over the wall, we were impressed not so much by the irony of their retreat, as simply by the energies displayed – impressed by the physical tension and dominance of Henry's stance (see Plate 3), which made his battle cry more credible and more com-pelling than Olivier could, sitting on a horse, or than Richard Burton could, placid with flat-footed poise, serenely staring into space (Plate 4). When Henry faced the audience to demand Harfleur's surrender (Plate 5), no doubt he put us in the victim's position, but, equally important, such staging permitted the full-throated and frightening volume which the speech requires, a vocal force impossible when Henry stands, as he so often does (Plate 7) at the feet of the Governor. When Oliver Ford-Davies capitulated from the upper circle, no one drew conclusions from the use of one actor for all the French-men who encounter Henry; no one knew it *was* one actor. But everyone experienced the strain and magnitude of voices across a gulf. For the city of Harfleur, we were given only a wall and the empty space between armies, but, since only the wall and the space count, we were convinced. This was not Olivier's fairy-tale Harfleur, but an empty space where heroism was the more heroic because the more real. The RSC staging made the words possible, made it possible to listen and believe them without being perpetually distracted by the inadequacy or superfluity of the representation, made it possible to listen to the whole of Henry's ultimatum to Harfleur, uncut, attending only to the cruelty of the language and to Henry's face.

We are repeatedly assured that modern audiences will not stomach rhetoric, yet modern audiences revelled in this the most oratorical of Shakespeare's plays, because for once the rhetoric was unashamed: it did not pretend to be anything else. In the breach scene of the 1968 John Barton production, Henry singled out the Boy, spoke the oration to him, the army 'overhearing'. In 1968, when Henry said, 'let [the eye] pry through the portage of the head / Like the brass cannon', the Boy tried to transform his face accordingly, to visualize the simile which should not be visualized: the audience laughed. The oration was treated not as oratory, but as a speech like any other. But, if we judge it as a speech like any other, it is a poor one, unnatural, manipulative. The only justification for its repetitions, its insistent imperatives, its simplicity of rhythm and thought, is passion, the passion of urgency and desperation. And Alan Howard's Henry was, more than any-thing, passionate. When at Harfleur he spoke, we were allowed to attend only to him, to Henry speaking, to Henry desperate, and in that desperation finding (because he had to) an unexampled and exhausting strength. Henry speaks to an audience without a face: to the absent Dauphin, to Scrope who exists only in so far as Henry creates him, to his unindi-viduated troops, to an invisible Harfleur, to Montjoy's absent masters, to God, to idol ceremony. Therefore we attend not in the least to his on-stage listeners, but to him, seeking the private man in the public utterance.

But perhaps the RSC did most for the play's heroism by resurrecting French dignity. If the French are weak, no one can take seriously the English danger and the English achieve-ment. After Harfleur, and for the only time, we see two conse-

cutive French scenes, the second full of anger, culminating in
the French King's invocation of his nobles. That speech,
magnificent in the theatre, makes no impression at all on a
reader, for the simple reason that it's a list. When a reader
reads a list, he tends to pay only a minimal attention to its
items; he quickly abstracts the principle of the list ('names of
French nobles'), he glances down the page to see how far it
extends, he reckons he has received the author's message and
need be detained by it no longer. This applies to all cata-
logues: to the list of French dead at Agincourt, to Macbeth's
list of dogs, to Malcolm's list of vices that he lacks. This
inattention will be even more marked in a reader coming to
the text a second or a seventh time, who will either skip the
list entirely or seek in its items some unsuspected principle of
selection, some unseen efficacy of detail, in which pursuit he
will of course be disappointed, as the list is only a list of the
names of French nobles. But a listener cannot make the actor
hurry over, or skip, the list; a listener has no choice but to
attend to each item, to give each weight, and from the weight
thus given to its items the list accumulates its growing force.
Because each item might well be the last, any such list is in
performance structured toward a climax, based upon an
ascending energy of expectation. But for the reader no such
structure will be evident, because he can see no ascending or
innate significance in the items themselves, and indeed there
is none. The emptiness of the speech for a reader is a measure
of its fullness for a listener. Earlier the French had dawdled,
talked calmly and of defence only, bickered, been upstaged by
Exeter. Now the French King creates in our imaginations a
French army of astounding potency. And after this magnificent French verse comes English prose; after the French
vision of Henry in a captive chariot comes English anxiety
over the conquest of – a bridge. For the first time, Henry asks,
'What men have you lost?' (III.vi.99). This scene, the first
Henry fails to end with a ringing couplet, the second consecu-
tive English scene to end sombrely, closes with the execution
of Bardolph, with Montjoy's defiance and Henry's reluctant
reply. (Here the RSC ended its first act.)

The French night scene, which follows, does parody an idea
of war, and we may in retrospect contrast it with the sombre
English meditations of the next scene. It does ridicule the

French. But it also shows them witty and human and appealing. And, when we next see them, they are again magnificient.

> – The sun doth gild our armour. Up, my lords!
> – *Monte cheval!* My horse! *Varlet, lacquais!* Ha!
> – O brave spirit!
> – *Via les eaux et terre!*
> – *Rien plus? L'air et feu!*
> – *Cieux!*   (IV.ii.1–6)

Exclamations do not read well. To a reader the words seem lame, the vacillation of French and English absurd. To an audience, the words matter less than the volume, pitch, tone, the tendency of the French to revert to French only for emotional outbursts. They are given in this scene two emphatic couplets, of a kind Henry is famous for, not because Shakespeare rewrote the scene and forgot to excise his original couplet ending,[37] but because Shakespeare intended the French to stir us, as elsewhere Henry stirs us. Nobility, horsemanship, light, air: all positive poetic values, as in for instance Vernon's famed description of Prince Hal.

Of the next French scene (IV.v) Coleridge wrote,

> Ludicrous as these introductory scraps of French appear, so instantly followed by good nervous mother-English, yet they are judicious, and produce the impression Shakespeare intended – a sudden *feeling* struck at once, on the ears as well as eyes of the audience, that 'here come the *French*, the baffled *French* braggards!'[38]

This is excellent, so long as we stress 'baffled' more than 'braggards'. Before the battle they were braggards, and we could relish the advantage our foreknowledge gave us, enjoy the disparity between their expectations and their destiny. But now, when they stand shattered by that same disparity, it is their bafflement that strikes us, that can move us. The French can be, should be and at Stratford were pitiable and admirable in their desperate courage. And the mix of languages, the tangle of confused voices and exclamations, contrast with Henry's reasoned sentences and commands, with the silent attention to Exeter's reports from the field, with Henry's decisive response. All these things are clearer in the theatre than on the page.

It is relatively easy to determine Shakespeare's material intentions: he wanted these words, and only these, spoken, in this order, by this character. It is by no means easy to determine Shakespeare's interpretative intentions. The value of a comparison depends on the security of its terms. We can say Shakespeare included certain words in his text, which the RSC excluded from theirs, and compare the responses created by the two different versions. But, though we can determine how the RSC interpreted the text, we cannot determine how Shakespeare wanted it to be interpreted. Happily, the relation between intent and effect can be approached from another direction. Because of Sally Beauman's book, we know what the RSC intended; because I had not read the book when I saw the play and because, at the eleven performances I attended, the vast majority of people in the audience had not read it, we can determine whether spectators interpreted the play as the RSC intended. Often, they did not, and the gap between what the company intended and how the spectators responded illuminates a range of recurring problems in the analysis of audience response.

Beauman's book must be used with some caution, as a statement of the RSC's intent. It was produced in three weeks. The commentary is often ironic, sometimes facetious, occassionally flippant. There are rare occasions when, consciously or not, it seems dishonest: for instance, it says that the list of French prisoners at Agincourt was cut 'to increase the impact of the reading of the list of the dead by Henry',[39] but as the list flatly contradicted the director's belief that Henry wanted to end the 'aristocratic game' of ransom, I rather doubt that the motives for omission were quite so straightforward. Because the people who produced the book are all professional actors, the book itself is a public performance, it constructs an image. Actors live by deceiving the public (including the scholarly public), and actors and directors are thus naturally loath to explain in too much detail how they deceive us. Terry Hands is personally quite frank about all this. But though one must be alert to the book's limitations and distortions, it remains of great value, especially when its account can be confirmed from other sources. In the examples that follow, it does represent, I believe, an accurate account of the RSC's intentions.

In judging whether an interpretation was communicated to the audience, one must first establish whether the cast expected it to be. This may seem a peculiar assertion. Alan Howard thought that Henry tried to model himself on Edward, Black Prince of Wales, and 'for this reason I asked for the surcoat to Henry's armour to be based upon that of the Black Prince'.[40] Of course, very few spectators could have known this, as Mr Howard was well aware; he mentioned it in the book because he wanted to tell us something about the meticulousness of his representation which we could not otherwise have known. Likewise, when Oliver Ford-Davies speaks of the fallen French at Agincourt 'trapped in their armour', so that 'what was designed to protect them, has become the instrument of their destruction . . . like men trapped in tanks or nuclear bomb shelters . . . dying inside the devices designed to protect [them]',[41] he knows that this image, though it works powerfully on the modern imagination, does not exist in the play, and will not be communicated to the audience. In both cases, these details are for the actor's own benefit, not for the audience; they help him into his part, assist in the metamorphosis he must nightly undergo. They are rungs of a ladder the actor climbs, then kicks away. (Of course, this can apply to authors as well, and their statements about their own work.)

But it is sometimes less easy to distinguish between the preparation for the part and the part itself. When Henry asked, 'Who hath sent thee now?' (IV.iii.89), Montjoy decided that his answer, 'The Constable', was a lie. (Actually, he has come of his own accord – to try to prevent the battle.) Oliver Ford-Davies says himself that he and Alan Howard did not 'telegraph it particularly, it's just there to be picked up'.[42] I know of no spectator who picked it up; I think no spectator could, unless it were telegraphed very particularly indeed. But this differs from the previous examples, because the actor's 'intention' is not simply an addition to the part, but an attempt to explain a contradiction or difficulty within the text itself. Montjoy 'makes his speech, and there is a rather odd sequence immediately after it. Henry says to him, "Who hath sent thee now?", which, if you consider it, is a peculiar question. And Montjoy says, "The Constable".'[43] The Constable, in the immediately preceding scene, had shown little disposition for diplomacy. This contradiction was made even more striking in the RSC production, because Montjoy was present in that preceding scene, and so we saw the French exit to the battle, confident of victory, without giving Montjoy any such instructions.

A. C. Bradley took an interest in just this sort of contradiction, in the notorious notes to *Shakespearean Tragedy*, and that preoccupation has been taken as proof of a bookish obsession with character. 'For of course in the theatre no one worries about Hamlet's age or Lady Macbeth's children.' But someone in the theatre does worry about such contradictions: the actor, who has studied the part, and must create a whole from its disparate elements. Bradley's method is the actor's method. Modern critics are rightly suspicious of Bradley, but some have developed an unjustified faith in the oracular pronouncements of actors and directors. I too believe Shakespeare belongs in the theatre; I too admire the multiplicity of talents which contribute to an act of collective genius, as any great production is; I too am personally curious about how actors manufacture their illusions. But that gratitude and admiration and curiosity should not obscure the disparity between an actor's experience of the play and a spectator's. It is the experience of the spectator that matters, and in Montjoy's case the spectators did not perceive the contradiction, and not perceiving it they had no reason to seek solutions for it, by inferring untold motives. We did not see the contradiction for a variety of reasons, but partly because Henry's question was merely exasperated. Just as the army is leaving for the battle, appropriately enthused, Montjoy arrives, interrupts the exit, breaks up the scene at what seems its natural rhythmical climax. Henry's question, by its tone, was saying, 'What are you doing here? Just let us get on with it!' At this exasperation the audience laughed. One was not even aware of an issue of motive being raised; the important thing was the question, not the answer, which we perhaps hardly heard, or immediately forgot.

But the contradiction would probably have gone unnoticed, even if Henry's question had not made us laugh. Audiences never notice, either, the contradiction between Exeter's remaining behind at Harfleur (III.iii) and his appearing at

Agincourt (IV.iii). Nor did audiences notice an even more glaring contradiction in the RSC staging of Agincourt. After the night scene, hearing Gloucester's call ('I know thy errand, I will go with thee'), Henry moved off stage left into darkness, apparently to join Gloucester. But in fact, as soon as he was out of the light, but still on stage, he lay down and covered himself with his cloak, so that when the lights came up on the next two scenes he seemed only another of the sleeping English soldiers, scattered about the stage. Then, when Westmorland (IV.iii) wished for more men from England, Henry appeared simply by sitting up, so that we recognized him. But, if audiences had reflected, they would have realized that Henry, while asleep on stage, could not himself have 'rode to view their battle', as we were told *only four lines before*. (The RSC cut lines 5–16.) I did not notice this contradiction myself until the eighth performance I attended; a friend of mine, who saw the play six times, never noticed it; prominent Shakespearian scholars I have asked never noticed it; and Terry Hands has told me that the RSC did not want anyone to notice it.

Why do audiences not notice such contradictions? Obviously, this is the same kind of problem we confronted with Viola. In the case of Montjoy and Exeter, the minor status of the characters largely explains our inattention. In a modern play, with half a dozen roles, we probably *would* notice; in Shakespeare's, with such a profusion of individuals, we are unlikely (and probably unable) to follow carefully the movements of each, and tend to take them on trust. In Henry's case, this explanation will not serve. *But we shall only perceive a contradiction if we juxtapose a present moment with an incompatible antecedent moment; how many spectators perceive a contradiction therefore depends on the probability of this present moment being juxtaposed with that one particular incompatible antecedent moment, and no other.* We shall only understand why spectators do not perceive such contradictions if we discover the principles of selection which govern the probability of such juxtapositions.

One might easily infer that, the greater the interval between the two moments, the less likely such mental juxtaposition becomes, and this principle obviously applies to Montjoy and Exeter. But in Henry's case one need only juxtapose his sitting-up with a remark made four lines earlier, yet audiences

did not make that juxtaposition. They did not do so because
no one on stage juxtaposed the two moments, or drew attention to their incompatibility; because Henry immediately
picked up Westmorland's remark and replied to it, so that we
were at once engaged in a dialogue, responding to Westmorland's surprise and to the content of Henry's speech, with no
time to think about Henry's presence. All these factors affect
the probability of juxtaposition; indeed, so does my earlier
observation about the number of characters in Shakespeare's
plays. Most important, audiences did not make the juxtaposition because the antecedent line was unlikely to strike
any spectator as important, when it was spoken, and it is our
evaluations of importance which determine what we shall
remember. As in Henry's exchange with Montjoy, what
matters in this scene is the question, not the answer. 'Where is
the king?' informs us of Henry's absence, which is important.
But, so long as the answer is vaguely plausible, we don't really
care where Henry is, so long as he isn't here. 'The king himself
is rode to view their battle' is forgotten almost as soon as it is
spoken.

An actor perceives such contradictions because his juxtapositions of one moment with another depend entirely upon
his presence during both moments, and his absence from the
interval between them – factors entirely irrelevant to the
experience of an audience. Moreover, the actor has a professional obligation to memorize certain portions of the text,
which means that he has available a mental transcript which
permits him to compare one moment with another. The
audience has no such transcript, and whether a spectator
juxtaposes the present moment with a past moment of course
depends on whether he remembers that past moment at all,
and the form his memory takes. The juxtapositions of a spectator depend on memory; those of an actor do not. Nor do
those of a reader.

A perceptual psychologist would have seen at once that the
contradiction between Henry's sitting-up and a remark
spoken four lines before was a problem in immediate memory
span:

A great deal of experience does not survive the instant of its
passing and is irretrievably forgotten the moment it is over.
. . . At each instant, it is best to be informed about the

detailed circumstances of that instant. But in the next instant, the circumstances of which we need to take account are different. It is not now necessary to retain every minute detail of immediately past circumstances; and indeed, if we did retain these details it would deprive us of freedom to consider the detailed requirements of the present moment.[44]

The psychologist, having assured us of the normality and indeed desirability of such oblivion, can also tell us that the length of our immediate memory span will be adversely affected by fatigue, consumption of alcohol(!), and age, and that it will be somewhat improved by education and general intellectual ability.[45] These factors will affect the ability to remember anything, but others explain why we tend to forget particular kinds of detail: for instance, our immediate memory will be severely impeded by distractions (such as the variety of stage business, as the English army woke up, during the first few lines of IV.iii) and by being surprised or startled – as when Henry sits up.[46]

The human capacity to retain detail is severely and physiologically limited. Therefore each spectator must select details to remember, and psychologists have investigated the principles of selection (the chief principle being our evaluation of importance, which will be based on a variety of factors). Finally, psychologists will remind us that, even if we have stored a fact in our memory, we may not recall it on a particular occasion, for recalling is itself an activity, which must first be motivated, and which will be governed thereafter by principles of its own.

The analysis of these principles of juxtaposition has a utility far beyond the significance of the contradictions themselves, for the same principles will govern a spectator's juxtaposition of lines and scenes and characters, juxtapositions which are regularly made the basis for entire interpretations of characters and plays. For instance, a spectator's reaction to Caesar's 'I am constant as the Northern star' speech will (as I have already noted) depend on whether he or she juxtaposes it with Caesar's vacillation in II.ii. My earlier explanation of why I did not make that juxtaposition myself can now be seen in a wider context. To the extent that a sentiment satisfies a pre-existent expectation (here, as to the classical dignity and magnitude of Caesar's character), it will appear self-sufficient;

it will not, like a *non sequitur* or an unexpected development, positively solicit a search for relation with other moments; it will not pointedly stimulate or motivate the machinery of active memory. Moreover, in this case the 'self-sufficiency' of the speech directly relates not simply to its content but also to its oratorical mode, a mode which (as *Henry V* demonstrates) satisfies hearers more readily than it does readers. And if in the first place the line does not demand juxtaposition with other moments, in the second it specifically encourages juxtaposition in a different direction: *forward* (to the impending assassination) rather than backward (to the vacillation of II.ii). Finally, if a spectator does make the particular connection with II.ii, how is he, as a spectator, likely to respond to it? There is obviously a contrast between the words here and the actions there; but this need not mean that the words here ring hollow, for the words here are accompanied by congruent action. The reader juxtaposes two passages as though they were coexistent, and deduces that one undermines the other; but the spectator juxtaposes a present moment with a past one, and as likely as not infers development rather than contradiction. Caesar vacillated then; he is constant now. Moreover, 'now' is not any old now, but a very particular one: Caesar's final now, the penultimate moment of his life. As we have already had occasion to remark, in connection with Viola, human beings naturally interpret character teleologically, fruition expressing essence (p. 79 above); hence a spectator-in-time responding here to a character-in-time will naturally interpret Caesar's final assertions and actions as a truer expression of his nature, his essence. ('Let me a little show it, even in this.') The spectator will in this particular case be further encouraged to this interpretation by the specific pattern of vacillation in II.ii (initial determination, change of mind, return to the initial intention), which is similar to the relation between II.ii and III.i (vacillation followed by determination), which mirrors the structure of the whole character (disappointment of expectation followed by satisfaction of it). An audience's response to these larger patterns does not in fact depend upon its conscious juxtaposition of II.ii with 'I am constant as the Northern star'; but those patterns can easily incorporate such a conscious juxtaposition, so that any spectator who does make it will be encouraged to see it in

terms of Caesar returning to and finally expressing his true
and noble essence.

Given the importance of such juxtapositions of moments
not only for interpretation, but also for understanding the
nature of the unity of a dramatic work, it may be useful to give
a few examples of supposed juxtapositions which are, it seems
to me, most unlikely to occur to an audience spontaneously.[47]

1 'Every reference to "ancestors" reminds the audience of
   the weakness of Henry's claim to the English throne.'
2 'No king of England, if not king of France' is reminiscent
   of Hotspur.
3 'Pistol "hath a killing tongue". So we might feel do Henry
   and the Chorus. According to the Boy: "They will steal
   anything, and call it purchase." They can use words to call
   a crime by a better name. Once more we may think of the
   bishop, the Chorus, and Henry himself.'
4 'On stage the whole scene [III.iii] looks and sounds like a
   senseless quarrel. With such a context, it is quite easy to
   examine the quarrel that Henry has raised with France
   with "suspicion".'
5 Catherine's 'introduction at this point ... relates this
   scene to the earlier argument between Nim and Pistol
   over Nell Quickly. .... All these arguments recall the foolish quarel over Nell that was finally settled with money.'
6 'Cambridge was out to do what Henry seems to be doing,
   to place a man, Edward Mortimer, on the throne because
   of his descent through the female line.'

Despite the author's lip-service to 'the audience', no audience
will make these juxtapositions. For the critic, unlike a spectator, apparently feels *a compulsion to compare*, having (as the
spectator does not) the leisure and the means to do so.[48] That
is, the critic assumes that these moments are not intelligible in
themselves, but only when related; that the appropriate principle for relating them is an abstracted conceptual similarity;
and that such comparisons will then form the basis for our
evaluations and responses.

But in each case the juxtapositions are in fact unlikely to be
made by an audience. We are not told that Cambridge intended to put Mortimer on the throne (II.ii.151–3), or anything
about the genealogical basis for Mortimer's claim, and, even if

we knew these things, the context does not encourage us to remember them, or relate them to the Archbishop's earlier speech. Edward the Black Prince *was* Henry's ancestor, and the word 'ancestors' (I.ii.102) itself summons up a distant relationship, skipping over the intervening generations; nor, again, does the context stimulate memories of Bolingbroke and Richard. If by chance the ending of II.ii reminds us of Hotspur, it will be because Henry displays there those stirring qualities which have so often in the theatre made Hotspur the hero of *Henry IV, Part One* – so that, even if we make the juxtaposition, we need not infer from it any criticism of Henry; indeed, the basis for the comparison makes such an inference highly unlikely. Pistol's 'killing tongue' is mentioned only for contrast with his 'quiet sword' (III.ii.33), and nothing suggests such a contrast in Henry's behaviour; moreover, the Boy means that Pistol has a *threatening* tongue, whereas, in order to be reminded of Henry's oration, we should need to translate the word as 'causing men to be killed'. Besides, the entire scene which precedes the Boy's speech has made us laugh because of the contrast between the exit Henry leads and the remaining behind of his 'irregular humorists', so that we are not immediately predisposed to seek similarities between them and Henry either in 'killing tongue' or in 'They will steal anything, and call it "purchase"' (III.ii.40–1). To apply this latter remark to Henry we must first conceptualize the entire war as a theft, and then disregard the distinction between Pistol (who steals something then pretends he has bought it) and Henry (who 'steals' something by pretending it was properly his to begin with). As for the 'Internationals' scene, the quarrel does not occupy the entire scene, but only a part of it (III.iii.61–80); no one comes to any harm; the entire episode encourages us to take pleasure in the idiosyncrasies of the characters, rather than harshly reproving their 'senseless' (but funny) bickering. As for the Catherine–Quickly juxtaposition, it requires us to compare (1) elements in the Chorus to Act III, (2) scenes III.iv and v, and (3) the final scene of the play, with (4) a brief episode in II.i; so that we must first combine all the Catherine material, disregard its manifest dissimilarities from the earlier episode, and on the basis of the similarities arrive at a judgement of – *Henry*.

The audience has neither the capacity nor the inclination for such activities. When Bardolph's 'On, on, on, on, on!'

immediately follows Henry's oration, we notice the contrast, because the two speeches are juxtaposed in time, similar in content, but dissimilar in detail (as in a metaphor). The same applies to the contrast between the exit of the Eastcheap regiment in II.iii, and the first line of the French King in the next scene ('Thus comes the English with full power upon us'), where 'Thus comes the English' describes the content of the preceding exit, but 'with full power' ludicrously misrepresents it. But the juxtapositions which the critic requires of us involve a separation in time, an abstracted similarity in conceptual content, and a (disregarded) dissimilarity of detail. Bardolph's line, by a juxtaposition in time, uses both the evident similarity and the evident contrast with the preceding speech; but the critic requires us simply to ignore the dissimilarities, and to use the (not evident but) abstracted similarity to overcome the separation in time. If audiences thought in this way, they would certainly notice the contradictions in Viola and Exeter and Montjoy and Henry.[49]

Directors can sometimes by visual or aural stimuli try to *force* an audience to juxtapose two moments. The attempts to do so often, perhaps usually, fail, but there can be no denying that they sometimes succeed. To take an instance from another play: in the 1979 RSC production of *Pericles* at The Other Place, Marina and the daughter of Antiochus were doubled by the same actress, and, as a direct result of this, when – immediately after the magnificent reunion of father and daughter – Lysimachus asked Pericles for Marina's hand (V.i.260–1), I was immediately struck not only by the cruel bad timing of the request, but also by its necessity: Pericles, unlike Antiochus, must be able and willing to give his daughter away, and the difficulty of the sacrifice was underlined by its timing. I don't know how many other spectators made the explicit comparion with Antiochus, but what matters is that one spectator certainly did, and as a direct result of the casting; one spectator, moreover, who had never made this particular juxtaposition when reading the play. Likewise, in Steven Berkoff's 1980 production of *Hamlet*, the actor who played Hamlet's Ghost doubled, visibly and remarkably, as Fortinbras – a pattern of doubling which gave the ending of the play extraordinary resonance, Fortinbras personifying the restoration of a legitimate order once embodied in Hamlet's father.

The question thus becomes: when is it legitimate for directors or critics to reinforce or underline such parallels? I will not presume to legislate an answer to such a question; but I do think that when a critic notices such parallels or presumes such mental juxtapositions, he is under some obligation to consider whether an audience would naturally make them; if not, he should say so, concede that his interpretation depends upon giving an extra theatrical emphasis, by no means inevitable, to certain parallels, and explain exactly how that theatrical emphasis could be achieved. Interpretations which disregard such simple criteria have no more validity than those of Charles Marowitz, whose versions depend almost entirely on just such unexpected juxtapositions, combined with an exaggerated emphasis on statements taken out of context.

The principles of selection governing the probability of juxtaposition determine whether a spectator will bring to bear, in interpreting one moment, the data contained in another; if he does not, he will not have sufficient data for the perception (let alone solution) of a contradiction. But such an insufficiency of data may arise in a variety of other ways as well. For instance, in the RSC production the Boy continued to carry Bardolph's mug after his execution;[50] but, as the mug was not large or unusual or conspicuous to begin with, even from the best seat in the house a spectator had no reason to distinguish that mug from any other, and no reason to note its continuing presence. Of Henry's encounter with Erpingham (IV.i.13–35) Hands wrote, 'It is interesting that for the first time in three plays an old man, a man of the previous generation, actually approves of Henry. It perhaps gives him courage in his further actions.'[51] How was this communicated? When Alan Howard said, 'God-a-mercy, old heart, thou speak'st cheerfully', he stressed 'old'. But no spectator could possibly derive Hands's interpretation from Howard's pronunciation of 'old'. We are also told that, by the middle of the second scene, the Archbishop had successfully 'shifted everybody away from proper contemplation of Church problems'[52] – everybody indeed, including the audience. The audience had ceased to contemplate Church problems at least in part because the RSC began the play in rehearsal clothes, so that Canterbury and Ely were not perpetually *present* to an audience in their identities as clerics. If a character is dressed like a bishop, then at any moment we may juxtapose his words with his clothes, to relate or contrast what he says to the interests or image of his profession. But, if a character is dressed like any other, we shall only be particularly and specifically conscious of his profession when it is called to our attention by speech or gesture; at any other moment, we can rely only on our memory of his profession, which will never be so strong as the perpetual visual stimulus of a costume. This applies to Ely particularly, as he is never named or identified as a bishop, so that, though his agreement with Canterbury was clear enough, we were never strongly or specifically aware of him as a man with 'vested' ecclesiastical interests. (Compare the problem of Olivia's costume, p. 67.)

The Archbishop's famous bee-speech, later in this same scene (I.ii.183–220), Hands described as 'the full medieval statement of paternal fascism', a hierarchic philosophy which Henry by play's end would abolish, and from which he here dissociated himself, by remaining isolated from the others during the speech.[53] This interpretation requires first of all that an audience perceive Henry's isolation, and then infer the significance and the cause of that isolation. As audiences have a natural and desirable tendency to listen to the character actually speaking, there are a good many people (myself included) who were not even particularly conscious of Henry's physical separation from the others. The decision to begin the play in rehearsal clothes was designed, and in part managed, to starve the eye, and so *force* audiences to listen to the words, in the long speeches for which this play is famous. To the degree that this intention succeeded, the intention that we notice Henry's isolation had to fail. Everyone in the audience saw Henry; he was in every spectator's visual field. But one was not *aware* of seeing him: he was on the periphery, not the fovea, of the retina.[54] This unawareness was the consequence of a perceptual decision about significance. Audiences watch the character speaking because (unless he is wildly upstaged) they assume that he is for the moment the most significant thing on stage. Usually the second-most-significant thing is the character addressed, in this case Henry, so one might expect at least a secondary attention to him. But one was hardly conscious of the speech being directed at Henry; it was virtually played to the house, as so many speeches in this play (rightly) were, and this extradramatic style of delivery simply increased a spectator's natural tendency to attend to the content of the words. The Archbishop and the nobles seemed to have a mental vision of that honey-bee kingdom, and encouraged us to create such a vision for ourselves. We would turn our attention to the man addressed when the Archbishop turned to him, as though snapping out of a dream ('Therefore, my liege . . .'). The spectator's decision that Henry was a relatively insignificant element of the visual field – no more significant than the visible lights and scaffolding, or the back of the head of the spectator in the next row – was further reinforced by the earlier choreography of the scene. Because of the size of the Stratford stage the actors were often as distant from one another, as isolated, as Henry was during the Archbishop's speech; Henry's spatial isolation thus did not seem unusual, and only by being unusual could it make a particular claim to our attention.

But even if spectators noticed Henry's isolation, how could they infer its significance or its cause? The isolation might in itself be no more than a way of emphasizing Henry, the leading actor, or of reinforcing the contrast between Henry's hesitation and the enthusiasm of his nobles. These are obvious answers, and a spectator could only have inferred a less obvious interpretation by carefully observing Henry's facial expression. It is, of course, unlikely that spectators would do so, even if they noticed Henry's isolation. But, as I had been forewarned by Beauman's book, in later visits to the play I took some care to watch Henry. Alan Howard look puzzled; he sometimes glanced sharply sideways at the Archbishop; he eventually put on a wry half smile. Now, even by watching Howard, and Howard alone, it would be exceedingly difficult to arrive at the specific content of Henry's thoughts, as described by Hands; for all those reactions might express no more than Henry's dissociation from the war-hunger of his court, rather than his rejection of the Archbishop's image of society. More important, if one concentrated to this extent upon Henry's expression, trying to interpret it, it became virtually impossible even to hear, coherently, what the Archbishop was saying. Perceptually, few people can do two things at once: either you attend to one task and slight the other, or by trying to attend equally to both to an extent you botch both.[55] If one did not hear the Archbishop coherently, one could not properly juxtapose his words with Henry's facial expression, and only by such juxtaposition could one arrive at

Hands's interpretation. But, even if we did all that this interpretation requires of us, how would we make sense of Henry's answer to Canterbury? For this 'full medieval state-ment of paternal fascism' apparently convinces Henry to attack France. Two obvious explanations of this decision present themselves: either Henry is persuaded by the content of Canterbury's speech (and the preceding debate), or he decides he cannot resist the court's unanimity of will. This second interpretation would in fact fit all the evidence the RSC provided. But Hands asks the spectator to ignore these obvious options, and choose instead a third: that Henry, appalled by the content of Canterbury's speech, decides that the system it glorifies must be dismantled, *by war with France*, just what the Archbishop and the nobles (= the system) want. This is simply an incommunicable interpretation.

If a spectator is not given sufficient data to enable him to arrive at a particular conclusion, he will respond in one of two ways. Most often, he simply arrives at a different and simpler conclusion. Repeatedly, the failure of the RSC to communi-cate particular intentions arose from the presence of a simpler alternative which would explain the data. Thus, after Henry's reply to his second embassy (IV.iii.79–126), Montjoy tore up his leafy branch, his 'badge of office'. According to Oliver Ford-Davies, 'I think, faced with what he sees of the English army, Montjoy realizes that his whole function, his whole world has become archaic. He cannot function any longer as a medieval herald.'[56] But, when spectators noticed this detail at all, they assumed it meant only that diplomacy was over, that the battle could not now be averted, that there would be no more truces. They assumed Montjoy was acting like a herald, not like a man who had suddenly decided he doesn't want to be one anymore. Again, at the beginning of III.vi, the heraldic canopy collapsed onto the stage, its grey underside covering part of the stage floor. But the wires holding it to the ceiling were still attached (see Plate 6), and during the scene the soldiers unhooked some of those supports, and reattached them elsewhere. According to Hands, 'The wire hauser supports for the canopy became leafless trees or undergrowth, being cleared by shivering archers.'[57] But to an audience the wires were just wires, with the actors repositioning them in preparation for some later scene-change. This non-naturalistic interpretation was encouraged by the stylized staging of the entire play, by the visibility of the lights and scaffolding, the production's insistence on the play as a performance. Again: this canopy did not cover the entire floor (see plate 6). According to Hands, 'Henry ... has the choice during the scene of joining the army on the canopy, or remaining isolated from it, downstage. For much of the scene he is off the canopy.'[58] One was certainly aware of Henry's isolation. But that awareness was purely spatial: it had nothing to do with Henry being on or off the canopy. For the RSC had taught us to interpret scenery as synecdoche. ('All art is synecdoche.') The wall at Harfleur, for the breach scene, did not cover the whole stage, or extend from wing to wing. We could see its edges: it was a wall standing in the middle of the stage. But we did not give its edges any real or symbolic significance; we simply realized that part of a wall was put there to stand for the whole. So with the canopy: its edges had no significance.

These examples confirm a simple but significant principle of economy: an audience will accept the simplest possible hypothesis which explains the data. 'The basic law of visual perception' is that 'any stimulus pattern tends to be seen in such a way that the resulting structure is as simple as the given conditions permit'.[59] Only when the simpler hypothesis fails will a spectator be driven to seek one more complex. (Incidentally, this is another reason for the failure of psychoanalysis in the interpretation of Shakespeare's characters: it requires us to think, intensely, about moments which do not demand a more complex hypothesis.) There is nothing lazy about this procedure. It is the method of science itself. Differences will of course arise over the precise conditions in which a hypothesis can be said to have failed the data, but in practical terms, as the preceding examples show, spectators apparently apply fairly similar criteria.

But if an audience is not given sufficient data to enable it to arrive at the intended interpretation, and if no alternative is readily available, it will often make no interpretation at all. That moment of the play will pass without meaning. The speed of performance does not leave a spectator time to puzzle out an explanation. This happened, for instance, with Alan Howard's stress on 'old'. It happened also with the business of Williams's glove (IV.viii.56–60):

> On 'Keep it, fellow', Williams refuses the money. Henry then tips the money . . . out of the glove, and on 'And wear it for an honour in thy cap', taps Williams with the glove on both shoulders, as if to knight him. 'Give him the crowns' became almost humorous. Having established his integrity, the money could be accepted by Williams, and was.[60]

I have yet to encounter anyone who understood what the tapping on the shoulders meant, or why Williams first refused the money and then, a line and a half later, accepted it. In fact, I have yet to find anyone who was bothered by his incomprehension of this sequence.

The success of the centenary production depended on what it communicated, not what it intended, and, though intention and achievement usually coincided, they did not always or necessarily do so. This might stand as a paradigm of the relation between author and creation. Traditional criticism is based, fundamentally, on intention; studies of audience response are based on effect. Usually the analyst of response assumes or asserts that the author's intention can be inferred from the response his work produces. But this is patently false. If it were true, no play could fail. It would be more accurate to say that every dramatist constructs a hypothetical audience, and that the success or failure of his intentions depends on the relation between his real and his hypothetical spectators. The RSC failed to communicate its intentions when it assumed that normal spectators could and would perceive elements which in fact they could and did not. To interpret the artist's intentions, we must reconstruct, as best we can, his hypothetical model. Most critics will of course fashion this in their own image. But, whatever the model may have been, and however we try to reconstruct it, we cannot assume it is identical with any real audience, or any collection of real audiences. The proper study of audience response must confine itself to empirical audiences, to the effect the work *does* produce (not what it should, or was meant to, produce). Living audiences can be studied; so can dead ones, in so far as history provides us with evidence of their responses. Moreover, we can reasonably assume, when the response of a living audience derives from factors which have not altered in the last four centuries (for instance, from the limitations of the human nervous system), that former audiences would have responded in the same way to the same stimulus. We should also be able to isolate factors which have changed since Shakespeare's death, and, by analysing and discounting their influence upon modern responses, we should arrive at a reasonably accurate hypothetical description of how Shakespeare's first audiences would have responded to his work.

But this still will not tell us what Shakespeare intended. If Beauman's book had not been written, if all the members of the cast were now dead and had left no record of their intentions, we could not by any means or with any certainty determine how Alan Howard and Terry Hands interpreted the content of Henry's thoughts during Canterbury's speech, for that interpretation could not have been communicated to any audience. Because the RSC has revealed its intentions, we can in this case measure the distance between intention and achievement. Of course Shakespeare did not record his intentions. But, even if Beauman's book had not been written, we might notice Alan Howard's odd emphasis on 'old', or the peculiar business with Williams's glove; or we might realize that the English soldiers were not repositioning the wire hausers merely in preparation for a scene-change, because in fact the scene was changed during the interval. We should be aware of something being done purposefully, without being able to determine its purpose. In such a case we are driven to postulate an intention, only because that intention was not fully communicated. This is perhaps a better paradigm of the critic's usual relation to an author's intent. The academic critic will be intrigued by precisely such moments, because they present him with a puzzle to be solved. Hence the modern fascination with *Troilus and Cressida* – or indeed, with any scene or passage or character which apparently fails. And, though the effort to reconstruct the author's intentions in such cruces often enough leads to absurdity, it has also often opened our eyes to great beauty. An author may legitimately puzzle us, thereby forcing us to seek a solution, the discovery of which delights us. Any delayed-reaction joke works in this way; so, on the level of plot, does a murder mystery; so, on the level of character, does the apparently irrational leap from one thought to another. An author may also legitimately puzzle us when the puzzle has no solution, as there is none for the riddle of the sufferings of Oedipus. But, having said this, it does not follow, whenever we are puzzled or disappointed, that the author meant us to be; nor does it follow that we are to blame, always, if we cannot grasp the author's intent, even when that author is Shakespeare. Finally, we must judge Shakespeare, as we have judged the RSC, by the achievement rather than the intent.

That achievement will be measured by the responses of audiences. But, as we cannot hope to observe the responses of every spectator in every audience at every performance, we must in practice arrive at a Platonic definition of the audience. 'The audience', as I define it, does not include spectators who, for one reason or another, will respond abnormally – as a professional torturer, after a hard day's work, would presumably respond abnormally to the blinding of Gloucester. But neither do I wish to limit myself to the lowest common denominator of response. Some audiences, as every actor knows, are more alert than others. Within any audience, some spectators are more intelligent and more perceptive than others, and they expect to be rewarded for this extraordinary sensitivity with extraordinary pleasure. Those who know French will enjoy certain scenes of *Henry V* more than those who don't. This disparity is normal, and there are many such disparities in any play, and the critic should try to locate them. But, in terms of our working definition, the ideal spectator to *Henry V* would have to know some French; he would have to sit where he could see Alan Howard's tears, after the surrender of Harfleur. But a significant minority of Shakespeare's audience could have been expected to know French, as part of the basic mental equipment it brought to the theatre, and, as soon as a character began to speak French, they would bring this knowledge to bear, reflexively, unconsciously. No such significant minority could be expected to know the genealogical basis for Mortimer's claim to the English throne; even those who did could only bring that information to bear if they were prompted, or motivated, to do so. But these differences between spectators are minute, by comparison with the differences between spectators as a class and readers (especially critics) as a class. Sometimes these differences matter little; but sometimes, as with *Henry V*, they are crucial. Any analysis of audience or reader response must be constantly alert to the difference.

However, the recognition of differences within audiences, and of ambiguities of text and performance which allow or create conflicting and ambivalent responses, returns us to the problem of hierarchy, the dramatist's ability or inability to control emphasis, to ensure that the ambivalences he permits do not endanger his overall structure, the general drift of sympathies his plot depends upon, the specific emotional climaxes where he wants an audience to respond, as far as possible, strongly and uniformly. The more complex, various, and powerful our responses to individual moments, the greater the danger must become of an audience losing its way. Even if we grant the validity of a modern interpretative strategy which argues that almost any work of literature is designed to deprive us of our moral bearings, still an audience must be collectively persuaded that this is indeed how it *should* respond; otherwise it will write down its confusion to the incompetence of the playwright or the production, or (as with the Archbishop's Salic Law speech) to its own unfamiliarity with the material.

We have therefore reached a point where the problem of controlling emphasis must be confronted. But at this point the methodology of the three preceding chapters breaks down, for we can no longer, in such complex cases, expect to find anything like critical or interpretative unanimity. It is precisely with regard to questions of relative emphasis that a critic's occupational strengths – his abnormal attentiveness, his abnormal familiarity with the text, his abnormal theoretical and articulate self-consciousness – most distance him from the responses of other spectators, and do so in a way that undermines the playwright's control of proportion and emphasis. Consequently, in attempting to describe the playwright's manipulation of emphasis through a complex succession of complex moments, I shall, almost inevitably, be forced to advocate one interpretation of a particular work at the expense of another; at which point the approach to drama through audience response will have become (what it is often accused of being) simultaneously 'reductive' and 'subjective'. Or, to put it another way, this approach to drama will then be capable of reducing the self-defeating, self-indulgent clutter of conflicting and incompatible interpretations, by demanding that the subjective responses of individual critics be subordinated to the objectivity of the audience as a whole.

5 Revolutions of Perspective: *King Lear*

> *The dramatist through working in the theatre gradual-*
> *ly learns not merely to take account of the presence of*
> *his collaborators, but to derive advantage from them;*
> *and he learns, above all, to organize the play in such a*
> *way that its strength lies not in appearances beyond his*
> *control, but in the succession of events and in the*
> *unfolding of an idea, in narration. . . . The theatre is*
> *unfolding action and in the disposition of events the*
> *authors may exercise a governance so complete that*
> *the distortions effected by the physical appearance of*
> *actors, by the fancies of scene painters and the misun-*
> *derstandings of directors, fall into relative insignifi-*
> *cance. It is just because the theatre is an art of many*
> *collaborators, with the constant danger of grave mis-*
> *interpretation, that the dramatist learns to turn his*
> *attention to the laws of narrative.*
>
> Thornton Wilder[1]

About *King Lear* there is no historical unanimity. Shakespeare's original, in whole and in perhaps every detail, is
greater than Nahum Tate's adaptation, yet against the unanimity of this modern verdict for Shakespeare must be set 150
years of seeming unanimity against him. Tolstoy preferred
King Leir. Complicating this dissension over the relative
merits of three versions of the myth is the fact that Shakespeare's play itself exists in two versions, the Quarto and
Folio, between them containing about 400 lines included in
one text but not the other, plus variants great and small in
what seems every line, often conspiring to agree only on what
is to us inexplicable. To this confusion has been added a third,
conglomerate text, the object of all modern criticism, but

boasting no authority greater than Theobald and the timorous inertia of his descendants. But even those who agree on the text and greatness of Shakespeare's play agree on little else. There is no unanimity about the effect of this play or its parts, and, if you deny even the existence of a particular effect, you will hardly be persuaded by an analysis of its causes. If Sir Isaac Newton had not secured assent to the proposition that apples fall from the tree to the ground (rather than falling from ground to tree), he most certainly could not have secured assent to his hypothesis as to the cause of the apple's behaviour.

The critical method I have heretofore employed, depending as it does on an evident consensus, cannot deal with *King Lear*: I must abandon the method or the play. I can escape from this dilemma only by lowering or altering the standard of consensus. For instance, I shall assume Shakespeare's superiority to Tate. Textually, it would be simplest to confine myself to Theobald's conglomerate, in one of its modern manifestations: Theobald represents the textual consensus. Unfortunately, my desire for simplicity must sometimes yield to my desire for truth. I believe the conflation is an editorial fiction; the consensus founded upon it has already been shattered.[2] In such circumstances, I have no choice but to consider all three texts (Quarto, Folio, conflation); where they produce substantially different effects, I have tried to elucidate or imagine those differences, in developing my argument.

As with *Julius Caesar*, I have limited myself to a scene consistently acclaimed, Lear's confrontation with Goneril in I.iv. But this scene requires methods of analysis much more complex than those which sufficed for *Julius Caesar*, which is a smaller achievement precisely because its greatest parts can be so isolated from the whole (though even there such isolation produces distortions). With *Lear*, to isolate is to dismember. In *Julius Caesar* I could focus on one scene to the exclusion of virtually everything else; with *Lear* I must subject much of Act I to partial examination, for the responses produced by scene iv fundamentally depend on responses produced by earlier scenes. But I nevertheless remain primarily interested in scene iv only: the rest of the act concerns me only in so far as it affects the hierarchies of emphasis in that scene.

My approach to *Julius Caesar* fails *Lear* in another and more important respect, for the consensus about this scene is much more problematic. Though probably only Tolstoy would deny its power, the degree of our sympathy for Lear and the progress of our loathing for his daughters remain among the play's most bitterly disputed issues. For many modern critics, if Goneril and Regan are as evil as preceding centuries believed, the play is no more than melodrama in verse. Nevertheless, there does exist a consensus about the power of this scene, about the intensity of the responses it creates, a consensus useful so long as its limitations are understood. (There is no such historical consensus for much of the rest of the play: for instance, the Gloucester plot, or much of the final scene.) The insecurity of this consensus makes *King Lear* a more difficult problem than *Julius Caesar*, or *Twelfth Night*, or – even – *Henry V*. But, on the other hand, what we have already learned from the assassination scene, from Viola, from the 1975 production should enable us to dismiss certain critical assertions, by showing that they derive from the application to drama of standards not germane to it. Of the variety of opinions about *King Lear*, some spring not from the valid ambiguities of the work of art, but only from misperception. An elephant remains an elephant, despite the verdicts of the three blind men.

An observer's reactions to the quarrel between Goneril and Lear (or to any quarrel) will depend upon his perception of the two antagonists before they quarrel, upon his perception of the issue, and upon his perception of the responses of the antagonists themselves to the confrontation.

If we imagine a continuum from total allegiance to Lear on one side, and to Goneril on the other, with neutrality between, an individual observer could occupy any position on this scale. But even observers occupying identical positions might in fact respond quite differently, since an observer who is intellectually committed might be emotionally neutral. If my sister is divorced by her husband on grounds of adultery, I may know my brother-in-law's action is justified, and yet feel more for my sister than for him, particularly if I have never known him well, or never liked him. The intensity of my feeling for my sister depends on the intensity of my perception of her, and of her suffering; though the husband's suffering may be greater, being distant it appears smaller. (Plato drew attention to this affective illusion; but being conscious of the illusion hardly impedes its daily operation.)

Our perceptions therefore depend on our perspective, and a dramatist can manipulate our perspective, as a painter can. The painter manipulates the laws of optics; the novelist manipulates point of view, and, though its laws are rather more complex, criticism has constructed a vocabulary enabling it to analyse the functions of a narrative voice. In drama there is no narrative voice, but the dramatist none the less controls our point of view, by controlling the narrative, by deciding what to show, and how and when to show it. All performers, so long as they are actually speaking, impose briefly their own perspective; they compete for our attention; they struggle to make our point of view theirs. Drama therefore seems the most impersonal of arts. No novel, whatever its manipulation of point of view, can achieve this seeming freedom, because there always exists a mediator between what happened and what we perceive, and even a play, read rather than performed, loses something of this illusion of freedom. A great play presupposes such liberty of theatrical interpretation, such competition among the cast: as in the classic hypothetical model (i.e. fiction) of capitalist economics, each participant pursues his own interest, yet each is guided by the unseen hand of the law of the market place. But it does not follow from this premiss that all interpretations are legitimate or useful, or that they can derive an ontological validity from the necessary ambiguity of the text. Grotesqueries of interpretation offer themselves as 'perspectives' on *King Lear*; they imply that the play is an object, which can properly be viewed from any vantage. But in fact the play is itself a point of view on an action, and interpretative arrogance derives from a false equation of the play and the play's action, or myth. The myth can indeed be viewed from any number of perspectives. Aeschylus and Sophocles and Euripides, in the Electra myth, have taken one story and made three plays from it, by observing it from different perspectives. In *King Lear* also, Shakespeare has taken a story and observed it from a created perspective, which he seeks to impose on his audience.

As the painter controls the disposition of space, so does the dramatist the disposition of time. Like the painter, the dramatist decides what to show; he conceals what he does not want seen; he draws attention to what has been left out, so that we supply it for him. But, unlike the painter, the dramatist also controls *when* we see what he shows us. We perceive the quarrel between Goneril and Lear in stages; our reactions vary and develop; one feeling succeeds another. What we feel at the end of I.iv is determined by what we have felt before, and when, and how intensely. Emotional states shade into one another. Therefore a dramatist must understand how one emotion turns into another, and therefore a critic must understand the present state of an audience before he can say how any given statement will affect them.

Let us momentarily assume that, though at first our feelings toward her are ambivalent, we eventually realize that Goneril is a fiend. In life, we could conclude she always was one, though we had not before perceived it, and from the later evidence of her true nature we could deduce the true interpretation of her otherwise-ambivalent past. In the theatre too there may come a moment during the performance when suddenly all her actions undergo a metamorphosis in retrospect: such moments, within the play, are magnificently dramatic. But readers and audiences, returning to the play, may be tempted to presume what they should discover, by bringing to bear at once the information they have acquired through previous exposures to the play. This fallacy, 'reading a play backwards', has been often enough condemned, but the fallacy has more manifestations than is usually supposed.

'Reading a play backwards' is a species of anachronism: it transfers something out of its proper place in a temporal sequence, into a time where it does not belong. A play, being a temporal sequence, is also subject to other species of anachronism, of which this is only the most familiar. (I am not now talking about historical anachronisms, which occur within the work itself, but about anachronisms in our response to the work.) For our previous experience of the play involves not only information, but also the emotions attendant on that information. A spectator who has been often moved to tears by Lear's sufferings may regard the Lear of I.i with an excessive, sentimental, anachronistic sympathy, which has no source and no function in that scene, at that time. Nineteenth-century interpretations and performances were particularly liable to such distortion. But, if anticipation may produce anachronisms, so may memory. The better the critic knows the play, the closer he comes to a simultaneous perception of all its parts, which will allow him to ignore the chronological imperative of performance. If, in *King Lear*, the critic can simultaneously perceive, in detail, scenes IV.vii and I.i, then the latter is no longer a distant background to the former; instead, two foregrounds are juxtaposed. His own knowledge of the whole has destroyed the dramatist's organization of perspective, and, as a consequence of his omniscience, he is confronted with a series of contradictions, which must be intellectually resolved into true or false, when in fact the dramatist never intended A and non-A to be juxtaposed.

Thus, critics have noticed that, in his speeches to Cordelia before their imprisonment (V.iii.8–26), Lear expresses the same desire for retreat from the world which motivated his follies in the first scene; they have also noticed that, here as in II.iv, Lear combines unreal threats against his daughters with a refusal to weep; this characterizing 'system of repetitions' persuades some critics that Lear has learned nothing. I find this conclusion wildly false to my experience of the play. It assumes that Lear's lyric expansiveness will recall a curt remark 3000 lines before ('To shake all cares and business from our age ... while we / Unburthen'd crawl toward death'), and that, in a play full of weeping and refusals to weep, full of curses, this curse and this refusal to weep will forcibly recall one (and only one) other, 1500 lines before. We must, moreover, in both cases be *conscious* of these parallels, if we are to judge Lear as the critics judge him. Having lifted background into foreground, the critics have then torn each passage from its emotional context, thereby combining anachronism with disregard for the dramatist's chosen perspective on each of these three moments. The critics assume that, because two passages are similar in conceptual content, they will provoke similar responses from an audience; that we shall morally equate Lear's resolve to make the best of prison with his voluntary and catastrophic decision to abdicate; that, because we condemned Lear's desire to retreat from responsibility, we shall likewise condemn his willingness to retreat from the suffering we have seen him endure since; that, if we do realize that Lear's wishes are now ironically fulfilled, we shall rebuke his inability to change, rather than rejoice in his happiness, or weep at the future Edmund has prepared for him; that in both scenes we watch coolly, reprovingly, even perhaps contemptuously, Lear's refusal to weep and his impotent threats. They assume, in short, that Lear's words in Acts I, II and V exist outside time, and can be extracted from the moment, from the emotions of that moment, to be scrutinized from any perspective and at any distance the critic selects. They assume that the play is itself an object, rather than a created perspective on an object.

The best-known and most successful critical exposition of this point of view is undoubtedly Robert Heilman's *This Great Stage* (1948), itself one of the best-known and most successful examples of the imagist school of the old 'New Criticism'. The book documents, by cataloguing, many of the play's verbal and intellectual preoccupations: the nature of Nature, the reasons for madness and the madness of reason, kinds of blindness, physical and intellectual and moral. No one would deny that the play eventually dramatizes and articulates each of these themes, but that articulation is not achieved until late in the plot's development, when Act III confronts us with Lear's real and Edgar's imagined madness, the storm and its heath, the blinding of Gloucester. An 'innocent' audience could hardly be expected to appreciate, at first sounding, the full significance of Lear's subordinate clause 'Where nature doth with merit challenge' (I.i.53), or Goneril's off-hand adverbial phrase 'Dearer than eyesight' (56), or Kent's hyperbolic accusation that 'Lear is mad' (146). None of these, in its immediate dramatic context, magnetically invests the words 'Nature' or 'eyesight' or 'mad' with the importance of a major philosophical theme. By the time these themes have been made manifest, in Act III, few spectators – if any – will remember, in the rush and magnitude of those later events, the play's first modest soundings of these three crucial words. On the other hand, no one who knows the play can read or hear the first scene again without perceiving and indeed savouring the aptness of the first restrained articulation of each theme. In each case critical 'anachronism'

genuinely increases our immediate pleasure in and appreciation of a moment of the author's play.

'The author's play' is a phrase fruitfully ambiguous.
Thomas Middleton's *A Game at Chess* – one of the greatest
Jacobean plays – begins with the declaration of a Prologue
that 'What of the game called chess-play can be made / To
make a stage-play shall this day be played', and in the 'play'
which follows we are at different times conscious of the 'playing' of individual actors, the 'playing' of individual characters,
the 'play' of the two unseen eternal adverseries who face each
other across the chessboard of the stage of the world, and
(above all these) the 'play' of the master dramatist himself.
When as veteran Shakespearians we relish that unobtrusive
introduction of 'Nature', what we relish is the author's own
technique, the artistry of his (chess) play: we learn nothing
about the proper interpretation of the characters or the action
of the drama of *King Lear*. We savour the first snatch of
melodies which will eventually develop into major musical
themes. The 'innocent' playgoer could not be conscious of
such touches, but they do I think nevertheless contribute to
his or her total response to the play. If we are not conscious of
such details, or rather of the pregnant relationship of such
details to later events, then they cannot influence our sense of
the action's specific meaning: meaning is the product of conscious interpretation. But the alliteration of ideas does
strongly contribute to our sense that the action *has* a meaning.
The increasingly conspicuous accumulation of allusions,
verbal and dramatic, to sight, to deviations from reason, to
Nature, prepare us to accept – as proper, indeed inevitable, to
this world – the stunning extremity of Act III. The violent
dramatization of those three themes in the middle of the play
then in turn lends an immediate emphasis and resonance to
every such allusion thereafter. Moreover, for the play as a
whole the mere density of such interlinking allusions powerfully reinforces our conviction of the unity of the fable. The
innocent theatre-goer need not be conscious, even at the end,
of those repetitions (or of Viola's), any more than an innocent
gallery-goer will notice the predominance in one painting of a
certain kind or angle of brush-stroke. An art critic might legitimately observe and admire the artistry of those brush-
strokes, just as the music critic might admire the artistry of the

casually introduced theme, or the literary critic admire the artistry of 'Dearer than eyesight'. But these things have no meaning. The individual images of eyes and blindness in *King Lear* have no influence on the play's structure, or our perception of it, until the scene of Gloucester's blinding, and the emphasis that scene gives to them cannot (in a performance) be retrospectively applied.

Individual productions might attempt to emphasize such images by purely theatrical means. Directors might insist that the cast stress certain words or images whenever they occurred (as Alan Howard stressed 'old'); non-naturalistic make-up could heavily highlight the eyes; a great heraldic eye, or a statue of 'Nature', might be interpolated into every scene, looming over the action; the play might be set, from the beginning, in a madhouse, like Peter Weiss's *Marat/Sade*. Some of these techniques would almost certainly fail, in that they would be appreciated only by spectators already aware of the relevant theme; others would succeed in highlighting early references to the theme, but only at the expense of the play's own structure. If the whole play is performed in a madhouse, or if real (acted) madmen occasionally erupt onto the stage, the full shock of Lear's madness, and of his encounter with Tom o' Bedlam, will be dissipated; if a great abstract eye dominates the set, Gloucester's horrific punishment will dwindle into predictable symbolism. All such attempts to insist upon the play's recurrent imagery labour to rearrange the hierarchies of the work itself: they either fail, or succeed only by subverting the action. A Van Gogh self-portrait may be unified by a pattern of brush-strokes; but even in Van Gogh brush-strokes are not the subject of the painting. They contribute to its unity and its texture, as do the images of *King Lear*. *King Lear* remains an enacted narrative: a textured and developing perspective on an unstoppable, irreversible action.

If we see *King Lear* as a created perspective on an object, then the object itself must be described as 'the Lear story' or 'the Lear myth', a simple plot outline which it would be possible to dramatize in a variety of ways. Any dramatization of that story, however, will have to face one major and very particular problem in perspective, a problem in the transformation of sympathy: a man clearly and monstrously wrong in the initial act of the story must eventually elicit, to a lesser or greater degree, our emotional and moral allegiance. At the level of narrative folktale or parable this problem hardly arises: so detached do we remain that our emotions are never actually engaged at all, and our intellectual allegiance can shift from one paragraph to the next. But a dramatist must make the revolution of perspective on the character plausible. Any playwright setting out to handle the Lear myth must soon face the technical problem of manipulating an audience's perspective (without seeming to), so that it sees Lear's rejection of or by his second daughter differently from his rejection of or by his first.

As virtually the whole of the play's stage history confirms that this manipulation of perspective can be successfully accomplished in the theatre, I shall confine myself, by way of illustration, to two of the more striking pieces of testimony. The first, one of the very few early allusions to the play, occurs in an elegy on the death of the actor Richard Burbage (1619):[3]

> Hee's gone & with him what a world are dead,
> Which he revivd, to be revived soe.
> No more young Hamlett, ould Heironymoe,
> *Kind Leer*, the greved Moore, and more beside . . . .

The italics are my own, and it must be confessed that this is the response of only one spectator; but one can hardly conceive of *any* spectator describing Paul Scofield's Lear as 'kind', and a certain school of modern critics would choke on the adjective. This single spectator, moreover (probably John Fletcher), is not only one who must have regularly attended the theatre, but one interested enough in it to want to write an elegy on a famous actor, and literate enough to do so; and he is also our only witness to the effect of the performance of the actor who created the role. The second piece of testimony is not about a famous actor but from one. The impact of David Garrick's Lear is well documented – he 'rendered the curse [in I.iv] so terribly affecting to the audience, that, during his utterance of it, they seemed to shrink from it as from a blast of lightning', making 'the Soul of every Hearer shiver'[4] – but Garrick's own judgement of the part, coming as it does not only from the technical experience of a great actor but from his observation of audiences as well, carries even more weight:[5]

> nay I think I might go farther, & venture to say that had not ye source of his unhappiness proceeded from good qualities carry'd to excess of folly, but from vices, I really think that ye bad part of him would be forgotten in ye space of an Act, & *his distresses at his Years* would become Objects of Pity to an Audience.

This time the italics are Garrick's own. Of course it can be objected that Garrick was acting Tate's adaptation; but this is what makes Garrick's conditional so important – *even if* one played Lear much more harshly in the first scene than Garrick did (which most modern critics would insist on), Garrick still felt that the revolution of sympathy would occur by the end of Act I. Since Garrick was acting Tate's adaptation (which omitted I.v), that means 'by the end of I.iv'.

An observer's reaction to the quarrel will depend upon his perception of the two antagonists before they quarrel.
We have seen Goneril twice before she enters in scene iv. In the first scene, on demand she expresses her love for Lear in a single seven-line speech; at the end of that scene, she speaks briefly to Cordelia, then privately to Regan. Her first speech tells me nothing. Goneril does not effectively exist until Lear names her, and she again ceases to exist when Lear turns to Regan. The actress may react to Lear's darker purpose; she may speak her speech haughtily, oilily, haltingly, however she likes; she may make its exaggerations seem either artificial or the usual hyperbole of love. Here – as I said earlier (p.77) – 'we can only recognize the necessity for choice, and the consequent variety of theatrical interpretation'. But only the third daughter matters; the first two exist to create a pattern for Cordelia to break (and if excessive elaboration interferes with our perception of this pattern, it distorts the scene). But at scene's end Goneril and Regan do interest me, because Cordelia has in the interim so insisted on the contrast between herself and her sisters, because they have not as yet responded to

events which must affect them deeply, because they are alone with the audience. Both sisters react similarly to Cordelia's farewell; in fact the Quarto and Folio differ on which speech to assign to whom, and it hardly matters. To the extent that I already admire, to some degree at least, Cordelia, their response to her is bound to disaffect me. In fact, I like Cordelia now more than when Lear banished her, not only because of the 'little faulty admixture of pride and sullenness in Cordelia's "Nothing"', of which Coleridge spoke,[6] but also because of the structure of the scene. Only after Cordelia's banishment does Kent intercede to defend her, and France marry her, dowerless: both elevate our estimation of her worth. Her rejection of mercenary Burgundy can be theatrically a triumphant moment.[7] We knew Lear was a fool to disinherit her; we did not realize how great a fool. But, when Goneril and Regan reject her, we know fully what they reject, and their coldness is the more notable after France's warmth, and Kent's.

Goneril and Regan have gained what Cordelia lost. If nevertheless they expressed regret and sympathy for her, we should feel their love had outweighed selfish satisfaction; but, when they show no sympathy at all, it is difficult not to feel they are happy to profit from her loss. Consider how differently the scene would affect us if Goneril and Regan spoke the following lines to Cordelia:

> *Goneril.* You see how full of changes his age is. The observation we have made of it hath been little. He always loved you most, and with what poor judgement he hath now cast you off appears too grossly.
> *Regan.* 'Tis the infirmity of his age; yet he hath ever but slenderly known himself.

The accuracy of these observations would not be altered; I have changed hardly a word. But, if spoken to Cordelia, they would express sympathy, reassurance, a desire to console. By condemning Lear they would endorse Cordelia. But, as it is, their criticism of Lear, after she leaves, makes it obvious that their criticisms of Cordelia did not spring from any deep filial loyalty. Again, if they had condemned their father in comforting their sister, we could discount and excuse their harshness, because of its admirable motive. As it is, they criticize the irrationality of Lear's actions only because they fear similar treatment themselves; as it is, since their professed motive is spurious, since hypocritical sympathy would have gained them much and cost them little, we can only conclude that they rebuked Cordelia to cause her pain, to gloat over her misfortunes, to kick her when she's down.

We might also consider how differently those speeches would sound in Cordelia's mouth. She, with cause to judge Lear harshly, never does, but leaves in tears, pleading with her sisters for his sake. Their criticism, after her concern, can hardly endear us to Goneril and Regan, who cite Lear's generosity to themselves as evidence of dotage; who express no gratitude or even satisfaction for what they have gained, but only anxiety for its preservation;[8] who show no love for Lear at all. We may not love him much ourselves, but we never pretended love. Cordelia's honesty makes their hypocrisy the more repugnant, and the accuracy of Cordelia's accusation of hypocrisy lends (illogically, but none the less) to her other accusations an immediate plausibility.

Goneril's second appearance, with Oswald in scene iii, more immediately affects the quarrel. At that point, there is no real reason to doubt the truth of her accusations. But the damning thing about this scene is that it exists at all: only omit it, as Tate did, and our reactions to the quarrel will radically change. In Tate, Goneril enters in scene iv just as Lear strikes Oswald, and she watches unseen as Kent trips him, then comes forward, immediately launching into her accusations. This stimulus gives her anger far more plausibility and spontaneity and sympathy than Shakespeare gives it: in Tate's context, 'Now, daughter, why that frontlet on?' becomes absurdly and infuriatingly naïve, if not disingenuous. But, in Shakespeare, Oswald is abused a hundred lines before Goneril's entry; Goneril does not witness it; we know, moreover, that Goneril engineered it. Scene iii lends conspiracy and malice aforethought to what would otherwise seem righteous indignation. Goneril's use of Oswald seems cowardly, particularly by contrast with Cordelia's direct defiance: not only in the cowardice of Goneril herself, rebelling through an intermediary, but in the cowardice of the form that rebellion takes ('weary negligence', walking away when Lear calls). The foreknowledge scene iii gives us not only weakens Goneril's own case, but strengthens Lear's, for instance lending a particular poignancy to his 'I have perceived a most faint neglect of late, which I have rather blamed as mine own jealous curiosity, than as a very pretence and purpose of unkindness'. That foreknowledge also predetermines our perspective on the quarrel itself. We know what Goneril means to do, hence our curiosity and interest focus upon Lear's reaction. We might have some interest in Goneril's reaction to Lear's reaction (particularly when his denunciations grow so violent), had not the third scene already informed us what that reaction would be. 'If he distaste it, let him to my sister.' Therefore, when Lear threatens to go to Regan, we know he is reacting just as she hoped and expected. Gonerils have been known to wax emotional when Lear threatens to leave; defenders of the lady have been happy to believe that her final words to him ('You strike my people, and your disordered rabble / Make servants of their betters') are a last desperate effort to get through to him – rather than, as they have always seemed to me, just another kick in the groin. But such defences of Goneril would be plausible only if scene iii did not exist. They belong to Tate's play, not Shakespeare's.

This is a crucial point, and one in some danger of being misunderstood. I am not claiming that an actress could not successfully and plausibly convey distress here, or even distress combined with rage, a pained viciousness (like Irene Worth's in the Peter Brook film); nor am I denying that, so interpreted, the moment will strike an immediate chord of recognition in most modern critics and (probably) most modern spectators. Nor need a spectator notice any particular contradiction between such sympathetic interpretations of this line and what we have earlier seen of Goneril in I.iii – the selective amnesia described in the previous chapter makes it most unlikely that a spectator would specifically juxtapose this line with the details of the earlier scene. Nor need such an interpretation jar with the rest of the play: it need be only another example of Shakespeare preserving moral ambivalence until our conflicting responses are resolved by a later, defining act. The moment in question is thus *actually* ambiguous, in that the performer can choose among alternative interpretations, which will in turn elicit different responses. But is the moment *intentionally* ambiguous? Was it ambiguous for the play's first audiences? I suspect not, for two reasons: first, because Shakespeare's manipulation of his material works against a sympathetic interpretation of the line; second, because (as I shall try to show in due course) such sympathetic interpretations of the line seem to me to arise from and depend upon a set of ideological assumptions which were not widespread at the time of the play's composition, though they are so now. It could always be claimed that Shakespeare himself anticipated those modern notions, but even if he did he could not have assumed them in his audience; he would have needed to encourage that perspective, rather than – as he does by his use of I.iii – discouraging it.

And what difference, one might ask, does Shakespeare's own intention make? None at all. In modern performance, or as an element in a moral parable (which is what most criticism makes of literature, in one way or another), a sympathetic interpretation of the line works well enough for the modern consumer. But, if we set out to understand how Shakespeare attempted to allow for ambiguities without letting them endanger an overall structure of developing reactions, then ambiguities of performance which Shakespeare intended or anticipated or encouraged must be distinguished, as far as possible, from ambiguities which have been imported by four centuries of subsequent ideological history. This ambiguity seems to me to belong to the latter rather than to the former category. However, the larger issue of our emotional responses to Goneril can be left in abeyance, for it depends on a great deal more than the existence of I.iii; all I want to point out, for the moment, is that the existence of I.iii does undermine much of Goneril's appeal for our sympathy in I.iv itself.

In the first scene, Goneril is peripheral and as yet relatively simple; Lear is central and complex. Before the quarrel begins, Goneril is alone on stage with a single character (who barely speaks, and has as yet no definable identity beyond the generic 'steward'), in a scene only twenty-two lines long (twenty-seven in the Quarto),[9] engaged throughout in a single activity ('Directions to Servants', *à la* Swift). Before the quarrel begins, Lear in scene iv is on stage for almost 200 lines in the company of a sharply delineated Gentleman, Kent, Oswald and Fool, the last of these being – Lear excepted – the play's most complex character; during this time Lear takes on a new retainer, demands his dinner and his daughter, reprimands and beats a servant, is abused and entertained by the Fool. This disposition of mass itself governs an audience's perspective. Goneril dominates our attention at the end of scene i and throughout scene iii, on both occasions preoccupied with the same problem. Lear, having dominated scene i, departs forty lines before its close, and does not return till scene iv. Consequently, at the beginning of that scene, it is difficult not to view him through Goneril's eyes, particularly as he supplements his train, strikes her gentleman (I.iii.1), demands in his imperious way and all at once Goneril, the Fool, Oswald and his dinner.

But, if it is difficult to avoid Goneril's perspective at first, it is equally difficult to retain it beyond the entrance of the Fool. Even at first, it is challenged by the return of Kent (with his own perspective, one we are predisposed to admire), by the equanimity and mildness of the Gentleman. And, if the Goneril of scenes i and iii impresses us chiefly by her sameness, with Lear we are most interested in the changes: from public to private man, from formal verse to prose. The very rapidity and elliptical density of scene i heighten this curiosity. If Lear bewilders us at first, we shall be the more interested in his reappearance; we accept the bewilderment of the first scene only because we expect the rest of the play to clarify it, to explicate the man. We thus expect scene iv to explain to us the nature of the man who made such a dreadful mistake; moreover, we are curious about the future of a man, any man, who has made such a mistake. At first, Lear seems entirely to have forgotten the past, which must strike us for its very unexpectedness. With his response to 'my young lady's going into France' (I.iv.73) we receive the first intimation of Lear's continued but subterranean preoccupation with Cordelia; after the Fool's entrance Lear's past, and his judgement on his own actions, become a prime focus of our attention. The more immersed we are in the complexities and nuances of Lear, the farther we move from Goneril's perspective, and the hundred lines between the Fool's entrance and hers decisively shift the balance, dramatizing a world of which Goneril knew and cared nothing. When she enters, we shall of course again conjure into memory what we recall of scene iii, but memory will itself dilute and attenuate the immediacy and strength of her case. And by now the momentum of the scene is against her, and we are watching from the Lear-Kent-Fool point of view. Because the Fool is funny, because in the hundred lines since Oswald's exit we have forgotten him and his mistress, Goneril is put in Malvolio's position, interrupting not only their party but ours too.[10] Her first words ('Not only, sir, this your all-licensed Fool'), in so far as they echo the complaints of scene iii discredit them: knowing what we now know about Oswald and about the Fool, for Lear to 'strike my gentleman for chiding of his Fool' (I.iii.1) – if we remember it – seems praiseworthy.

So much we may infer from the structure of events. But an observer's predisposition toward Lear in scene iv will also depend on Lear's behaviour in scene i.

Lear's part in that scene falls into three convenient sections: (1) his abdication, the love-trial, and his disinheriting of Cordelia; (2) his banishment of Kent; (3) his disposal of the bride. But before any of these can be analysed, some mention must be made of the differences between Quarto and Folio, especially in Lear's first speech.[11] Where the Quarto reads,

> and 'tis our first intent
> To shake all cares and business of our state,
> Confirming them on younger years

the Folio alters and expands to

> and 'tis our fast intent
> To shake all cares and business from our age,
> Conferring them on younger strengths, while we
> Unburdened crawl toward death. Our son of Cornwall,
> And you our no-less-loving son of Albany,
> We have this hour a constant will to publish
> Our daughters' several dowers, that future strife
> May be prevented now.

Later, the Folio adds two more lines:

> tell me, my daughters,
> *Since now we will divest us both of rule,*
> *Interest of territory, cares of state,*
> Which of you shall we say doth love us most?

It will be seen that all these changes explain and clarify Lear's behaviour. The change from 'of our state' to 'from our age' substitutes a personal motive for a political; 'while we unburdened crawl toward death' adds a personal motive where there was none. Balancing these personal additions is the extended reference to Albany and Cornwall, and the prevention of future strife, while the simple shift from *years* to *strengths* implies a recognition of their superior ability to govern. The change of two other words also alters slightly the nature of Lear's abdication. Q's ''tis our first intent' implies, at its simplest, that he is speaking first of the abdication, then of the love-trial and Cordelia's suitors; *first* might also mean 'primary, chief'. F's ''tis our fast intent' implies instead that he will not be dissuaded from this intention, that his mind is made up, though he expects to hear (may already have heard) objections. This personal intransigence is reinforced elsewhere by the Folio's added reference to his 'constant will' (above), and by the added 'I am firm' (later). The second change, from 'confirming' to 'conferring', occurs again at line 81, and slightly alters the emphasis, from the legal and ceremonial confirmation of decisions already made beforehand (as appears from the first six lines of the play) to the King's act of donation itself, which will be central to succeeding scenes.[12]

The final two-line addition seems to me related to these others: in 'cares of state', for instance, it reasserts a motive omitted by the alteration of 'cares . . . of our state'. By its position it proclaims that Lear is demanding professions of love *because* he is renouncing power; it asserts a political motive for a personal act. Familiarity has perhaps dulled the force of this *non sequitur*, which can imply Lear's recognition of his own power or weakness or both: because I still have power, I can still demand this of you; or, I shall only give up power if assured of your love; or, I know you will not love me so much when I am impotent, so love me now this one last time. As with Viola, Shakespeare creates the vacuum, and forces us to fill it. That vacuum involves us in the *active* contemplation of

Lear's motives, an attention the Quarto does not encourage. More particularly, the two added lines, like the other Folio changes, intertwine the political and the personal: throughout the speech, the Folio gives us personal motives for political acts, and political for personal.

The addition of these motives for the abdication does not necessarily justify or excuse Lear's behaviour. Indeed, quite the contrary, for it is far easier to take the Quarto as a myth, in which the decision to abdicate is a necessary given, is in the Aristotelian sense 'outside the plot'. In the Folio we are told why Lear abdicates, why he demands the professions of love, and therefore we are free to judge, are required to judge, the adequacy or inadequacy of his motives. In the Quarto, if we find Lear's actions incredible, we can only blame the implausibility of the story or the incompetence of the playwright; in the Folio, we are invited to blame Lear himself.

These changes are supplemented elsewhere in the scene by the Folio's new emphasis on the political significance of events. Albany and Cornwall and the prevention of their future strife are given a new and initial prominence. Just before Cordelia's 'Nothing', the Folio adds another reference to the competition between France and Burgundy for her hand (lines 83–5) – important not only in keeping the political context in the forefront of our consciousness, but also because it again illustrates Lear's intertwining of political and personal, in that he seems to value Cordelia at least partly as a political asset, seeing her not only as his daughter but as a key to 'the vines of France and milk of Burgundy' as well.

But the most important alterations of this kind concern Kent. In the Quarto, his advice to 'reverse thy doom' and 'revoke thy doom' both clearly refer to Cordelia's disinheritance; in the Folio, 'reserve thy state' and 'revoke thy gift' refer, just as clearly, to Lear's abdication. The Folio changes are in this instance the more remarkable because Kent's outburst is obviously prompted by Lear's treatment of Cordelia. The Quarto thus has a more evident logic and coherence; I nevertheless prefer the Folio. I do not notice the contradiction, let alone object to it, partly because the change of a few words alchemizes their context ('reserve thy state, / And in thy best consideration check / This hideous rashness'), but chiefly because the Folio Kent voices an objection which has been troubling me, and presumably the rest of the audience, an objection which would certainly have troubled a Jacobean audience. If Lear's abdication stands outside the plot, as in the Quarto, then of course no one on stage will draw attention to its absurdity. But, because the Folio makes the absurdity Lear's, we expect and desire someone to voice our incredulity. Psychologically, Kent, his restraint overcome by Lear's outrageous treatment of Cordelia, could easily find himself expressing other indignations which have nothing to do with her, but which might otherwise have been successfully suppressed. The effect of Kent's criticism is to force Lear again to make the decision to abdicate, before our eyes, resisting advice to the contrary. In the Quarto, the decision has been made beforehand (when, under what circumstances, we do not know), and has apparently been accepted without demur, from the manner in which Gloucester and Kent discuss it and the fact that during the entire first scene no one objects to it. Of the Quarto Lear it is possible to believe he has been duped; we see the Folio Lear dupe himself. In the Quarto, Lear 'confirms' his abdication, and we later hear of a 'Lord that counselled' him to do so (I.iv.140–1); in the Folio, his 'conferring' of the kingdom on his daughters becomes, instead, 'hideous rashness', which his counsellor strongly criticizes and which no one recommends. As before, the Folio makes Lear responsible for his behaviour, and thus open to even greater condemnation.

A third group of changes in the Folio concerns Lear's personality. First, most simply, he is given more lines. Of the first fifty lines in the Folio after Lear's entrance, nine do not appear in the Quarto, all nine belonging to Lear, and thus increasing his already marked domination of the scene. Not only are his speeches longer; they are denser, partly because additions are for the most part incorporated in existing sentences, making them longer and more complex, but also because the Folio packs more meaning into the same number of words, as when 'younger years' becomes 'younger strengths' or 'merit doth most challenge' becomes 'nature doth with merit challenge'. These Folio changes are accompanied by a pruning of the Quarto's colloquialisms.

[Go to, go to!] Mend thy speech a little.   (I.i.93)

[Well,] Let it be so.   (108)

[Go to, go to!] Better thou hadst not been born.   (233)

(In the first example, Folio substitutes 'How, how, Cordelia' – Lear's first use of her name, and very telling.) By virtue of such exclamations, the Quarto Lear is closer, marginally, to the testy old man of nineteenth-century interpretations. Similar considerations may lie behind the change from 'The map there' (Q) to 'Give me the map there' (F), or that from 'Nothing can come of nothing' (i.e. it is a universal law that nothing comes of nothing) to the Folio's 'Nothing will come of nothing' (i.e. I will not let anything come of nothing). All the alterations in this third category seem to me directed toward creating a more titanic Lear. This impression must, of course, influence our responses to Lear in any text of the first scene, but the Folio heightens it, so that our initial responses to Lear are, more clearly, responses to Authority, in its abstractest manifestation.

One's response to Authority, whether of absolute parent or absolute monarch or absolute God, is compounded necessarily of admiration, rebellion and fear. When Lear curses Cordelia, I cannot help admiring his power and the eloquence which expresses it, as I admire them in Oedipus cursing Polyneices: nor can I help fearing anyone or anything who makes things happen simply by saying them, who has the power so to turn word into deed that he can extinguish me with a sentence, as Oedipus does Polyneices; nor can I help rebelling from his error toward Cordelia, just as I rebel against the extremity of Oedipus's reaction to Polyneices. I respond to Lear as to Authority – but with this complication, that Lear proceeds to divest himself of his prime characteristic, of his identity. (Hence our intense curiosity in scene iv.) But the proportion of admiration, rebellion and fear will vary, and so, since one's responses to Lear depend on one's responses to Authority, responses to Lear will *necessarily* vary, within this predetermined range. The variations are simply multiple responses to a single trait – as we saw in the characterization of Viola (p. 76).

But the differences between Quarto and Folio, however important or informative, remain differences of detail: structurally, the two texts agree, and we may now return to the structural analysis with which we began. Lear's role in this first scene falls into three sections. Of these, the first, though only about one hundred lines long, includes the abdication and the love-trial and the disinheriting of Cordelia, and has attracted more attention than all the rest combined.

Critics sometimes claim or assume that Lear's initial actions are incredible. But kings have been known to abdicate; Charlemagne sundered his own kingdom between his sons; a father asks his children if they love him, and gives them treats for saying yes. *King Lear* has never seemed a fairytale to me, certainly not if 'fairytale' implies some mitigation of Lear's fault, as it clearly does mitigate Cymbeline's. Some critics also claim that the ritual and ceremony of the first scene are a vanity and an affectation. In some minds, no doubt, and in some moods, all ceremonies seem affectations – or, if not all, at least those of other people. But to me it seems natural enough that occasions of such magnitude should be organized and accompanied by ritual: that is, by an agreed, premeditated, formal insincerity. And audiences generally like ceremony, for its own sake; indeed, the critical dismissal of *Henry V*'s theatrical popularity, on the grounds that it testifies to nothing more than the play's susceptibility to spectacle, takes this love of spectacle for granted. It thus seems to me that an audience is initially most unlikely to regard the actual ceremony of this opening scene censoriously, however much it objects to the actions so ceremonialized.

This formality makes possible the dramatic economy of this crucial scene: it contributes to the theatrical magnification of Lear and Lear's authority, since he controls the ritual; it creates an impression of premeditation, or organized forethought, which extends from the form to the content, so that Lear's abdication does not seem 'done upon the gad'; it creates a powerful formal pattern and expectation, thereby increasing the energy of Cordelia's rebellion; finally, it lessens any initial suspicion or distaste I might feel toward Goneril's and Regan's volubility, for such rituals are by definition insincere, while on the other hand *increasing* my distaste for them in retrospect (after Cordelia has exposed the hypocrisy of the form itself). I do not mean to say that the nature of the ritual encourages a positive initial response to Goneril and Regan, only that it prevents a negative one, thus further contributing to their initial emotional anonymity. Lear's trial of love is of course humiliating, but Goneril and Regan are (apparently) not humiliated, though I feel they should be, a feeling intensified by Cordelia's rebellion. Cordelia *would* be humiliated, but she does not comply, thereby sparing Lear the hatred of the audience – which he would certainly provoke if we had to watch his daughters' pained humiliating embarrassment. When Cordelia weeps at scene's end, her tears illumine the callousness of her sisters; if she wept here, her tears would make intolerable the callousness of her father, who is already quite callous enough.

One's responses to the central confrontation between Lear and Cordelia will always depend at least partly on one's age. I do not subscribe to the post-Coleridgean denigration of Cordelia (as a means of mitigating Lear's fault) or to her canonization (as a means of magnifying it). In the theatre through that litany of 'Nothing' I can feel little but the most physical amoral excitement at the confrontation, a vicarious thrill in her rebellion. The Folio is surely right to have prolonged that moment. Between 'Nothing' and the curse, most of the words are Cordelia's; Lear asks questions; I am told nothing of his thoughts. I stand on Cordelia's side looking at Lear, not knowing how he will react. Shakespeare does nothing to prepare us for the intensity of Lear's outburst, and Tate debases the play by doing so – by emphasizing, so ploddingly, so diligently, Lear's 'choler' and 'rashness', which preparation cheats Lear's outburst of half its power. To tell us, as Tate does, that Cordelia *wants* to be disinherited, not only forewarns us of Lear's reaction but actually makes it welcome when it comes. Even for a modern audience, knowing what will come, the attention is still directed at Lear – perhaps now even more so, as we savour his approach to the great moment. Until the outburst itself, our attention is largely amoral; afterwards, we shall judge him, but now we simply watch, expect, desire the excitement of a violence we can condemn.

The Folio, which goes to considerable lengths to give new motives for Lear's abdication, gives none for the disinheritance. Why does he do it? – What else could he do? Lear's reaction, though obviously wrong, is immediately intelligible. Cordelia calls his bluff; he has either to surrender the game, or

play his cards. I have already tried to describe my reactions to
Lear's speech; I should add that, during it, I am entirely
committed to Cordelia's perspective. But the first ambivalence has already been sounded, when Lear asks, 'But goes thy
heart with this?' (105). And after the curse, in Lear's next
speech, Shakespeare decisively complicates the issue. 'I loved
her most' – in an instant, for an instant, Cordelia seems
cruel.[13] 'Let pride, which she calls plainness, marry her.' Not
only does Lear's criticism of Cordelia stick, but in the second
speech he is angry, frustrated, disturbed, as he had not been in
the first, with its long cold sentences and precision of allusion.
If before we responded to him as an embodiment of Authority, now we cannot help responding to him partly as a man, in
pain. The sequence of these responses is fundamental to our
experience of the scene. Shakespeare creates one perspective,
then catapults us into another.

The Kent episode, which follows, articulates and intensifies
my disapproval of Lear. Coleridge saw Kent's intervention as
a fine contrivance 'to lessen the glaring absurdity of Lear . . .
forcing away the attention from the nursery-tale the moment
it has answered its purpose, that of supplying the canvas to
paint on'.[14] But what Kent does is object vociferously to 'the
glaring absurdity of Lear', thereby redirecting our attention to
the nursery tale. The more clearly Kent tells Lear of his
mistake, the more guilty Lear becomes: what might have been
forgiven as unthinking reflex in a moment of rashness
becomes instead an elected blindness to the truth, issuing
finally in the tyrant's removal of a man he does not want to
hear. Coleridge – and this could be said of other critics –
describes Tate's play better than Shakespeare's, for in Tate
Kent says virtually nothing about Lear's 'glaring absurdity',
speaking instead in generalities, or being interrupted before he
can name specifics.[15]

> Be Kent unmannerly when Lear is mad:
> Thy youngest daughter –
> *Lear.*   On thy life, no more!   (I.i.152–3)

But Tate in his ineptitude also illustrates the perspicacity of
Coleridge. Kent does lessen Lear's absurdity, not by distract-
ing attention from it, but by justifying Lear's over-reaction.
When Shakespeare's Lear says, 'Kent, on thy life, no more',

he has already listened to ten lines in Kent's bluntest and most infuriating manner. Throughout, Kent engages in a thrilling but dangerous species of repartee, each of his speeches picking up Lear's last words and twisting them to his own purpose. No doubt this partly explains the exhilaration, even joy, which Kent arouses in an audience. His last and most extreme defiance carries this repartee into the realm of action, not language, by accepting Lear's act and redefining it:

> Kill thy physician, and the fee bestow
> Upon the foul disease.

Lear responds to Kent with an ascending series of threats; Kent deflates them all, carrying our vicarious rebellion a step further than had Cordelia. Now, when Lear invokes his deities, what had before been awesome Kent makes ridiculous. Even after his banishment, Kent is not beaten, but in the equanimity of his couplets delivers his judgement on them all. Kent's manner in parrying Lear's threats exposes what was only implicit in Lear's reaction to Cordelia, Lear's final act being in both cases the same – but with Kent we see him driven to that act by the impotence of his alternatives. He banishes Kent because that is the only way he can shut him up. He must do something, and he has nothing else to do – as with Cordelia. Kent thus not only magnifies Lear's error, but begins to strip him of the awe which has till now clothed his impotence. 'What wouldst thou do, old man?' Of course, Kent is daringly rude, but he reminds *us*, as much as Lear, that the great King is a man, and an old one. But Kent's very vehemence, and the wit which so exhilarates, justify and excuse Lear's reaction: Lear is reacting not only to Kent's advice, but to Kent's manner, and we may endorse the advice and enjoy the manner, while yet recognizing its injudiciousness.

Kent magnifies Lear's error and diminishes Lear's authority, but the third section of the scene brings to a head our antipathy, even contempt, for Lear. Before France and Burgundy he relishes coldly humiliating Cordelia, treating her as a thing for sale: a considered and happy cruelty far uglier than anything he has yet done. He takes pride in proving that, by not loving her, he can prevent anyone else from loving her. When finally she breaks her long silence to defend herself, he

can only say, 'Better thou / Hadst not been born, than not
t'have pleased me better'. (A line terrible because it isolates, in
its cruellest form, a sentiment few parents have not felt.) But,
if this third section extrapolates from the second in magnifying Lear's fault, it also further diminishes his authority. For in
the end Lear has done Cordelia no harm: in spite of Lear,
France loves her, marries her, gives her a land whose richness
and expanse surpass any gift Lear himself could make. 'Thou
losest here, a better where to find.' Therefore we need not
worry for Cordelia's future. Kent will return to England, to
Lear's own presence, by scene iv, thus completely negating
Lear's punishment; Cordelia leaves the stage in triumph.[16]
This seems to me the prime function of Burgundy, a character
seldom discussed, often wished away and sometimes omitted,
who raises a variety of bothersome questions in decorous
minds, such as why this duke is given precedence over a king.
Burgundy exists, I think, to increase the triumph of Cordelia's
union with France. Cordelia is actually saved from Burgundy
by the very disinheritance with which Lear meant to punish
her. As the Fool will later say, 'this fellow has banished two
on's daughters, and did the third a blessing against his will'. By
scene's end Lear has been made effectively powerless, before
his abdication; we all conspire to triumph over him in the
moment of his most inexcusable cruelty. But Lear has also
been made harmless. The final conversation of Goneril and
Regan strongly suggests that he has succeeded only in harming
himself.

The progress of my emotions toward Lear in scene i can be
crudely schematized thus: from an initial confrontation which
will arouse strong but disparate emotions (varying with the
age and political inclination of each spectator), the emotions
are gradually resolved as Lear's own conduct becomes more
repugnant and intolerable, while sympathy with his opponents increases; at the same time, Lear becomes steadily less
harmful to anyone but himself. Since it soon becomes apparent that those to whom he has entrusted his future harbour no
superfluity of benevolence towards him, by scene's end interest is already shifting to Lear as sufferer. No doubt to an
extent we welcome the prospect of that suffering, as revenge
for his malefactions here, but the emotional appetite for such
punishment has already been partly, perhaps largely, satisfied

by the structure of the first scene itself. Certainly, the 250 lines between his exit and his reappearance in scene iv will cool and distance our animosity, allowing simple curiosity to come to the fore.

So much for the first scene; so much for the perspective created by Shakespeare's disposition and arrangement of his material. But there remains – what is fundamental – Lear's behaviour in the first half of I.iv, the reactions it will provoke from an audience, and the influence those will have on our judgement of the quarrel. In this scene our reactions to Lear are largely a function of our reactions to Kent, Oswald, and the Fool. Kent and the Fool between them speak ninety-seven of the scene's first 169 lines (114 of 185, in Q), and, though Oswald says little, his silence is itself assertive, precipitating the scene's first crisis. To the extent that Oswald's conduct is insolently provocative, Lear's reaction will be justified. Is it insolent?

'Who am I, sir?' (I.iv.78). By definition, in a rhetorical question not only is the answer self-evident, but so is the questioner's motive. We know the answer Lear wants, and know why he wants it: as the premiss for a lecture on the duties of servants. Polonius asks Hamlet a similar question, 'Do you know me, my lord?' (II.ii.173). Presuming as it does that Hamlet is *non compos mentis*, this question is insulting, and Hamlet's scurrilous reply seems fit retribution. But Lear knows Oswald knows him, and his question is not provocative, except in so far as any rhetorical question invites a rebellious answer. Oswald in answering refuses to respect the rhetorical question. He first disobeyed by ignoring a question and leaving the room; now he disobeys by not complying with Lear's intended format for their conversation. Instead, he defines Lear by reference to his daughter (rather than his own authority, or name); by a declension of possessives, Lear goes a progress through the guts of an Oswald, for Lear is Goneril's father, and Goneril is Oswald's lady: ergo, Lear is Oswald's. '*My* lady's father.'

Oswald's second reply, 'I am none of these, my lord', might in itself engage our sympathies, as a dignified and quiet denial after Lear's enraged abuse. But his next four words transform in retrospect the tone of these, by introducing the designedly facetious explanation that Lear can only have mistaken him for someone else. When he says, 'I beseech your pardon', Oswald is not apologizing for his conduct, but means instead, 'Sorry, you have the wrong chap.' Oswald apologizes for *not* being the slave, cur, whoreson dog Lear thinks he is addressing, and this reply (like Polonius's question) carries the imputation of mental incompetence. Oswald introduces what will become a prime tactic against Lear (and Kent): the simple refusal to take their indignation seriously.

'I'll not be strucken, my lord.' This is admirable: its independence, its assertion of freedom and dignity, its insistence upon bounds beyond which masters may not go in reprimanding servants. But this seeming independence is belied by the knowledge of Oswald's servility which scene iii gives us: he disobeys upon command. But, even were it genuine, his is a species of independence less admirable than Kent's: Kent criticized Lear, but never denied his authority, for Lear's sake enduring a punishment far more severe than a slap on the face. Whether such comparisons occur to us during Oswald's speeches depends on the blocking of the scene, but that we will eventually make them is guaranteed by the fact that Kent himself does so, intervening (on his own initiative) to defend his master from the insolence of a fellow servant. Immediately after having been struck, Oswald declares, 'I'll not be strucken', and the ridiculousness latent in this contradiction Kent makes explicit by adding, 'Nor tripped neither', and tripping him.

If they were innocent, Oswald's replies would deserve my sympathy; if he were witty unwittingly, I should be amused. If Oswald, a clown, had wandered on stage in the midst of Lear's fury, been suddenly and inexplicably accosted, answered as best he could ('My lady's father?'), been bewildered by Lear's lunatic reaction, and tried to excuse himself by the quite reasonable suggestion that Lear has mistaken him for someone else – how completely my responses would change, without changing a word of this dialogue. But, in such a construction of the scene, I should laugh because of the discrepancy between my awareness and Oswald's, should laugh at and appreciate Oswald's *innocence*. Shakespeare has ensured that

Oswald cannot be innocent. Nor does it seem to me entirely accidental that in three brief speeches Shakespeare twice channels our sympathies for Oswald in directions that have been carefully doomed in advance, so that the one favourable interpretation possible is advanced only to be vetoed (in the same way that, with Viola, criticisms were only voiced by a person or in a context which discredited them).

To Oswald's insolence Lear responds first with sarcasm, then incredulity, taking as often the form of a dumbfounded indignant repetition of what he has just heard ('He would not!' – 'My lady's father!'), then anger, expressed first in curses and then physically. This escalation of feeling, here neatly delineated into stages and compressed into a few lines, is capped by a kind of *deus ex machina*, Kent, who, having been silent and essentially invisible for forty lines,[17] unexpectedly resolves the deadlock in Lear's favour, thereby satisfying and relieving the emotional tension. Lear's responses to Oswald – sarcasm, incredulity, anger – will be repeated in his confrontations with Goneril and with Regan, and in Kent's later confrontation with Oswald in Act II. These emotions, elaborated and intensified, depersonalized also, expressed by Kent and the Fool as well as Lear, become the major emotional chord of the play's first movement. But, in the subsequent sequences, there will be no *deus ex machina*, no resolution. Lear's anger, though no less violent, will not be permitted a physical outlet: Goneril and Regan will not be strucken. In those later confrontations, our sense of Lear's turbulent frustration derives at least in part from the immediate satisfaction given his anger here and in scene i. Lear's reaction to Oswald thus helps us understand his greater anger with Goneril, and the intensity of his frustration, the difficulty he must have in controlling himself. He curses her so violently partly because he cannot strike her, as he struck Oswald. This episode creates a subtext for the next.

Kent's tripping Oswald from behind might serve as a paradigm of the uses of farce. Oswald is now contemptible, our mutual butt, hoist on his own illogic. Simultaneously, my admiration for Kent is confirmed by the decorum and finality of his intervention. Moreover, Kent's endorsement of Lear virtually ensures our own. Kent's actions might easily be performed by another character, by 'Caius', but in that case we should probably regard him more critically. At the beginning of scene iv, Kent's disguise creates the usual comic discrepancy between Lear's awareness and ours; at the end of the play, that discrepancy becomes tragic, Lear's failure to recognize him depriving Kent of his long-awaited, much-deserved reward. But in the interval the discrepancy hardly exists:[18] Kent and Caius are identical in function and nature, so we are not made conscious of Kent concealing himself. Because it does not intrude on our attention, the disguise convention does not seem inappropriate to tragedy – Tolstoy, to make it so, must keep *reminding* us that Kent is in disguise[19] – and it serves an important function: the disguise itself expresses and confirms Kent's loyalty, and our affection and respect for Kent predetermine our perspective on 'Caius'.

Nahum Tate's Kent also trips Oswald.

> *Lear.* Now, who am I sir?
> *Gentleman.* My lady's father.
> *Lear.*   My lord's knave –
>   *Strikes him.*
>   *Gonerill at the entrance.*
> *Gentleman.* I'll not be struck, my lord.
> *Kent.* Nor tripped neither, thou vile civet-box.
>   *Strikes up his heels.*   (I.ii.27–30)

Easily but thoroughly Tate has undone the emotional structure, thereby diminishing the satisfaction of Kent's climax. Tate's Oswald gives Lear less provocation, and by omitting Lear's indignant repetition Tate not only alters Lear's character but also makes Oswald's remark and its insolent implications less emphatic. (The simplest effect of Lear's incredulous repetitions is that they give an audience two chances to take in the full meaning and connotation of the words.) Tate's Lear resorts immediately to physical violence, without further verbal or visual ('Do you bandy looks with me?') provocation. Tate minimizes Oswald's offence, and makes Lear's reaction more unreasonable; by bringing on Goneril he not only interrupts the escalation of tension but also distracts us from Kent's revenge and radically alters our perspective. Because in Tate Oswald does not return on his own initiative, but is *'brought in by Kent'*, Kent's intervention later loses both its surprise and its sense of climax. In Tate, the

words which accompany the tripping are an entirely gratuitous insult; in Shakespeare, they are directly related to
Oswald's conduct, and to the tripping itself (a fate appropriate
enough for a 'football player'[20]). Shakespeare's Lear, unlike
Tate's, afterwards profusely thanks Kent, twice – and, consi-
dering the ink spilt in praise of the 'Thank you, sir' in Lear's
last speech, his gratitude here surely deserves more critical
attention than it has received. The intensity of Lear's gratitude to the good servant balances his anger at the bad, and he
praises Kent for actions we too applaud, just as earlier in the
scene he had accepted Kent into his train for qualities an
audience admires, indeed the very qualities Kent displayed in
scene i. It has been often enough remarked that Kent's fidelity
is itself high praise of Lear, but, equally, Lear's praise of Kent
cannot but redound on his own head.

Kent's intervention effects a crucial simplification of the
issues and emotions of this quarrel: the confrontation between
Lear and Goneril (two complex natures, each in some ways
distasteful) is first waged by proxy through Kent (who secured
our admiration in scene i, and has certainly done nothing to
lose it) and Oswald (whom Coleridge declared 'the only
character of utter unredeemable *baseness* in Shakespeare'[21]).
Virtually all Tate's changes work to prevent this simplification, for, though Kent remains no less admirable and Oswald
no less contemptible, our responses to the servants are dissociated from their masters. Tate's Oswald – within five lines
dragged in by the collar, struck by Lear, tripped by Kent –
invites our contempt for his weakness and effeminacy, rather
than for the insolence Goneril had commanded; in Tate scene
iii is omitted altogether. Tate's Kent is admirable not so much
for his loyalty to Lear or indignation at Oswald's insolence as
for his manly scorn for such a powderpuff: Tate thus omits
Kent's long speech to Oswald, and Lear's gratitude. In any
case, the very presence of Goneril prevents us from feeling the
Kent–Oswald confrontation as an image of the Lear–Goneril
one: the larger issues immediately confront us.

Here and throughout the scene, Tate improves Goneril,
making her case more reasonable, weakening Lear's, strug-
gling to redeem her exactly as modern critics have done.
Modern criticism derides as sentimental or melodramatic any

interpretation which too thoroughly blackens Lear's daughters, and yet the sentimental melodramatic Tate has done his best to find excuses for them, often the very excuses paraded by their latter-day apologists. Sentimentality is the refusal to believe in evil, in irredeemable evil. Whether the impulse spends itself in normalizing Goneril, or securing a happy ending (real or allegorical), it is the same impulse. Melodrama is melodrama not because it so sharply distinguishes good and evil, but because its good and its evil are neither of them credible. As Arthur Miller wrote, in his 1957 introduction to *The Crucible*,

> my own – and the critics' – unbelief in this depth of evil is concomitant with our unbelief in good, too. . . . I think now . . . that I was wrong in mitigating the evil of [Danforth] and the judges he represents. . . . from whatever cause, a dedication to evil, not mistaking it for good, but knowing it as evil and loving it as evil, is possible in human beings who appear agreeable and normal. I think now that one of the hidden weaknesses of our whole approach to dramatic psychology is our inability to face this fact – to conceive, in effect, of Iago. . . . We are so intent upon getting sympathy for our characters that the consequences of evil are being muddied by sentimentality under the guise of a temperate weighing of causes.[22]

A recurring fallacy of modern criticism, expressed in the very titles of such essays as *'King Lear*: A Study in Balanced and Shifting Sympathies' (Block) and 'Shakespearian Tragedy and the Mixed Response' (Honigmann), is the assumption that Shakespeare is great because he always balanced the claims of competing sympathies, mixing our responses, never permitting the uncomplicated emotions of stereotype. I should not wish to deny the complexity and fluctuation of our responses from moment to moment. But it does not follow that the sum total of these individual complexities will be a mixed or balanced response; indeed, as with Viola, the complexities may be only the requisite preparation for a plausible and committed simplicity. Nor does it follow that our responses to every single speech or act or character in a complex pattern must be themselves complex. A complex pattern can be constructed of simple elements; a set of complex elements can form a simple whole. As in the visual arts, 'Subtle complexity can be obtained by combining geometrically simple shapes; and the combinations, in turn, may be held together by a simplifying orderliness.'[23]

Oswald can again serve as illustration. He is three times the butt of our contempt: here; in Act II when Kent pours on him magnificent abuse; in Act IV when he is killed ridiculously, having been cudgelled over the head repeatedly while Edgar dances around him just out of sword's reach.[24] Of all the evil creatures in this play, only Oswald invites contempt, and in the economy of the play's emotion it is vital that he do so. Many have remarked on the division of the characters into camps good and evil, but the variety of the good and evil is as remarkable, and instrumental to the variety of our emotional response. Edmund, Goneril, Regan, Cornwall, Oswald between them draw from us, what no one in isolation could, the full range of our reactions to the existence and nature of evil. In this *symphonie du mal*, Oswald plays contempt, and the virtue of his loyalty to Goneril in Act IV cannot mitigate his conduct earlier, for the impact of that later loyalty depends on shock, on a sudden kaleidoscopic shifting of our perspective on the character, illuminating in retrospect the whole of his behaviour. Any softening of his nature in Act I, in anachronistic deference to what we later learn, will only dilute the force of his later-day virtues, and deprive the play of its emotional structure and variety. For Goneril and Regan, as well as Oswald, in Acts IV and V are transformed by an alteration of perspective. 'O the difference of man and man!' – there is a line worthy the heroine of a Restoration comedy. 'An interlude!' has in it a fierceness I am forced to admire, a heroic hardness immediately confirmed by her suicide.[25] If Goneril bids for my admiration, Regan in the competition for Edmund becomes almost pitiful. From the start Goneril has her beaten; she cannot even wheedle the letter from Oswald; she begins Act V pleading again, this time with Edmund, for a faithfulness we know he does not mean to give; she dies poisoned. Edmund too in Act V regains his humour, candour, courage; 'yet Edmund was beloved' opens a window on his soul; he tries to save Cordelia.

Shakespeare permits his villains this access of virtues at

play's end because by then our conviction of their evil will not be weakened by such qualifications; our moral certainty can survive complication. Moreover, as Lear ceases to be an agent in the main plot, it becomes structurally imperative to widen and vary our responses to the other principals; otherwise, the play would become emotionally monotonous, and the deaths of the final scene uninteresting. With Edmund and the sisters, as with Oswald, premature sympathy simplifies the play, by making its characters more complex.

The Fool is not only a more complex character than Kent or Oswald; his relationship with Lear is also more intimate, more complicated, and more important to our evaluation of Lear himself. Upon entering, he first pointedly ignores Lear for ten lines – precisely Oswald's offence. Yet Lear is not angry. This tolerance, the colloquialism and eagerness of Lear's greeting ('How now, my pretty knave! How dost thou?'), Lear's earlier desire to see him, Lear's having 'noted . . . well' that the Fool has pined away since Cordelia's banishment: all immediately testify to Lear's affection for the Fool. This affection is displayed at once, after his equally open gratitude toward, and pleasure in, Kent. For the first time, we see Lear expressing what we might call love, not to one person but to two.
After ignoring Lear for ten lines, the Fool procedes thus:

> How now, nuncle! [feigned discovery]. Would I had two coxcombs [pause; doubletake, looking back and forth from Kent to Lear, then down at his one coxcomb, uncertain whom to award it] – and two daughters [evasion, pretending he did not intend to imply Lear was a fool].
>
> *Lear.* Why, my boy? [Obviously, we think, so the Fool could give one to each daughter – but no:]
>
> *Fool.* If I gave them all my living, I'd keep my coxcombs myself [Lear is not simply a fool, but a double fool].

The rapidity of these logical connections is dazzling and typical. The answer to the riddle, 'Would I had two coxcombs and two daughters', seems obvious; the Fool sets up obvious answers, then supplies unexpected ones – in fact, the very obviousness of the decoys magnifies the surprise and sting of the real. Lear is not 'deliberately acting as a stooge',[26] but the victim of an ancient comic routine. Part of the wit of the routine is that, eventually, you may set up an obvious answer (which your stooge will disregard, knowing your ways), then give that obvious answer, ridiculing your partner for having missed it. Once your audience expects the unexpected, you can surprise them by supplying the obvious, the one thing they no longer expect. Further variations on this technique will be played in scene v.[27] When the Fool asks, 'Canst tell how an oyster makes his shell?', we assume the question is a riddle; afterwards, by claiming ignorance, he turns it retro-actively into a genuine interrogative, as though he were simply inquiring about the facts, like a naturalist. Again:

> *Fool.* The reason why the seven stars are no mo than seven is a pretty reason.
> *Lear.* Because they are not eight.
> *Fool.* Yes indeed, thou wouldst make a good Fool.

Here Lear supplies the obvious answer, which the Fool then endorses, congratulating Lear on his qualifications as a fool. But had Lear *not* given the obvious answer, he would have been lambasted for his ignorance. However you answer, you cannot win.

The Fool's first speeches also illustrate his dexterity in shifting audiences, a fluidity central to his style. He per-forms to Kent, for Lear, all the while playing to the au-dience as well, and he can shift audiences at will.

> *Lear.* A pestilent gall to me.
> *Fool.* Sirrah, I'll teach thee a speech.
> *Lear.* Do.
> *Fool.* Mark it, nuncle.

The Fool nowhere else calls Lear 'sirrah', but he does so ad-dress Kent, and I thus think it probable he speaks the first of these speeches to Kent. Besides, were the first speech ad-dressed to Lear, there would be no need to add, 'You listen too, nuncle' (which is how I would paraphrase the last line).

The point of Lear's reply is that the Fool did *not* address him, yet Lear knows perfectly well that the Fool's promised speech will be aimed at himself. 'A pestilent gall to me' contrasts with the imperative 'Do' in a way altogether typical of Lear's relationship with the Fool.

> Have more than thou showest,
> Speak less than thou knowest,
> Lend less than thou owest,
> Ride more than thou goest,
> Learn more than thou trowest,
> Set less than thou throwest,
> Leave thy drink and thy whore,
> And keep in-a-door,
> And thou shalt have more
> Than two tens to a score.

We have every expectation of meaning from this speech. So far, the Fool has said nothing without an obvious satiric point. 'Mark it, nuncle' makes us even more suspicious of, and alert to, ulterior implications (particularly if the Fool has been addressing Kent, in which case he now admits that Kent is only his cover for an attack on Lear, which he wants the victim to hear). The form – a series of moral injunctions in the Drab manner – and the clarity of the opening couplet both intensify such expectations: the first commandment propounds an ethic ('be more than you seem') which accurately describes the Fool's own satiric practice, and again encourages us to seek for significance beneath the seeming surface. But, though the speech stimulates and demands this search, it also, I think, quite deliberately frustrates it. Witness the reaction it elicits: 'This is nothing, Fool.' The Quarto gives this reaction to Lear, the Folio to Kent – which makes it difficult to interpret the line as an ironic reflection on the naïveté of the speaker. In either mouth, it echoes the bewilderment and frustration of an audience who like Kent and Lear have been led to expect something, then been given nothing. For, though the Fool's speech begins clearly enough, it rapidly ascends to nonsense. There cannot be more than two tens to a score, and attempts to rationalize this absurdity by reference to pounds and shillings, or 'a score of money', only illustrate the strength of the impulse toward meaning.

To begin with, modernized texts unanimously obscure a central difficulty in the entire sequence. The third word of each of the first six lines is spelt, in the original texts, 'then'. 'Then' was then a normal spelling of 'than'; but it could also, as easily and as often, represent no more than the modern 'then'. Whether this ambiguity asserts itself depends entirely on the actor's delivery:

> Have more, then thou showest;
> Speak less, then thou knowest;
> Lend less, then thou ow[n]est;
> Ride more, then thou goest;
> Learn more, then thou trowest;
> Set less, then thou throwest.

By the final line, this interpretation of 'then' seems to produce nonsense – but, as we shall see, 'than' produces nothing better.

But, even if we ignore or choose to subordinate this alternative interpretation of 'then', most of the other key words in the speech do or should tie commentators in knots. The difficulties begin long before the last line. The Shakespearian 'owe' covers the same linguistic territory as modern 'owe' and 'own', and, despite editorial unanimity in asserting the provenance in this passage of the latter, both make sense, though they produce different readings: either 'lend less than you own' (so you will have reserves to fall back on, should your debtors default) or 'lend less than you owe' (better a borrower than a lender be, so that you can default on your creditors). The difference is between prudence and fraud. As for the next line, it makes sense enough, as *goest* usually has the limited sense 'to walk', but at least the flavour of paradox remains, for the broader meaning of the word – 'to move, to pass in any manner'[28] – produces nonsense. (The Fool cultivates just such incongruities elsewhere, as in the phrase 'thou bor'st thine ass on thy back o'er the dirt', where *ass* must mean 'donkey', but where I am none the less startled by the surrealist image of a man carrying his buttocks on his shoulders.) The next line is rather more difficult. Though usually glossed as 'Don't believe all you hear', that interpretation requires us to assume *learn* = 'hear'.[29] But *learn* is of course not normally used in that sense, nor does Schmidt provide any parallels for this particular construction. Certainly, at the start of the line, we have no reason whatever to take *learn* in that specialized sense. (It might even mean 'teach': *OED,v*.4.) *Trow* also has several meanings, and, though there can be no doubting that one or more of them fit, the uncertainty of *learn* does not make it easy, initially, to know which meaning of *trow* to select, and, until we define *trow*, we cannot retrospectively decide on the proper (limited) sense of *learn*.

'Set less than thou throwest' has confused commentators most of all. *Set* elsewhere means to stake money, usually to match another man's bet.[30] *Throw* means 'to throw dice';[31] a gambler throws the dice *for* a particular stake. How, from this evidence, does one derive the paraphrase, 'Don't stake all your winnings on a single throw' (Muir)? The Furness Variorum cites, 'Keep on throwing, but set nothing', without giving a context to which it would be appropriate: you cannot win money without staking some. Furness also cites a variant of Muir's interpretation ('Set a less sum than thou hast won by thy last throw'), the last six words of which must all be inferred from *throwest*, as well as Elizabeth Griffith's 'never set equal to *the stake you throw for*' (my italics), which makes good gambling-sense, but is again difficult to infer from the Fool's single verb. M. C. Bradbrook privately suggests that a person could set less often than he threw if he were winning, in which case the stake and/or winnings from the last bet could remain on the table, and so not need to be 'set' (there) again; but, aside from the fact that this ingenious interpretation requires a very particular and (even to a gambler) hardly inevitable sense of *set*, the significance of this practical advice still remains obscure. Does the Fool mean 'only continue to play if you keep winning'? Could the lines convey that meaning, even if it were intended? And, if they could, wouldn't that be an argument for abdication (which the Fool can hardly intend)?

What all these interpretations suggest is that, though the line seems strongly to make sense, and to imply a particular gambling-context, *what* sense and *which* context are not self-evident. Let us assume the line means, on the simplest interpretation of each word, 'Stake another man less [often] than you throw'. In hazard, a very popular dice-game of the period, one man threw the dice, while everyone else at the table staked him. If he won, he took all their money; if he lost, he had to pay each of them off. The man throwing the dice, though he had more to win, thus also had far more to lose, so it would not have been self-evident, even to a Jacobean audience, that it was wiser to throw than set. But the caster did have one advantage – he could cheat. As the pamphlets of the period make clear, cheating, or the suspicion of cheating, was inseparable from the game, from any game of dice.[32] But only the man with the dice could cheat. Ergo, it is better to throw than to set. But to understand the line a spectator must first find a specific context, in which one man throws while another bets but need never throw, and then infer from this context the explanation (cheating) which solves the apparent paradox. But, even granting that we deduce this meaning, the relation of this line to the rest remains puzzling. The Fool leaps without warning from instructions on how to gamble (and, implicitly, how to cheat), to injunctions against drinking and whoring, its sister vices. After a series of apparently serious moral injunctions, in heavily emphatic parallel clauses, when we are expecting a climactic assertion of the heavenly reward, the deserved eternity and bliss which such prudent earthly conduct will earn, we get instead an accelerated nursery-rhyme rhythm and the ludicrous reward of 'more / Than two tens to a score'.

These are ambivalences designed not to enlighten, but to bewilder. The very monotony of the rhymes hypnotizes, making it increasingly difficult to concentrate on the content at all, and the content itself becomes increasingly difficult to follow. Even the pattern of the stanza contributes to this bewilderment, for, instead of the more–less–more–less–more–less one would expect, we get more–less–less–more–more–less – which of course produces a pattern of its own,but one less immediately recognizable, and of less help in organizing our attention to the movement of thought. If we could discern that movement, we could fit each new impression into a system, an order; we could discard any ellipsis or ambivalence or eccentricity in the lines themselves, by reference to a context, to the superstructure of the Fool's speech, which would inform us which elements were mere irrelevancies. But that superstructure never becomes clear. Without it, ambiguities leave the mind frustrated rather than stimulated, unable to discern alleged relationships rather than delightedly alerted to new ones. This speech signally fails to supply what the play as a whole so clearly does: a perspective on its progress, a hierarchy of emphasis.

In the absence of such a hierarchy, we become the victims of an old comic routine, transposed from the physical to the mental world: 'Here, take this ... and this ... be careful, these are irreplaceable ... hold this a minute, would you? ... this too ... one more ... oh, here's another' – until finally the stooge is so overburdened that he cannot move and, eventually of course, drops everything. Psychologists have shown, again and again, that, when confronted with such a sequence, unless we succeed in constructing a formula to unite all the items, we 'drop everything'.[33] The auditor struggles to keep hold of the Fool's commandments, waiting for the key which will suddenly unite them – and, instead, when we expect the solution, the Fool produces nonsense and anticlimax. Hence the irritation of 'This is nothing, Fool.'

One of De Quincey's finer paragraphs concerns this very phenomenon, though he is talking generally and about what he regards as a vice of style:

It is the suspense, the holding-on of the mind until what is called the ἀπόδοσις, or coming round of the sentence commences; this it is which wears out the faculty of attention. A sentence, for example, begins with a series of *ifs*; perhaps a dozen lines are occupied with expanding the conditions under which something is affirmed or denied; here you cannot dismiss and have done with the ideas as you go along; for as yet all is hypothetic; all is suspended in air. The conditions are not fully to be understood until you are acquainted with the dependency; you must give a separate attention to each clause of this complex hypothesis, and yet, having done *that* by a painful effort, you have done nothing at all, for you must exercise a reacting attention through the corresponding latter section, in order to follow out its relations to all parts of the hypothesis which sustains it. In fact ... each separate monster period is a vast arch, which, not receiving its keystone, not being locked into self-supporting cohesion, until you nearly reach its close, imposes of necessity upon the unhappy reader all the *onus* of its ponderous weight through the main process of construction.[34]

If this is true of a reader, how much more so of a mere listener – especially when, as it emerges, no keystone is ever forthcoming.

A reader can govern the speed and direction of his reading, as an auditor cannot; he has time to puzzle out the lines, time to attempt to relate them; he needn't worry about storing the sequence in his memory while he awaits the key, because for the reader the text is itself an infallible memory, available on demand. Even if we imagine the Fool pausing after each line, to allow his audience time to decode the line, and appreciate its ambiguities, by such delivery the Fool only increases the burden on the spectator's memory, while at the same time emphasizing the importance of each commandment. J. D. Wilson, whose interpretation has many adherents, asserts that the speech 'bids Lear be everything a Fool is not: canny, close-fisted, unsociable, strait-laced, in short a miser or usurer whose sole aim in life is to make money "breed" '. This interpretation asks us to believe that one rides rather than walks only in order to save shoe leather; that the proverbial 'Believe not all you hear', which Wilson himself cites in explicating 'Learn more than thou trowest', is cynicism fit only for usurers; that the Fool's injunctions against drinking and whoring are ironic, amounting in fact to criticisms of Lear for being 'strait-laced'.[35] But, even if you admit Wilson's gloss is absurd, you will probably return to the speech, you will probably seek to arrange the evidence in some coherent patten, because you too share the conviction that a meaning and a pattern must exist. So do I. So do Lear and Kent. The speech preys on our credulity. For, however we interpret the lines, what have gambling and drinking and whoring to do with Lear? They fit the rest of the play, no doubt; they anticipate Poor Tom's confessions and commandments; 'keep in-a-door' anticipates the storm. Such tentacles of allusion to past and future not only justify the presence of the speech, but also contribute to our conviction that it must mean something. But this relevance to the larger context does not alter the bewilderment the speech produces in its own immediate context.

The Fool's injunctions all relate to the need for caution, watchfulness, security, and this advice fits the Fool's interpretation of Lear as an unwary fool who has put himself in the hands of knaves. But this explanation is itself anachronistic, a symptom of 'reading the play backwards', for as yet we have little evidence for the Fool's interpretation of Lear in this way – an interpretation significantly different from our own, at this point. For till now the play has encouraged us to see Lear himself as the wrongdoer, and we enjoy the Fool's initial wit for that very reason, because he stings and punishes Lear. Besides (and this is the merit of Wilson's gloss), a proper caution is almost indistinguishable from selfish, canny close-fistedness. Throughout the speech, we are unable to decide whether the Fool genuinely recommends such conduct, or not.

The nature of the Fool's poetry can be illustrated by two poems, each similar to and dissimilar from Shakespeare's: the first from Florio's *Second Fruites* (cited by Muir as a parallel to this passage), the second from Nahum Tate, in a speech he invented for Poor Tom.

> The bottom of your purse or heart,
> To any man do not impart.
> Do not give yourself to play,
> Unless you purpose to decay . . .
> Shun wine, dice, and lechery,
> Else you will come to beggary.

> Whilst Smug plied the bellows
> She trucked with her fellows,
>   The freckle-faced Mab
>   Was a blouze and a drab,
> Yet Swithin made Oberon jealous.
>
> (III.iv.36–40)

The first is what commentators have tried to make of the Fool's speech, everything geared to the communication of a simple moral lesson. The rapidity incites us to boredom; we learn the game, find it too elementary for our tastes, cease to listen. The second produces the same consequence by different means, for Tate has simply thrown together items without logical connection to create an easy chaos, and, since for such a method any particular will do, we quickly accept the general message and cease to attend to details. Shakespeare instead perpetually promises and perpetually denies definition. He creates chaos by the marshalling of particulars which clearly relate to one another, but how they relate we cannot discover. The imaginative unrest created by this technique is characteristic of the Fool.

The speech should create unrest, but of course it does not. Because so much Jacobean speech has lost its significance for us, we usually no longer recognize true nonsense. We generally assume instead (as in the Archbishop's Salic Law speech) that the meaning which once was has been obscured by time; we sit bored in our seats, assured that scholars could explicate the joke or the profundity for us, and indeed in their commentaries they attempt to do so. But there is no joke here. If there were, our intellects would be placated: 'oh, it's just a joke'. Shakespeare does not permit that dismissive solution.

Lear only speaks sixty words (seventy in the Quarto) during the Fool's entire performance. But the imaginative unrest, the disequilibrium, created by the Fool's speech is of a piece with his recurrent comic method, its fluidity of logic, its structuring of a game Lear cannot win, its shifts of audience. All these tactics stimulate a working of the mind, but will not let that working rest, will not allow the stability of a conclusion. The Fool bewilders reason: ours, and Lear's – for it is Lear he attacks, Lear who attempts to understand him. The structure of the dialogue encourages us to observe how Lear reacts to the Fool, to watch Lear attempting to follow him, to imagine Lear *thinking*. Like Solzhenitsyn's General Samsonov: bewildered, the mind labouring to think things through, perpetually distracted, the surprise of accusation provoking defensive hostility and, at the same time, a renewed effort to understand.

We appreciate the Fool partly for the dexterity of his comic guerilla war, striking by surprise, from behind, or cockily to Lear's face, all the while preserving his pretence of innocence. Like Cordelia, he impresses us with his courage in flouting the old man, especially as he has apparently nothing to gain from it, acting solely from love of Cordelia and of Lear himself; and, of the two, love of Lear dominates. Only twice does the Fool reprimand him for Cordelia's sake, once explicitly ('has banished two on's daughters, and done the third a favour against his will'), once implicitly ('Can you make no use of nothing, nuncle?'). He chiefly criticizes Lear for giving away his kingdom and trusting his two daughters, seven times explicitly (nine in the Quarto) before Goneril's entrance. After her entrance all his jibes are aimed at her, or at Lear for having trusted her. The Fool emphasizes the harm Lear has done himself, and in all his satire describes him as a fool: not a knave, not a man who mistreated others for his own profit, but a self-made fool, who can expect to suffer for his folly. The Fool thereby advances the revolution of perspective, from Lear as malefactor to Lear as sufferer, which was promised by the end of scene i.

The Fool, at the very bottom of the social hierarchy, is what we would call 'the little man', and for that very reason we delight in his comic victories over authority. This partly explains the emphasis on Lear's whip, and the repetition of 'boy' and 'sirrah' and 'nuncle', all reasserting the power of Lear, his superiority in the social hierarchy. Subversive Fool runs under the whip of Authority and wallops the old man's arse, then skips away with a smile and a subservient bow – whereupon the upper classes remark on the extraordinary sense of humour in the lower classes. We relish this performance because we are all, ourselves, someone else's lackey. Why then do we not take a similar subversive pleasure in Oswald? Because we are all, ourselves, someone else's master, and from our lackeys we expect and demand and feel we deserve obedience and respect. Shakespeare arranges for us to see Oswald from the perspective of Authority, and the Fool from that of Rebellion. Both reactions depend on and extend our relationship with Lear in scene i.

The Fool demarcates the boundaries of proper disrespect. Lear may only permit from the Fool what he would not from Kent because he needn't pay much attention to the criticisms of an idiot. If both Kent and the Fool spoke in scene i, if Lear allowed the one but not the other, we should have to impute the distinction between them to some such reasoning. But in fact Lear *now* allows criticisms he would not allow *then*, which encourages us to impute the distinction to a change in Lear. As with Caesar, 'the spectator juxtaposes a present moment with a past one, and as likely as not infers development' (p. 149). For Lear does attend to the Fool's criticisms, as he did not (at the time, at least) to Kent's. His brief contributions to the dialogue take three forms: encouragement of the Fool, and active participation in his riddles; exclamations of pain when the Fool scores; threats when the Fool goes too far. These three responses occur repeatedly and in no discernible pattern, making it impossible to simplify Lear's reactions to a progress from permission to outraged pain to threats of punishment, but creating instead the impression that all three coexist, almost simultaneously, in Lear's mind. His last words to the Fool before Goneril's entry again threaten him, but only *if he lies:* that is, if he stops telling the truth, which Lear finds so painful. We may not approve of Lear's threats, but if (like Orsino's) they are symptoms of pain we will understand them, and, if he allows the Fool to hurt him, if by implication he admits he deserves such punishment as the Fool supplies, we will sympathize with his pain, pain intensified by self-condemnation.

An observer's reaction to the quarrel will depend on his perception of the two antagonists before they quarrel, and Shakespeare with great subtlety and consistency predisposes us to see the quarrel largely from Lear's perspective – or, rather, from Kent's or Cordelia's perspective, who though they know Lear's faults nevertheless seek to understand him, and certainly prefer him to Goneril.

An observer's reaction to the quarrel will depend also on his perception of the issue. But his perception of that issue will necessarily be influenced by his predispositions toward the antagonists, and, though the presentation of the issue might alter or even reverse his prejudices, to do so it would have to overcome a heavy initial bias. Arguments which convince a neutral observer do not convince an interested partisan. Yet, obvious as this proposition is, critics assume that we must (and in the theatre do) weigh Goneril's grievances with impartiality and calm, solely on their judicial merits. This absurdity has been perpetrated not only by Bradleian critics (who continue to commit the documentary fallacy, seeking the REAL truth behind the dramatist's partial presentation of events), but by anti-Bradleians as well, who will have nothing to do with mere character criticism (i.e. with an observer's perception of the antagonists before they quarrel), and who therefore seek to judge the moral issue in a fictive, pure and microscopic isolation.

Goneril accuses Lear's train of gross misconduct, encouraged and abetted by Lear himself; Lear denies the truth of the allegation, and denies Goneril's right to make it, even if it were true. We are required to judge an ethical question and a question of fact.

We can only judge the question of fact by what we see of his train's conduct on stage – which means in fact the conduct of the one knight who speaks, a decidedly mild-mannered and respectful creature from the gallery of Shakespeare's anonymous gentlemen. Those who desire to make Lear's train odious must therefore invent odious business for the ninety-nine silent knights. In doing so, they do not fill a vacuum which the text leaves ambiguously empty, but directly defy the text, which clearly intends for the silent ninety-nine to be represented by the one who speaks. The director of a large modern company can fill the stage with knights, so that their sheer numbers suggest the chaos and inconvenience of which Goneril complains. But Shakespeare did not have 100 extras, and his stage would certainly have been no more crowded in scene iv than in scene i. On an unlocalized stage, an audience could have no inkling that Goneril's palace might be smaller than Lear's, or less able to accommodate such numbers. This leaves, as the only possible substantiation for Goneril's claim, the conduct of Kent and the Fool, of which I have already spoken. The evidence does not support Goneril's accusation of fact; it does not even begin to approach the weight which would be needed to overturn our prejudices.

Moreover, the scene minimizes the entire presentation of the issue, concentrating instead upon the preparation for the confrontation and the reactions it provokes, particularly Lear's, and this slighting of the issue further damages Goneril, who has most to gain from a full presentation of rights and wrongs. Consider, for instance, Tolstoy's summary of the issue:

> She demands of her father that he should diminish his retinue, that he should be satisfied with fifty courtiers instead of one hundred. At this suggestion, Lear gets into a

strange and unnatural rage, and asks, 'Does any here know me? This is not Lear . . .'[36]

Of course this is inaccurate: when Lear asks these questions, Goneril has not yet even demanded that he disquantity his train, let alone specified fifty. To motivate Lear's fury by direct reference to Goneril's specific numerical demand makes his reaction seem ridiculously excessive. Lear reacts first and primarily to Goneril's tone and Goneril's accusations; her demand that he diminish and reform his train thus comes as the last straw, which provokes his decision to leave. Even then, Goneril does not mention a number. From her point of view, to do so now would be tactically inept; from Lear's point of view, since he rejects her interference on principle, to ask her to specify a number would be superfluous; from Shakespeare's point of view, to mention a number now would distract our attention from the principle and turn the actual number of retainers into a debating-point. Once the number becomes negotiable, rather than Lear's inviolable right, then to quarrel and curse over the retention of one man becomes ridiculous. And if one can go, why not another? – a progress of diminution whose inevitable end Shakespeare exposes in Act II. But here too much attention to specifics weakens attention to the ethical issue, Goneril's right to make such demands, and to make them in this manner.

Nevertheless, the number fifty must somehow surface, and so Shakespeare has been driven to a circumvention of reality, solving his problem by an imaginative leap which never troubles audiences, though it has often troubled critics: Lear simply exits, then enters again, saying, 'What! fifty of my followers at a clap! / Within a fortnight!' We assume, readily enough, that off stage he has been informed of Goneril's specific intentions, though how or by whom he has been informed, and whether she may already have dismissed half his men, we do not pause to question (partly because of the surprise of his re-entry – as with Alan Howard's sitting-up in *Henry V* IV.iii). The number is thus broached, and the revelation of the number in this way turns it to Lear's advantage, for now we see the hypocrisy of 'a little to disquantity your train', translated into (what Lear finds incredible, presumably what drives him back on stage) the dismissal of fifty, of half, of fifty 'at a

clap' (rather than a slow and decent diminuendo), of fifty
'within a fortnight' (though till now the scene has given no
hint of the interval since his abdication, implying if anything a
rather prolonged one). Goneril makes no reply.

However, it is misleading to take too seriously the accusations against Lear's train. In scene iii, Goneril mentions them
only once ('His knights grow riotous'), even then in a context
and a fashion ('his') which implies Lear's responsibility for
their conduct. She directs the remainder of her criticisms in
that scene at Lear himself. In scene iii we have as yet little
reason to doubt Goneril, for she has no motive for lying to
Oswald, and her complaints that Lear himself behaves with an
intolerable imperiousness are intrinsically credible: the very
first scene demonstrates as much, and the fourth does nothing
to contradict this impression. But, when the confrontation
comes, Goneril accuses not Lear but his entourage. Though
she does accuse him implicitly of responsibility for their
conduct, she does not, until the very end, fault his own ('You
strike my people'), as she had faulted it repeatedly and
strongly in scene iii. To my knowledge, no one has even
noticed this change in Goneril's tactics; presumably we were
never meant to notice it. If audiences did, audiences could
postulate reasons for it ('she is trying to spare his feelings', 'she
cannot bring herself to accuse him directly') – just as, if
audiences had noticed the contradiction in Alan Howard's
sitting-up four lines after we had been told that he was viewing
the enemy's battle formation, they could have invented
reasons for that ('in the confusion on the eve of battle, there
are conflicting rumours about the king's whereabouts'), or
even seen it as an important theme ('the English army searching for its leader'), or as evidence of an ironic interpretation of
Henry ('while the day, his friends, and all things stayed for
him, Henry went off and – slept'). But, as, in both cases, the
discrepancy seems not to have caught our collective attention,
such explanations have no hope of communicating themselves.

But though we may not notice the change in Goneril's
tactics, nevertheless we do experience scene iv differently as a
result of it. If Goneril levelled her criticism there at Lear's own
conduct, there could be no disputing the issue of fact: Lear
does carp and quarrel, strike her gentleman, upbraid her and

her people on every trifle, and so on. Moreover, if he wished
to dispute the issue of fact, he could only do so by praising his
own character, in the way he praises his knights (lines 261–4).
In his own mouth, testimony to his own virtues would of
course be suspect; it would, besides, be less admirable than
indignation in the defence of others. By shifting her main
attack from Lear to his train Shakespeare severely weakens
Goneril's credibility, for, even without the speeches of the one
mild-mannered knight, we have no *a priori* reason to think ill
of them, particularly as Goneril in scene iii spends little of her
initial credibility attacking them. The extravagance of her
later accusations provokes involuntary disbelief. Her case
against the knights also lacks the sincerity of an open outburst
against Lear, who clearly remains her real target. Even if scene
iii did not tell us as much, the organization of her speeches in
scene iv would: the first beginning with his retinue but rapidly
turning on Lear; the second directed entirely at Lear; the third
reprimanding Lear, then criticizing his retinue, then threatening Lear; the fourth combining criticism of his retinue with
her strongest, most explicit attack on Lear himself ('You strike
my people'). Goneril thus appears to malign the knights only
as a means of getting at Lear, as Lear himself deduces. The
structure of events thus encourages us to second his deductions, which might otherwise seem merely a paranoid's effort
to evade the true issue (just as the structure of events in
Twelfth Night makes Viola seem intelligent, and Malvolio
seem ludicrously deluded, for each jumping to the same
conclusion).

More important, Goneril's insincerity – which scene i led us
to suspect, which her premeditation and her use of Oswald
have confirmed – colours her entire presentation, not only in
the manifest hypocrisy of such phrases as 'your good wisdom'
and 'these dispositions which *of late* transport you' (compare
her dialogue with Regan in scene i), but also in the very
length, the premeditated syntax, of her speeches.

Not only sir, this your all-licensed Fool,
But other of your insolent retinue
Do hourly carp and quarrel, breaking forth
In rank and not-to-be-endurèd riots.
Sir, I had thought, by making this well known unto you,

To have found a safe redress, but now grow fearful
By what yourself too late have spoke and done,
That you protect this course, and put it on
By your allowance, which if you should, the fault
Would not scape censure, nor the redresses sleep,
Which in the tender of a wholesome weal
Might in their working do you that offence,
Which else were shame, that then necessity
Will call discreet proceeding.

Compare Tate:

Sir, this licentious insolence of your servants
Is most unseemly; hourly they break out
In quarrels bred by their unbounded riots.
I had fair hope by making this known to you
T'have had a quick redress, but find too late
That you protect and countenance their outrage.
And therefore, sir, I take this freedom, which
Necessity makes discreet.   (I.ii.35–42)

Tate cuts it by half, turns it into four elementary sentences
(where Shakespeare had only two). Shakespeare's first sentence, a statement of fact supporting four assertive moral
adjectives (two of them compounds), Tate reduces to a flimsy
moral assertion, leaving the statement of fact to be implied
from the predicate. In Shakespeare their quarrels break forth
into riots; in Tate, their riots breed quarrels. In Shakespeare,
Goneril fears, by what Lear 'too late' has spoken and done,
that he *puts on* their course; in Tate, Goneril herself finds 'too
late' that he *protects* it, both changes shifting the emphasis
from Lear's own conduct and initiative. Tate dispenses with
the formality of such constructions as '*this your* all-licensed
Fool' (compare '*other your* new pranks' and '*this our* court', in
her third speech) and 'which else' (repeated in her third
speech). He simplifies the artifice of Goneril's vocabulary, of
compound adjectives such as 'all-licensed' (i.e. licentious) and
'not-to-be-endurèd' (i.e. unbounded), of such a verb as 'disquantity', in her third speech (where Tate writes 'lessen').
Metrically and syntactically, Tate replaces the muscular
with the facile: of seven full lines, four have their caesurae

after the fourth syllable, another after the sixth; the striking enjambment of 'which' serves no purpose; the first four phrases are each a line and a half long.

Each detail, each word or phrase or rhythm, Tate makes intrinsically less interesting, but it must also be conceded that he produces more natural speech, language of a kind a historical Goneril might well have used. If nevertheless we prefer Shakespeare, in fact persist in believing that Shakespeare has created words more appropriate to Goneril, it is because Shakespeare in a handful of lines has communicated certain traits of mind, which normally we could only have perceived through prolonged acquaintance with Goneril's words, Goneril's actions, Goneril's all; so that Shakespeare's deviations from the lingual norm each have meaning, each conveying something of a character's own deviations from the norm of unindividuated being (which is of course not a norm at all, having never existed except as an intuited statistical mean). With Goneril as with Viola, each deviation is justified, not by its semantic likelihood in a context, but by its fitness to the whole of the character, by its intimation of motive. Poor Tate only transcribes what any (or at least, many) of us might have said, so that at play's end we know perhaps no more of Goneril than we might know of anyone after two hours of sporadic eavesdropping. The complexity of Shakespearian speech is another instance of an artist compensating for the inherent deficiency of his materials, here the unnatural intensity of the moment compensating for the unnatural brevity of a play.

Shakespeare makes Goneril's speech seem *written*. It will seem so particularly after the disjunct and impromptu prose of the Fool; it will seem so, too, because we expect it to, because we know Goneril manufactured this crisis to create an opportunity to speak. Whether Goneril actually wrote it out in advance does not matter, for by 'written' we mean *premeditated*, and from premeditation we deduce intent. From the seeming premeditation of Goneril's words we deduce that she fully intends each one, each nuance, each provocation, each cruelty of phrasing; that she has considered, at some length and in cold blood, how her words will affect Lear, and that she intends them to affect him as they do. This cannot be said, for instance, of Lear's quarrel with Cordelia, or the famous quarrel between Brutus and Cassius: the cruelties they speak can be forgiven, by one another and by the audience, because we feel they were not fully intended, and we feel they were not fully intended because they were not premeditated, but the accidents of anger. The artifice of Goneril's style makes her seem, by contrast, responsible and accountable for all she says.

Critics who remark on the triviality of the ostensible issue in this scene state or imply that Lear thus has small cause for such extravagant wrath, and indeed, when he curses Goneril, the disparity between stimulus and response must strike any observer. But strategically the ostensible triviality harms Goneril more than Lear. In Edward Bond's adaptation, Lear abuses his subjects, conducts a neurotic foreign policy, and finally, to set an example, personally executes an innocent man, on stage. If Goneril's accusations had that degree of intrinsic magnitude, if they harnessed our own moral or emotional energies, they might overcome our predispositions; they might even make a virtue of her premeditation, if we could see it as a willed determination to resist her father, in defence of a moral principle. Goneril is the prosecutor: if the charges are trivial, she, not the defendant, suffers in our estimation.

Triviality characterizes all the assaults on Lear: Oswald's impertinence, Goneril's accusations, the stocking of Kent, the mere entrance of Oswald, Goneril and Regan holding hands. These actions, like Northumberland's neglecting to kneel in the presence of Richard II, are active expressions of disrespect. Richard II, like Lear, began the play by alienating our sympathies with an arrogant display of power; Richard II, like Lear, regains our sympathies in being denied even the appurtenances of respect. But, since Bolingbroke in fact deprives Richard of his crown, Northumberland's disrespect is only the objective sign of a far greater assault upon the King; the neglecting to kneel is symptomatic only. In *King Lear*, such disrespect becomes itself the central assault on the protagonist. In nightmares, I am not maddened, nor my heart broken, by the depradations of tyranny and war, but by someone I love refusing to open a door, or walk with me across the park. The child denied a toy cries and continues to cry, not for the forgotten toy, but because the refusal heralds a division between the child's ego and the world. As the naked child ages into armed adulthood, the original terror of that recognition is masked by familiarity and repetition, but terrifying it remains. I cannot make anyone love me. I cannot make even my own children love me. Lear thus is driven mad by Goneril and Regan holding hands.

I should not contend that audiences are or should be conscious of this psychological mechanism. Our reactions to Goneril in scene iv are heavily influenced by the premeditation and conspiracy of scene iii, yet the play does not ask us to reflect upon, or even notice, the degree to which premeditation affects our judgements of guilt. *Oedipus Tyrannus* and *Oedipus at Colonus* do ask us to reflect upon that principle; *King Lear* does not. The critic must always distinguish between the great structure of assumptions which the work of art uses, as invisibly as it can, and the few it deliberately lifts into consciousness: between the geometry of a Raphael and the geometry of a cubist. Raphael's silently influences our perception of his subject; the cubist declares that geometry *is* his subject. Moreover, because the play (unlike the painting) develops through time, it may inch its assumptions into consciousness gradually – which contributes to the seeming impersonality of great drama, for the issues thus appear to emerge, unsought, from the material itself.

The cubist dictates the visual issue; he exposes his own consciousness, to alter ours. Shakespeare also dictates the issues, but seems in doing so only to expose the consciousness of his characters. In scene i, Lear monstrously over-reacts to Cordelia's 'most small fault'. But in scene iv I am inclined, audiences are I think inclined, to accept Lear's valuation of the magnitude of the issue, at least partly because no one explicitly challenges it, and Goneril herself has already implicitly endorsed it, in the preceding scene. Even so, when he curses her I cannot help feeling he has gone too far; I cannot but be reminded of his disinheriting Cordelia. But throughout Act II, while I become more and more committed to Lear's assessment of the seriousness of the confrontation, Lear's opponents insist increasingly upon its triviality. As the disparity between these two evaluations widens, since I must concede the material triviality of the issues it becomes imperative that I explain their spiritual importance, though I can no more do so than Lear himself. My agitation escalates as Goneril and Regan count down from fifty to twenty-five to ten to five to one. Only then, when they have narrowed the issue to its smallest possible significance, when I feel it at its very greatest, does Lear discover for himself and for us the principle which has all along governed his and our reactions: 'O reason not the need!' Among the satisfactions of that great speech is its resolution of our own agitation, so that we may at once and forever reject Goneril's evaluation of the issue's magnitude. Shakespeare motivates Lear's insight, by making the audience need it as much as Lear, so that we at once understand why he arrived at it, and triumph in his seeing the solution we could not. The cubist himself declares the issue; Shakespeare declares it through Lear, having beforehand ensured, through his control of perspective, that when it rises into Lear's consciousness it will satisfy ours.[37]

The triviality of the ostensible issues is psychologically fundamental to Lear and to the audience. In *Titus Andronicus*, whose affinities to *King Lear* are well known, the causes of the protagonist's madness are hardly trivial: the murder of a few sons, the rape and mutilation of an only daughter, the amputation of his own hand in jest. Consequently we respond first to the acts themselves, and only secondarily to their effect on Titus. In *King Lear* we are brought to see the same evil, greater evil, in acts familiar and familial. Evil reveals itself not in the act, but in the motive of the act.

In the archaic culture whose last and greatest expressions were *The Oresteia* and *Oedipus Tyrannus*, guilt was a property of the crime, not the criminal: the crime was conceived as an object, which stained indelibly whoever touched it. Intent was therefore immaterial. After all, whether the crime was committed deliberately or accidentally made little difference to the victim. But already, in the fifth century before Christ, this philosophy of guilt was being gradually superseded, in law and in tragedy, by one which required a conjunction of criminal act and criminal intent. At Colonus, Oedipus insists upon his innocence, because the incest and parricide were unintentional: he is still polluted, but no longer guilty. This compromise, though legally it continues to govern the administration of justice, philosophically was shattered by Christ, who drove the underlying principle to its necessary conclusion: guilt is a function of intent, and so criminal intent, even if never consummated in a criminal act, itself constitutes sufficient condition for guilt, including the final guilt, damnation. Guilt is anterior to the act, rather than its consequence: he who lusts after a woman in his own heart commits adultery. Christ is primarily concerned not for the victim, but the sinner, and the crime itself is only a material manifestation of spiritual evil. The preoccupation of Christian tragedy has therefore been the nature of a character's essence, of his 'soul', rather than the nature of the act. Spiritual evil need never be articulated by an act of equal magnitude; indeed, on the contrary, the magnitude of the evil will lend stature to the act, which may itself be trivial. Hence, for Goneril and Regan to close their doors against their father, to shut him out in the rain, betrays a malignity of soul as terrifying as Clytemnestra's.[38] Nevertheless, Shakespeare still preferred to give the soul's potential an ultimate and congruent expression: Iago stabs Roderigo, Cornwall blinds Gloucester, Regan murders the good servant from behind, Goneril poisons her sister. These acts are so satisfying (dramatically), not only because of their obvious structural value, in conveying climax, but also because they prove the accuracy of our earlier ethical estimates, thus securing a hatred first founded on surmise. As Kenneth Burke said, 'the essence of a thing can be defined . . . in terms of its *fulfilment* or *fruition*'.[39] But by Ibsen's time these apocalyptic horrors have been dispensed with, as unnecessary and outside ordinary experience. Hedda Gabler does no more than burn a manuscript, however often she may claim to be burning a baby – but so terrible a woman is capable of burning the baby, and what she is capable of matters more than what she actually does.

The philosophy of guilt has in this century undergone a further revolution, with predictable consequences for modern criticism. If guilt is a function of intent, then we are all guilty, as Christ well knew. But Christ's principle, though accepted theologically, was ignored legally and practically, a contradiction seized upon by Freud (among others), who drove Christ's principle to its necessary conclusion. For, if we are all recidivists in the psychopathology of everyday life, then we differ from the mass murderer only because he is less able to express (and so relieve) the evil of his nature in trivial ways. Moreover, that inability is the product of his genetic inheritance or his environment as a child, and in either case we cannot blame him for it. The criminal is conceived as handicapped, and for his handicap we are to pity him (or, since he acts upon desires we suppress, to admire him for his liberation from taboo). Christ saw the actual crime as the manifestation of a corrupt self; Freud, Marx, and the modern world see that corrupt self as itself the manifestation of a corrupt society. Guilt is now anterior not only to the crime but also to the criminal. All crime thus becomes political. So does all tragedy.

The consequences for criticism of such a philosophy of guilt are not far to seek. I have already quoted, in relation to Viola, Arthur Miller's proposition that 'how to dramatize what has gone before' is 'the biggest single dramatic problem', an emphasis shared by modern critics and modern directors as well as modern playwrights. Goneril and Regan are no longer regarded as responsible for the evil of their own souls. Instead, Lear himself, as father and as king, must be guilty for what they are, since they are merely the heirs of his chromosomes, the products and the victims of his home and his society. Therefore, in the 1976 Royal Shakespeare Company production, a nervous Regan, called upon to speak, began to stammer, exasperating her tyrant father, who finally stamped his booted foot to stop it, allowing her hurriedly to finish and then collapse with relief. The ceremony of state and the structure of the family were decidedly Victorian; Lear himself, a male Victoria, chewing a cigar, in the pompous vestments of the late Austro-Hungarian empire, became the symbol of a repressive and decaying culture, in fact the very culture Freud psychoanalysed (see Plate 8). By such historical and psychological allusion, the audience was encouraged to conclude that Lear had driven his daughters to their neuroses. Lear thus becomes personally responsible not only for the follies of scene i, but for all evil in his world, all suffering. This guilt the play does not and cannot exorcise; under the burden of it, critical sympathy for Lear collapses; without such sympathy, the play itself collapses. In the theatre this did not happen, because in the theatre the allusions largely disappeared after the first scene; one forgot about them; their implications ceased to govern one's responses to Lear. Where they did recur, as in Act II when Cornwall and his party appeared with evening dress and cocktails, they actually increased sympathy for Lear, by making him an outcast from that society which we today find so unsympathetic. But, though in the theatre Lear's antecedent sins are evanescent, and disappear once you cease to assert them, the critic has the power to continue this indictment of Lear's past indefinitely. From this perverse constancy, this unremitting rectitude, arises the belief that the central issue of the play is (or should be) what made Regan's heart so hard, and the conclusion that the storm scenes fail because they do not answer that question, or because the spectator, having little sympathy for Lear, simply loses interest in his madness.[40]

One will sympathize with such criticism, in so far as one shares its philosophical assumptions. But it begins from a perspective radically different from any that Shakespeare could have expected from a Jacobean audience. If we assume that Shakespeare shared our own ideological assumptions, then we give him the benefit of intellectual 'immortality', and can exploit his cultural authority to endorse our own beliefs – but only at the cost of distorting his own models of reality. If, on the other hand, we recognize his intellectual and artistic integrity (and our own), then we must also recognize that his fictions, his 'hypotheses', are in part modelled upon postulates we no longer accept. If criticism denies the existence of this dilemma, then 'the dramatist's manipulation of the audience' does indeed become morally pernicious – because one artist's model of reality, his constructed 'hypothesis', has been given the cultural authority of a fact. In those circumstances, as in medieval science, saving Aristotle has become more important than saving the phenomena.

An observer's reaction to the quarrel between Goneril and Lear will depend upon the responses of the antagonists themselves to the confrontation. From the first the confrontation precipitates a personal crisis in Lear. His reaction may conveniently be divided into two parts: the first, and more complex, from Goneril's entrance to her third speech; the second, and more powerful, from that speech to Lear's exit.

With Goneril as with Cordelia, Lear responds to disobedience by disclaiming his paternity; but, while with Cordelia we see only the result of this process, with Goneril we witness the movement of thought which precedes it, from 'Are you our daughter?' to 'Your name, fair gentlewoman?' to 'Degenerate bastard!' Lear's articulation of this process not only makes his reaction more intelligible, but also implies that Lear has now himself become conscious (or is becoming so) of what was before only impulse. 'Are you our daughter?' This question implies an antecedent syllogism: you cannot be my daughter, because Lear's daughter would not treat Lear in this fashion. This is Lear's ethical postulate, and leads to a second line of thought: perhaps you are Lear's daughter, but perhaps I am not Lear. Goneril has herself suggested this in replying to Lear's first question, when speaking of 'these dispositions which of late transport you from what you rightly are'. This doubt, once entertained, cannot be dispelled. (I know I am Gary Taylor, and not Napoleon, partly because others recognize me as Gary Taylor. What if they began to treat me as though I were Napoleon?) 'Does any here know me?' Lear chokes on his own rhetorical question, for he requires social recognition and confirmation not only that he is Lear, but that he is a particular Lear, a man with certain rights and privileges. His self-definition is not descriptive but normative: it too rests on the ethical postulate. Because Goneril denies that postulate, Lear must eventually choose between belief in an ethical principle and belief in reality, and choosing the former he goes mad.[41]

'Your name, fair gentlewoman?' virtually repeats 'Are you our daughter?' But in the interval Lear has answered his first question in the negative. 'Are you our daughter?' is a rhetorical question, intended to remind Goneril of her filial duties. 'Your name, fair gentlewoman?', with its mock gentility, is instead in the style of the Fool's feigned recognition of Lear, after ignoring him for ten lines: though it implies a moral rebuke, its immediate intention is ridicule.

Lear's adoption of the Fool's style relates to another peculiarity of this sequence: the fact that the Fool, not Lear, first responds to Goneril's two speeches.

For you know, nuncle,
   The hedge-sparrow fed the cuckoo so long
   That it had it head bit off by it young.
So out went the candle, and we were left darkling.

May not an ass know when a cart draws the horse? Whoop,
Jug! I love thee.

The Fool creates a pause before Lear's reaction, a pause during which our own attention will be focused on Lear, in anticipation. The mere fact of the pause makes Lear seem less rash
than in scene i; it alerts us to the act of *Lear thinking*, engaged
in thoughts he does not express but whose nature we infer
from 'Are you our daughter?' Our attention to Lear's
unexpressed antecedent thought makes that question less
unnatural than it might otherwise seem. The intervention of
the Fool not only allows Lear to be seen thinking; it also
allows us to think – for, remove the Fool (as Tate does), and
we are immediately swept up in the alternating escalating
passions of the antagonists themselves. After Goneril's third
speech, the Fool does not intervene again, and the removal of
his comic buffer zone structures the escalation of the quarrel.
At this early stage Shakespeare deliberately restrains the
impetuous acceleration and excitement, by allowing the Fool
to create these pauses. Moreover, by placing the Fool between
stimulus and response, Shakespeare allows us to consider
whether the stimulus justifies, and why it provokes, Lear's
peculiar response. A modern dramatist would probably leave
all this to the stage direction '*Pause*'. Though for a reader such
a direction might interrupt the dramatic illusion, in the
theatre the effect would be much the same – except that
Shakespeare's pause has a distinct content. The Fool comes,
unnaturally, between stimulus and response; he passes moral
judgement on Goneril, thereby anticipating and justifying
Lear's reaction; he interprets the real issue as filial obedience
and love, thereby anticipating and justifying Lear. The
parable of hedge-sparrow and cuckoo describes a parent feeding children *who are not its own*, thus anticipating the reasoning implicit in 'Are you our daughter?' The Fool's criticisms,
here as earlier, strike at both parent and child, but for quite
different reasons, taking in fact the form Lear's own thoughts

do, eventually: Lear is a fool (like the hedge-sparrow, the horse, the shadow, the obedient father) for having trusted such a knave as Goneril.

It will be seen that the Fool begins with straightforward choric commentary, clearly intended to guide our moral responses to Goneril's preceding speech. In each case, he follows this with a deliberately obscure quip, of indeterminate reference and intent, for, though Jug and the candle may have relevance to the play as a whole, at this point they only bewilder. This bewilderment has three functions. It conceals Shakespeare's own moral commentary from the audience; it distracts the Fool's own on-stage audience from responding too harshly to his criticisms, by remindling them he's only an idiot; it creates a limited chaos.[42] For the Fool to speak at all disturbs the natural sequence of events. On stage, the Fool and Lear both demand our attention, so that the initial incongruity of such a line as 'May not an ass know when a cart draws the horse?' (depending again on the ambivalence of 'ass') may puzzle us even further, when we are only half-attending to the Fool. Moreover, in each case the most bewildering of the Fool's remarks comes just before Lear speaks. Having personally acquired considerable experience of the confusion created for an American theatre-goer by British accents, I can describe in some detail what happens when a listener does not quite grasp what has just been said on stage. Mentally one tries to go back over the preceding words in order to puzzle a meaning out of them, but in the meantime, of course, the dialogue continues, and consequently, not only is it impossible to decipher the preceding words, but even those which follow (however straightforward) require an effort of concentration to be understood. This failure to penetrate the meaning of a phrase leaves a residue of frustration and impatience – though, if it happens too often, if we conclude the words *have* no worthwhile meaning, we simply cease to search for one, and so cease to be frustrated. Likewise, if we decide the meaning eludes us only because the accents are British, or the language Elizabethan, or because the Fool alludes to the refrain of a lost ballad, we can contentedly ignore the difficulties. We can also ignore them if we decide Shakespeare was trying to be funny – in which case, our frustration is vented on the dramatist, for failing to make us laugh. But the confusions here seem to me deliberate: like 'Have more than thou showest', they create in the minds of an audience a disorientation which mirrors and anticipates Lear's own. In both cases, even as we concentrate on the Fool's puzzles, we are also and simultaneously conscious of Lear himself, thinking.

Not that audiences consciously realize that Lear feels as they feel. In fact, once audiences do so, the Fool's confusions will cease to frustrate: they may be dismissed, because we know their function. But, though the audience does not yet associate its own mental confusion with Lear's, as the play proceeds this disorientation more frequently and more emphatically associates itself with Lear, explaining (at least in part) why we find it natural that Lear goes mad. Consider to what lengths Shakespeare must go to motivate the madness of Titus Andronicus. Even so, most readers and spectators find it less convincing than Lear's. Lear loses his sanity for reasons less extraordinary, and consequently Lear's madness is the more frightening, because the nearer our own lives.

The Fool's presence has one other effect: it helps deprive the confrontation of any intimacy. From the moment Lear turns to Cordelia, until Kent's intervention forty lines later, the other characters on stage virtually disappear; but, in the quarrel with Goneril, as soon as the Fool drops out of the scene Albany enters it. The reactions of a third party continuously impinge on our attention. I never feel any communion at all between father and daughter. With Cordelia, there is an intense intimacy despite the public character of the scene; with Goneril, there is none, despite its ostensible domesticity. Lear negotiates with Cordelia, and will with Regan; he makes allowances, offers opportunities of escape. Not so with Goneril: the sarcasm begins immediately. Lear never gives Goneril a chance. Whether she deserves one may be doubted; certainly he gives her none. But perhaps for that very reason, because there is never the least communion between them, Lear does not here seem to throw away or to repudiate so much.

After Goneril's third speech begins the second phase of Lear's reaction, alternating between self-reproach, wrath, and self-pity. All three emotions are available to the actor; much of the theatrical excitement and emotional realism of the scene derives from their juxtaposition and interrelation. Nevertheless, one can discern, particularly in the dominant tone of Lear's three long speeches, a broad movement from reproach to wrath to pity. After his initial violent outburst ('Degenerate bastard!'), self-reproach dominates, taking the form of open repentance for his conduct toward Cordelia. The logic, by which Goneril's accusations force him to acknowledge his mistreatment of Cordelia, is clearly implied and easily inferred, though never stated: Goneril's behaviour makes Cordelia's seem, by contrast, a 'most small fault'. But the logic of Lear's self-reproach is perhaps less important than its emotional consequences, for Lear's repentance significantly increases an audience's sympathy and esteem for him, at the very moment he rejects his second daughter.

During Lear's curse, the crest of his wrath, no spectator will have the leisure or presence of mind for detailed memories of scene i, but juxtaposing Lear's curse there with his curse here neatly illustrates the different emotions the two speeches convey and stimulate.

> Let it be so. Thy truth then be thy dower:
> For by the sacred radiance of the sun,
> The mysteries of Hecate and the night,
> By all the operation of the orbs
> From whom we do exist and cease to be,
> Here I disclaim all my paternal care,
> Propinquity and property of blood,
> And as a stranger to my heart and me
> Hold thee from this for ever. The barbarous Scythian,
> Or he that makes his generation messes
> To gorge his appetite, shall to my bosom
> Be as well neighboured, pitied, and relieved,
> As thou my sometime daughter.
>
> Hear, Nature! Hear, dear Goddess, hear!
> Suspend thy purpose, if thou didst intend
> To make this creature fruitful.
> Into her womb convey sterility.
> Dry up in her the organs of increase,
> And from her derogate body never spring
> A babe to honour her. If she must teem,

> Create her child of spleen, that it may live,
> And be a thwart disnatured torment to her.
> Let it stamp wrinkles in her brow of youth,
> With cadent tears fret channels in her cheeks,
> Turn all her mother's pains and benefits
> To laughter and contempt, that she may feel
> How sharper than a serpent's tooth it is
> To have a thankless child. Away, away.

The first seems unnatural because it suppresses an appropriate emotion; the second, because it hysterically exaggerates
that emotion. The first has calm, an ordered magnitude; the
second is shrill. The first, in its first line, summarizes (and so
makes immediately intelligible) all the suspended elaborations which follow. But the rationale of Lear's second speech
is withheld until its end: 'that *she* may feel' (what I feel). With
Cordelia Lear may be wrong, but only with Goneril does he
begin to seem mad. The withholding of his motive till the end
also serves to close the speech on its most pathetic note, so
that Lear's exit immediately afterward becomes an act of
disguised weakness, the retreat of a man overcome by his feelings. By contrast, the first curse ends not on its most pathetic
but its most horrific note. Lear's curse in scene iv is an act of
desperation; the measure of his desperation is the measure of
our sympathy. Lear is no longer the abstract of Authority, but
a mere and particular father denied any authority over his
children.

With Cordelia, Lear is wrong. With Goneril, he is right, but
immeasurably more extreme, so that we recoil from the
violence of his expression of emotions we may share. In his
impotence, he demands more: vehemence is inversely propor-
tional to power. To an extent, this must make his rage
pathetic, but it also – and simultaneously – makes it more
frightening. In disinheriting Cordelia, Lear invokes a power
he undoubtedly possesses, but a recognizable and limited
power, the power of political and familial institutions. In
cursing Goneril, deprived of the authority of those institutions, Lear invokes a power he may not possess at all, a power
any man might or might not possess, simply because it is not
defined or recognized or regulated by human institution. A
curse, particularly of such verbal 'authority', disturbs us

precisely because we cannot be entirely sure whether the one cursing has the power he claims.

Tate rearranged Lear's speeches so that this curse immediately preceded his final exit. Many actors have preferred it there, for by all accounts Lear's second speech is more powerful than his third, and would thus produce a more effective exit. But Shakespeare follows the wrath of the second speech with the pity of the third, so that pity dominates our final impressions of Lear in this scene. We have already seen Lear's wrath; his self-pity, and the pity it engenders in us, are new, introducing an emotion which will dominate Lear's next two scenes. In the place of a powerful – but in some ways redundant – wrath, Shakespeare puts Lear's tears, his shame at his own impotence to restrain them, his fury when even his own body refuses to obey him, his humiliation when his eyes confess a pain his pride would deny, his pathetic assurance of Regan's love, his effort to wound Goneril or rouse her jealousy by praising Regan, his final threat to reassert his authority as King, by way of regaining his authority as father.

Lear first left the stage after his curse, but almost immediately returned.[43] In one sense, Shakespeare has given him two exits from the scene, each powerful. Any actor will appreciate the theatrical advantages, but there are psychological ones too, which an anecdote will perhaps make clear. After a fire drill, a class of schoolchildren were re-entering the school, rather noisily perhaps, when the headmistress (a nun) emerged from the door and loudly berated them for their behaviour; she then turned and disappeared into the building, only to emerge a few moments later, without further provocation, continuing her harangue, then disappearing again – only to appear yet again, after the children had quietly returned to their room, repeating and intensifying her wild denunciation of their earlier behaviour. Afterwards, several teachers remarked privately on the peculiarity of her behaviour; not long after, she suffered a nervous breakdown, stopped teaching, and withdrew from the convent. Her behaviour in the fire drill was first thought peculiar, and later seen as symptomatic of her impending breakdown, partly because of the triviality of the provocation, and the wild excess of her language. But, if she had spoken three times as long on her first appearance, this might have been thought excessive, but not so peculiar as the repeated entrances and departures. When she left, one assumed she was finished, but with each reappearance, it became clearer that this conventional explanation for her behaviour was inadequate, and that each time she left she was in fact attempting by an act of will to control her own emotions (which she realized were in excess of the occasion), that when this effort failed the intensity of her feelings compelled her to return, each reappearance more frenetic than the last precisely because she had in the interim failed to regain control: the emotion, temporarily dammed, broke through all the more violently. Likewise, though Lear only leaves and reappears once, and, though he has apparently or possibly suffered further provocation in the interim, the scene is usually staged as though he were repeatedly *about to leave*, but never quite making it out the door, each time returning for a further attack – until, after what seems the finality of his great curse, he does at last leave, only to return moments later. Even a reader, I think, senses this repeated movement and return:

> Saddle my horses; call my train together.
> – Degenerate bastard! I'll not trouble thee.
>
> Prepare my horses!
>
> Go, go, my people!
>
> Away, away!

Always on the brink of going: by such simple means, Shakespeare delicately suggests the disintegration of Lear's mind.

To the confrontation between Goneril and Lear he reacts with pain; she does not react at all. If she is hurt, her words never show it, and to that extent her pain must *seem* more distant and less significant than Lear's. If we want to focus on Goneril, we must imagine she is visibly pregnant,[44] or that, in the words of a nineteenth-century prompt-book, she 'is very much agitated during curse and at the End Shrieks & rushes to Lear imploringly who throws her off – She falls into Albany's arms & faints – Ladies and pages cluster round her'.[45] Goneril does not speak to Lear after Albany's entrance, nor respond to any of his speeches; twice she addresses herself to Albany, in reference to Lear, on both occasions displaying only a tactical regard for her husband's support. His recurrent amazement and concern for Lear further discourage an audience from attending to the hypothetical sorrows of Goneril. Goneril's tactical objective (Albany's acquiesence) continues to dominate her speeches after Lear's exit.[46]

We may call Goneril cold, or stoical, or realistic, but, because she displays no emotion which could stimulate an answering emotion from ourselves, an audience will naturally feel for Lear more strongly than for her, even if it were convinced Goneril is right. But Goneril's absence of emotion does not simply neutralize our responses: it positively alienates. She shows no awareness of Lear's pain, which has been so powerfully communicated to us. Admittedly, Lear himself shows no awareness of his daughter's feelings. But, as she displays none, the oversight is pardonable; indeed, we may not perceive any oversight at all. But to fail to notice Lear's pain requires a willed inattention to suffering. In so far as she notices his feelings at all, she can feel for them only contempt: they are, to her, dotage, no more. Pity and contempt are complementary reactions to a single stimulus, weakness, and Goneril's contempt may express a repugnance we all feel. In performance, some Lears provoke this uneasiness more than others, particularly in the details of their senility, which may easily provoke embarrassment or contempt. But the text itself does not encourage us to imagine a debile Lear. On the other hand it does insist on Lear's age, and Lear's age is, in performance, like the Archbishop's ecclesiastical costume in *Henry V*, something perpetually present, which the actor can forcibly bring to our attention at any moment, which we ourselves may freely juxtapose with any moment, any word or action. Garrick identified '*his distresses at his Years*' as the crucial determinant of an audience's sympathy for Lear; certainly, for a spectator 'his Years' are a constant visual stimulus, where for the reader they (and the sympathy they might engender) are only intermittently and intellectually present.

I find Edmund's contempt bracing and admirable; I recoil from Goneril's. Edmund infectiously enjoys his own contempt, consciously exaggerates it, wittily expresses it. No one thinks of Goneril here as witty: mirthlessly and curtly she denigrates individuals (where Edmund mocks ideas and institutions), even including us among her implied targets, in so far as we feel the least sympathy or pity for Lear's 'dotage'. Edmund instead confides in us, so that we relish his machinations, his manipulations, his *acting*; we respond to his plotting as a performance, and delight therefore in its ingenuity and accomplishment. The juxtaposition of I.ii and iii heightens this contrast between Goneril and Edmund, and the contrast – which cannot, except retrospectively, affect our responses to Edmund – does influence our responses to Goneril. To see this we need only imagine how differently we should respond to scenes iii and iv if Goneril, like Edmund, first explicitly and directly to the audience spelt out her plans for getting the old man out of the house, explaining as well how intolerable he had been around the place, parodying for us his domineering manner, and then – either standing aside, or up above – oversaw an abbreviated version of scene iv, assuring us that she had set on Oswald, confirming that Lear reacts just as she'd expected, and finally (with a parting 'Now must I play my part') putting her 'frontlet on' and confronting Lear with 'Not only, sir, this your all-licensed fool . . .'

In imagining how differently the same sequence of events could have been dramatized, it becomes obvious how complete is the dramatist's control of perspective, how differently he has presented Edmund and Goneril, how fundamentally that difference affects our responses to the two, how inconspicuously the contrast itself helps distance us from Goneril. The interpolation of the subplot in scene ii influences our perspective on scene iv in several other ways as well, all quietly contributing to the same revolution of sympathies. Gloucester and Edmund both explicitly generalize the basic issue as 'parents vs. children'; that in turn further encourages us to see the quarrel in scene iv in the same terms, rather than as a dramatization of a dispute between host and guest, or between two individuals at odds over a matter of manners – two alternative perspectives, equally valid, which would tilt our sympathies toward Goneril. Gloucester moreover *does* seem a fool; we watch him being duped; we see him turning against a completely innocent son, who has in truth offered him no provocation whatsoever. Lear, by contrast, may have made a dreadful mistake in scene i, and may be repeatedly mocked by the Fool, but dramatically he never seems a fool; we never see him duped (even in scene i); Cordelia and Kent *did* deliberately and dramatically provoke him. Lear's explosion of wrath against his good child is exhausted in one scene; Gloucester's is sustained over several. And Gloucester's error begins after Lear's, so that in scene iv Lear's repentance is juxtaposed with Gloucester's persistence. Finally, Edmund turns against a father who treats him callously in scene i, and who shows him no extraordinary generosity beforehand; Goneril abuses the father who gave her all.

'I.e. by the end of scene iv we're already pretty much on Lear's side.' A rather bathetic conclusion, no doubt, to sixty pages of analysis. But that is precisely my point: that such conclusions do not matter, that in themselves they tell us less than nothing about the greatness of a work of art. What matters, what gives us pleasure, is the emotional and intellectual richness of the individual moments that contribute to those conclusions, the process by which we arrive at them, the experience of which they are the transitory culmination – and we are interested in that culmination only because it becomes itself an ingredient in the experiences which follow. These dense and complex contributory moments not only contain the real greatness of the scene; they also form, individually and in combination, the only secure basis for generalizations about our responses to it. Thus, anyone who, by offhandedly asserting that '100 knights *would* be inconvenient', thinks he has dealt a crippling and irrefutable blow to sympathetic interpretations of Lear, does a grotesque injustice to the multiplicity and interdependence of our emotional and moral responses to this scene. Conclusions can only be reached by an analysis of moments, and conclusions are only valuable in relation to the analysis of subsequent moments.

But we embarked on the analysis of this scene from *Lear* not only for the scene's own sake, but in order to explore the dramatist's creation of a hierarchy of emphasis. The fruits of that exploration cannot so easily be summed up. An observer's reactions to the confrontation between Goneril and Lear depend upon that observer's perception of the characters before they quarrel, his perception of the issues about which they quarrel, and of the characters' own reactions to their quarrel. Since most drama depends, in one way or another, upon confrontation and conflict, most plays should be amenable to analysis in terms of these three questions. But the first and third of them force us to find a way to discuss dramatic character, how it is created and how we respond to it. As I have tried to show in describing Viola, 'character' is created largely by sensitive accretion rather than psychological or moral analysis, by striking juxtaposition rather than long-distance coherence, by immediate impact rather than intellectual consistency. Most modern critics, however, prefer not to discuss character at all; when they do discuss it, they usually attempt to abstract the 'unity' of a character, rather than attending to our developing responses to it.

Critics tend to emphasize the second question, about issues, sometimes to the virtual exclusion of the first and third. Shakespeare by contrast often pays it little attention – as in *Caesar*, where we are told nothing about Publius Cimber, the ostensible subject of the dispute in the Senate. Moreover, as we have seen by experimentally addressing her sisters' words to Cordelia, or putting them in her mouth, the same words, the same moral and intellectual assertions, affect an audience very differently depending on who speaks them, and to whom. A critic committed to the moralization of literature judges characters by means of an intellectual judgement about the abstract veracity of what they say; an audience more often judges the veracity of what is said in terms of who said it, when, to whom, and why. Audiences are, properly, more interested in people than themes. And this intellectual bias of the critic accounts also for the tendency to insist upon the tendentious content of comedy (whether the Fool's, or Fluellen's, or Catherine's) rather than its establishment of mood, affection, chaos, or character, or its contribution to a larger, developing emotional structure.

Most important, spectators' perceptions of any issue will largely depend upon the perspective from which they approach it. I began this book by describing a play as a 'hypothetical model'; I began this chapter by calling a play 'a developing perspective on an unstoppable irreversible action'. These definitions can be combined: a play is the working model of an hypothesis; the hypothesis takes the form of the enactment of a progress of perceptions. Like the psychologist flashing numbers on a screen, the dramatist controls not only what we see, but when and how long we see it. The dramatist's control of emphasis depends upon the fact that the model is constantly 'moving' (in both senses). The pun on 'moving' is not simply accidental or contrived: it encapsulates two elements of all dramatic representations, elements which readers are likely to neglect or underestimate. A play is not simply a passive object which we actively interpret; it moves, and in the process moves us. The manipulation of emphasis should therefore be described in terms of different aspects of movement. Like any moving object, a play has *direction*; it traverses *distance*; it has *velocity*; it has *mass*; it has *impact*; it moves in *space*. These interrelated categories will account for most of the techniques described in the preceding pages.

The importance of direction is implicit in the importance of character: our responses to any development will be crucially affected by our existing emotional allegiances to the participants. But those responses will also be affected by the other assumptions and expectations an audience brings with it, since all of these contribute to the vantage point, the direction from which an audience views any action. These assumptions can range from grand ideological postulates (about the pathological character of nationalistic or sexist jokes, for instance, or the nature of guilt) to particular pieces of information (that Oswald will, at Goneril's behest, 'put on ... weary negligence'; that Lear's new servant is in fact Kent in disguise). Human beings tend to see what they expect to see, and a Jacobean spectator brought up on folktales about King Lear's one good and two bad daughters will likely see Goneril as a wicked daughter, unless the dramatist overwhelmingly discourages that expectation. Likewise, when Goneril herself describes Oswald's directed conduct as 'negligence' and as coming 'slack of former services', when an anonymous gentleman then speaks of 'a great abatement of kindness', an audience will tend to see what follows as neglect (Lear's interpretation) rather than a return to decorum (Goneril's).

But the 'direction' from which we approach or perceive an

action can be emotional as well as intellectual. We have already seen this in the Archbishop's speech in *Henry V*, when the failure to get a laugh at one point resulted in a subsequent failure to get a laugh at others. An audience's mood will determine its receptiveness to certain kinds of development: hence the structuring of oratorical crescendos in *Henry V*, the satisfaction produced by Lear's climactic 'O reason not the need!', and the hostility toward Malvolio and Goneril when each interrupts an onstage party. An audience tends to approve of actions which satisfy its own theatrical expectations, regardless of the intellectual or moral merits of the action itself. Caesar at last lives up to our expectations in the scene of his assassination; Lear, at the climax of the quarrel with Goneril, again produces the superbly impressive theatrical rage which we had seen in I.i, which we have been expecting to see again ever since Goneril announced her intention to provoke a confrontation, a rage of which we are reminded by his physical abuse of Oswald and his threats to the Fool ('Take heed sirrah: the whip').

We can appreciate Lear's rage against Goneril not only because it is theatrically impressive, but because of the distance between I.i and I.iv. Shakespeare could have organized Act One very differently: I.i could have been followed by Kent's return and soliloquy (I.iv.1–7), then by I.iii and the remainder of I.iv, leaving out the Fool entirely and postponing Edmund's scene until after Lear's confrontation with Goneril. This arrangement would not only deprive an audience of the perspective which the subplot lends to the main plot; it would also, more importantly, reduce the distance between Lear's rejection of Cordelia and his rejection of Goneril. The distance between these two events allows an audience to respond differently to the second. More generally, of course – as we have seen in both *Twelfth Night* and *Henry V* – mere distance is the most important of many methods by which the dramatist obscures contradictions and discourages inappropriate analogies.

Since we are talking about movement in time, the 'distance' between two moments depends to some extent upon the velocity at which the action travels. The play's pace in any given scene also affects an audience's capacity to absorb and reflect upon detail. To some degree a director and cast determine the pace of any performance; in particular, the exact pacing of individual speeches or actions or reactions – what the theatrical profession calls 'timing' – rests wholly upon the performer. But in another sense the dramatist, as I have tried to show, can and does control the velocity of the action as a whole. In *Henry V*, the Archbishop began his explanation of Henry's claim to France slowly and intelligibly; his sudden acceleration half-way through, during the hardest part of the argument, was designed by contrast to make the content impossible to follow. In this case, the contrasts and uses of pace were the work of an individual actor; but elsewhere similar effects are dictated by the dramatist. The assassination scene begins with a flurry of interlocking action; it then slows down during Caesar's speeches to the Senate, allowing us to attend to every intellectual nuance of this tense, significant penult. Likewise, Lear at the beginning of I.iv is in a hurry, and his hurry determines the pace of the scene: issuing orders in many directions, rapidly interviewing Kent, dispatching attendants, receiving reports. But by the time the Fool enters the scene has lost the pressure of urgency, and we can simply attend to the intellectual interplay between jester and master. We are, of course, vaguely aware that a confrontation with Goneril impends, but for the time being we are entirely absorbed in the present, in riddles. This part of the scene encourages, indeed demands, more mental alertness than any other; it also presents Lear as a fool who has placed himself in the power of hypocrites. When Goneril enters, the Fool again, by his interventions, at first slows the quarrel down, letting us take in Goneril's accusations, commenting on them in a particular way; but by the time of Lear's two great outbursts, the buffer zone has been removed, we are given little time for reflection, we must simply respond to the power of Lear's passion. Caesar's speeches are a deliberate pause before an expected climax; Lear's are the climax itself. Caesar is arguing and we listen to his arguments; Lear is cursing and weeping, and we respond emotionally, not intellectually. The pace of the play encourages us to *think* about Caesar's speeches, but to *feel* Lear's.

The impact of a physical object is a function of velocity and mass; the impact of individual moments of a play is altogether harder to calculate. But no one would deny that Goneril's short scene with Oswald (I.iii), like Artemidorus's short scene alone (II.iii), has relatively little impact: we perceive both as scenes in which little happens, scenes which merely feed us neat gobbets of information and prepare us for a later, more interesting and important moment. We carry from these scenes the information which is their *raison d'être* (Goneril can no longer tolerate Lear's conduct; she wants a confrontation; she wants Oswald to provoke it; she does not care whether Lear leaves), but otherwise they leave no vivid or lasting impression. Kent's soliloquy, which follows, is similarly neutral. But after this 'rest', this relaxation of attention, the entrance of Lear again fully engages our faculties, as we attend to Kent's encounter with Lear, wait for the confrontation with Oswald and eventually Goneril, and scrutinize the play's protagonist, who made such a remarkable impression in the first scene. In short, we regard Lear's portion of I.iv as more important than Goneril's earlier short scene: it has more impact partly because we expect it to, partly because more happens in it, partly because it is unpredictable – Oswald's first and second entrance, the Fool's, Goneril's, Albany's, Lear's re-entry, all coming at moments when we do not expect them.

These decisions about significance and importance, these levels of attention, obviously affect the impact of different episodes, and as a result help to determine the relative priority we attach to any item of information. The relatively uninteresting character of Goneril's scene of exposition weakens her claims on our dramatic allegiance, whatever the merit of her arguments. The impact of her case is likewise reduced, in the central confrontation itself, by her own coolness. Lear's emotion generates an answering emotion in us; Goneril's apparent emotionlessness generates a corresponding distance in an audience. Goneril, in fact, here positively repels human approaches, whether of the Fool or her father or her husband; and since, as with Viola, the character's relationship with an audience is of a piece with her other relationships, in a real sense Goneril tends actually to repel us, too.

Impact is therefore partly a function of interest: if we wished to sustain the physical analogy, we might say that the impact of the oncoming action will be greater, the greater the force of the curiosity and interest which goes out to meet it. Goneril's earlier scene, and her general coldness, fall upon a static or even retreating audience; Lear's actions and speeches collide with an audience leaning forward (often physically as well as spiritually) to meet them. Nor is it difficult to explain why, in general, Lear interests us more than Goneril. Lear is already multi-faceted; Goneril is merely two-faced. Like Viola, Lear is a figure of layered complexity; like Orsino, he is a character whom we expect to change fundamentally, before the end of the play. Moreover, Lear is the character all the other characters watch and attempt to affect – not only in the first scene, but throughout the play. Whatever the merits of Lear's perspective on events, everything encourages us to attend to it, to try to envisage it, more than we do Goneril's.

Impact is partly a function of mass, and one of the dramatist's most obvious means of controlling emphasis is by the distribution of mass. Because the speed and security of all perception depend upon redundancy, upon an excess of information directing us to one conclusion, the sheer bulk or mass of impressions we receive from any one character, or set of characters (Lear's entourage), heavily affects our point of view. As I have said, the distribution of mass in Act I of *King Lear* predisposes us to see the eventual face-to-face confrontation between Lear and Goneril from the perspective of Lear's party. But the idea of dramatic 'mass' can also help to explain an essential difference between readers and spectators. A reader is only conscious of Lear's age abstractly, or when the text calls particular attention to it; for the spectator his age is perpetually present, like the Archbishop's ecclesiastical costume, and hence makes a much more significant contribution to an audience's responses. Garrick insisted on the importance, in producing sympathy for Lear, of '*his distresses at his Years*'; both of these elements make more impact upon a spectator than a reader. In reading the text we merely infer Lear's distress; in watching the play we see it. The repeated perception of the king's age and pain is, from the critic's point of view, redundant; but it keeps making a single point over and over again, mere repetition ensuring that it cannot be overlooked or underestimated in the theatre.

Like all other moving objects, a play moves in and through a particular space: in this case, a theatre of some kind. The nature of this special space affects, as one would expect, our perception of the object's movement. It is a place where we go to watch a show, a prearranged series of designedly impressive actions; hence we are, in the theatre, far more receptive to the attractions of ceremony and spectacle than we might be when reading in the intimacy of a living room, or in the puritanical functionalism of a library. But it is also a large empty space which must be filled by the players' performances: we therefore admire the vocal power which can fill and command that space, whether in King Henry's orations to his troops or King Lear's outbursts and imprecations. We go to the theatre expecting, and ready to relish, verbal extravagance; we are thus relatively disinclined to pass moral judgement upon it. The armchair critic suffers from no such inhibitions.

The dramatist's manipulation of emphasis might therefore be described in terms of his control of the direction, distance, velocity, mass, and impact of an hypothesis moving through a very particular kind of space. At least, any adequate description of how an audience responds to particular moments in that movement must take account of all these factors, and must at the same time resist all of the associated occupational prejudices of the academic reader. I believe that anyone who could achieve such a description would indeed have succeeded in catching Shakespeare 'in the act of greatness'.

6 Inconclusion

There are plenty of moments – scenes, characters, productions – where a consensus of response could be made the starting-point for an analysis of the dramatist's stimulation of his audience. *King Lear* itself contains four more such scenes: Lear's rejection by Regan (II.iv), the blinding of Gloucester (III.vii), Lear's reunion with Cordelia (IV.vii), and the play's ending (from Lear's re-entrance with Cordelia in his arms, until his own death). The problems of analysing these scenes get progressively more difficult: any satisfactory analysis of the later ones would entail a satisfactory analysis of the earlier, and a successful description of all four would not only necessitate a description of our responses to the entire play but also raise almost every issue in the burgeoning and intractable controversy over the nature of tragedy. Since Aristotle, tragedy has been defined in terms of its final emotional effect upon an audience, and, whatever the validity of that definition, any attempt to describe the totality of our emotional responses to the ending of *King Lear* could hardly avoid grappling with it.

But it would also be possible, and perhaps in most ways preferable, to turn away from *King Lear* altogether, in a search for moments more tractable to analysis. Because (as for I.iv itself) the existing consensus testifies only to the power, not the interpretation, of those later scenes of *Lear*, any thorough analysis of them would (like the preceding analysis of I.iv) become embroiled in critical controversies of the most divisive nature. The chances of carrying out such an extended analysis successfully would be much better if it could draw upon the evidence of other examples, other moments, of a less debatable nature: the character of Malvolio, for instance, the funniness of Falstaff, the 'Pyramus and Thisbe' episode in *A Midsummer Night's Dream*; or, of more obvious relevance to *Lear*, the quarrel scene in *Julius Caesar*, the character of

Feste, the deaths of Romeo and Juliet, the character of Richard III, the reunion of Pericles and Marina, the final scene of *The Winter's Tale*. For all of these (and many more) there would be widespread agreement about both the strength of the effect and its general nature. One problem which certainly needs sustained attention – and for which any one of several of the preceding examples would serve as a convenient point of focus – is the mimesis of emotion: how much of it is in the text, how much is left to the performer, how the emotion of the performer relates to that of the spectator. Equally important, this technique allows us to analyse failure as well as success, and the failures (so long as almost everyone agrees they *are* failures, at least theatrically) should be instrumental in helping us to account for the impact of the agreed successes. The unsatisfactory endings of *The Two Gentlemen of Verona, Romeo and Juliet* (after the lovers' deaths), and *Timon of Athens* have a good deal to tell us about the overwhelming power of the ending of *Lear*.

No doubt this is a roundabout way to arrive at an interpretation of *King Lear*, or any play. Of the engrained biases of literary criticism as a profession, one of the most disabling is impatience. This springs from more than the familiar economic imperative, 'publish or perish'; equally compelling is the need, in preparing articles for journals, to keep them short, and to give them the maximum possible claim to importance. This need is itself born of the explosion in the sheer bulk of criticism published every year: with so many voices clamouring for attention, editors are legitimately concerned not to let any one contributor hog the available page-space, while contributors are themselves legitimately anxious to get a hearing, partly by raising the pitch of their voices. To this market seventy-page discussions of a single scene – discussions, moreover, which aim only to confirm commonplce reactions – hardly recommend themselves.

But there are good reasons to resist the institutional incentives to find quick solutions. The best is that no one believes the quick solutions anyway. The attempt to describe and analyse the widely accepted impact of individual fragments of plays indisputably brings us closer to the actual moment-by-moment experience of the work of art; it releases us from theory into practice, from the pursuit of unknowable and impalpable intellectual intentions to the study of discernible and definable effects. This does not mean that criticism will ever become 'scientific', or that in some future happy/ miserable consummation critics will all agree, and agree too that everything worth knowing is known. But this approach at least promises a way of looking *at* great drama, instead of through it; a way of talking about literature without turning it into a dilute and scatter-brained compartment of philosophy; a way of celebrating, directly, what brings us back to Shake-speare again and again: his power over us.

Notes

CHAPTER ONE: PASSING PLEASURES

1. Virginia Woolf, 'Jane Austen at Sixty', *The Nation,* 15 Dec 1923, 433; repr. in *Jane Austen: A Collection of Critical Essays,* ed. Ian Watt, Twentieth Century Views (1963) p. 15. (The phrase quoted does not appear in the version of this essay in *The Common Reader.*)
2. I owe this anecdote to Theodore Redpath, Wittgenstein's interlocutor on that occasion.
3. References to *Julius Caesar* and *Henry V* are keyed to the Oxford Shakespeare edns, by A. R. Humphreys and myself, respectively; for all other plays I adopt the line references of *The Riverside Shakespeare,* ed. G. Blakemore Evans (1974), though I have modernized them myself. The texts of *King Lear* create special problems, which I discuss below.
4. The most recent book-length studies of response in Shakespeare are Peter Bilton, *Commentary and Control in Shakespeare's Plays,* Norwegian Studies in English 19 (1974); Larry S. Champion, *The Evolution of Shakespeare's Comedy: A Study in Dramatic Perspective* (1970) and *Shakespeare's Tragic Perspective* (1977); Bertrand Evans, *Shakespeare's Comedies* (1960) and *Shakespeare's Tragic Practice* (1979); and E. A. J. Honigmann, *Shakespeare's Seven Tragedies: The Dramatist's Manipulation of Response* (1976).
5. Jean Piaget, *Play, Dreams, and Imitation in Childhood,* trs. C. Gattegno and F. M. Hodgson (1951). For a summary of this aspect of this difficult book, see Susanna Millar, *The Psychology of Play* (1968) pp. 50–1.
6. Ian M. L. Hunter, *Memory,* rev. edn (1964) p. 78.
7. M. D. Vernon, *The Psychology of Perception,* 2nd edn (1971) pp. 149, 166.
8. Norman Rabkin, *Shakespeare and the Problem of Meaning* (1981) pp. 33–62. In my Oxford Shakespeare edn of *Henry V* (1982), I suggested that the disparities in interpretation noted by Professor Rabkin 'probably tell us more about the nature of discursive literary criticism' than about the play (p. 1). Amusing confirmation of this conjecture has been supplied by reviews of

the edition. As the dustjacket itself proclaims, I argue 'for a complex view of Shakespeare's presentation of Henry'; yet one reviewer (*Glasgow Herald*, 2 Oct 1982) accuses me of being 'Henry's apologist', while another claims that I 'prefer' an 'unsympathetic presentation of Henry' (*Times Higher Education Supplement*, 12 Nov 1982). In this case there can be no doubt about the author's intentions, since these reviewers are talking about my intentions, not Shakespeare's; yet the two reviewers, standing at opposite ideological poles, interpreted my equator in radically different ways.

9. Vernon, *Psychology of Perception*, p. 4.

CHAPTER TWO: 'JULIUS CAESAR': THE NOBLEST
MOMENT OF THEM ALL

1. *Johnson on Shakespeare*, ed. Arthur Sherbo, *The Works of Samuel Johnson*, VII (1968) 62.
2. Samuel Taylor Coleridge, *Shakespearean Criticism*, ed. T. M. Raysor, 2 vols (1930) I, 224.
3. I am using 'scene' loosely, here and throughout, as my analysis does not include the entirety of the scene, as defined by the usual formal criteria. A certain arbitrariness of definition is inherent in the study of moments. We must begin and end somewhere, but, as the only logical beginning and ending are those of the play itself, any other division will inevitably be more or less unsatisfactory, and based (as mine here is) on a fairly subjective sense of the limits of an 'episode' or 'movement'.
4. For full documentation of its theatrical success, see John D. Ripley, *'Julius Caesar' on Stage in England and America 1599–1973* (1980).
5. *Narrative and Dramatic Sources of Shakespeare*, ed. Geoffrey Bullough, 8 vols (1957–75) V, 85. Ann Pasternak-Slater, in *Shakespeare's Stage Direction* (1982), argues that we must assume that Shakespeare intended the same action that he found in his source. Aside from the absurdity of this as a general principle, nothing in the dialogue alerts us to such a role for Metellus; it is Casca who is to be 'the first', a direction surely superfluous if Metellus must, by the time Casca strikes, already have initiated hostilities with his 'sign'. Moreover, Metellus Cimber's role, in the scene as Shakespeare wrote it, is to 'prefer his suit to Caesar'; after initiating the subject of discussion, he then fades from the dialogue, as the other conspirators press forward. An audience could hardly be expected to attend to an unprepared 'sign' by a minor conspirator whose place in the

dialogue has already been usurped by other and more important characters.

6. For Tieck's description of the 1817 production, see *Julius Caesar*, ed. H. H. Furness, Jr (1913) p. 440. For the two Gielgud performances, I rely on personal experience. The assassination has been performed slowly or ritualistically in other productions; but these are the only ones where I can testify to an audience's response.

7. For instance, Norman Sanders in the Introduction to his New Penguin edn (1967): 'the alienation of sympathy toward [Caesar] is built up by Shakespeare until the moment he is struck down as he stands, still asserting his superhuman "fixity", which is to be disproved by the view of him as very much a man of flesh and blood' (p. 30). Likewise T. S. Dorsch in the new Arden edn (1955): the conspirators' suit 'provokes Caesar into such extravagant expressions of arrogance that all sympathy for him is alienated' (note to III.i.55–7). In the same vein, 'What touches us ourself shall be last served' draws from both editors only the assertion that Caesar's assumption of the royal plural 'alienates' us – ignoring the selfless *content* of the speech, and assuming furthermore that the subjects of a longstanding and popular monarchy would have regarded Caesar's use of the royal plural as arrogant and dangerous.

8. *Narrative and Dramatic Sources*, V, 83, 173.

9. Ibid., p. 101.

10. Vernon, *Psychology of Perception*, p. 33.

11. See *The Complete Works*, ed. Peter Alexander (1951) p. 983: '*They stab Caesar. Casca strikes the first, Brutus the last, blow*'; Humphreys adopts my more economical formula.

12. 'Whilst damnèd Casca, like a cur, behind / Struck Caesar on the neck' (V.i.43–4).

13. This is a fundamental principle, analysed in a variety of contexts: see Vernon, *Psychology of Perception*, pp. 25–31, 36–9; Hunter, *Memory*, pp. 68–9; George A. Miller, *Psychology: The Science of Mental Life* (1962) pp. 166–9.

14. See the long note on this passage in Humphreys's edn or the Furness Variorum.

15. *The Dramatic Censor* (1770) II, 3.

16. See Ripley, *'Julius Caesar' on Stage*, pp. 125 (Booth), 94 (Macready), 98 (Phelps), 258 (Papp), 272 (Nunn).

17. Stanley E. Fish, *Self-consuming Artifacts: The Experience of Seventeenth-Century Literature* (1972) p. 400.

18. The fullest discussion of the crux is J. Dover Wilson's 'Ben Jonson and *Julius Caesar*', *Shakespeare Survey*, 2 (1949) 36–43.

19. Ben Jonson, *Works*, ed. C. H. Herford and Percy Simpson, 11 vols (1925–52) VIII, 583–4 (spelling modernized).

20. I say '*substantially* as Jonson *reports* it' because the textual issue has been unnecessarily complicated by Jonson's slightly misreporting the first part of the Folio line. But this is hardly surprising: Jonson in these notes was obviously relying on his memory; he was in this respect similar to the agents responsible for what are now generally recognized as memorial or 'reported' texts, and he was therefore likely enough to make some minor verbal substitutions. The point of Jonson's criticism is the impossible contrast between 'doing wrong' and 'just cause'; the key words are therefore 'Caesar', a negative adverb, the verb 'to wrong', and 'but with just cause'. Jonson has done no more than substitute one negative adverb for another (never/not), misremember the tense of the verb (did/doth), and omit the to-him superfluous imperative 'Know' (which, if he had only heard the line, he might easily have interpreted as 'No'). The effect of these changes is, incidentally, to make the contrast even more glaring, 'Caesar did never wrong' being a much more absolute assertion than 'Caesar does not (now) do wrong'. But these simple and very common memorial errors do nothing to impugn Jonson's authority for the four extra words, 'but with just cause'; for without those words there would have been no reason to remember, or cite, the line at all. Likewise with his compression of the dramatic context. No one in the scene actually says 'Caesar, thou dost me wrong'; which has led some scholars to conjecture further corruption in the Folio text. But such a claim is clearly being implicitly made – as Caesar himself recognizes. Jonson's description is a legitimate paraphrase of the relevant aspect of the context. But, again, his only interest in recalling that context at all, however imperfectly or even dishonestly, was the striking contrast in the line in question, which had so offended his sense of decorum.

21. Norman Sanders (New Penguin, 1967) accepts the Jonson addition, and Dover Wilson (New Shakespeare, 1949) defended it; but other modern editors continue to print the Folio text.

22. This would be unlikely, if the Folio text of this play were set from a prompt-book (the traditional view). But Fredson Bowers, in 'The Copy for Shakespeare's *Julius Caesar*', *South Atlantic Bulletin*, XLIII (1978) 23–36, has challenged this, arguing that it was set from an intermediate manuscript earlier than the prompt-book, in which case it might not have included any final verbal revisions.

23. See for instance M. C. Bradbrook's allusion to the *Hamlet* passage in *Shakespeare: The Poet in his World* (1978) p. 161.

24. A recent example of such inspired casting occurred in the Royal Shakespeare Company's 1981 season, when Tony Church combined a triumphantly successful Polonius with an equally illuminating York in *Richard II*.
25. The Folio reads 'lane' of children, but Dr Johnson's emendation, graphically very easy, has been almost universally (and I think rightly) accepted.
26. It is for this reason, partly, that I chose not to discuss the Forum scene, which is of course even more famous than the assassination. A good deal more could be said about that scene, but the kind of detailed analysis I here wish to illustrate would have to include much rehashing of familiar insights, and it seemed best to concentrate on relatively virgin material. The quarrel scene, another attractive candidate, not only comes later in the play, but also depends so much upon our responses to character that it seemed useless to consider it before the problems of character-portrayal were explicitly confronted.

CHAPTER THREE: WHO IS VIOLA? WHAT IS SHE?

1. Levin L. Schücking, *Character Problems in Shakespeare's Plays* (1922) 173–6. Schücking and his kind, of course, do not represent contemporary critical orthodoxy. But such critics do raise a number of relevant and unanswered questions about the artificiality, the irreality, of dramatic characters, questions which critics interested in themes and images naturally ignore, but which any investigation of response must eventually face. Hence my rather unusual attentiveness to the misguided opinions of these rather old-fashioned critics – my interest being in why we all agree that they are misguided. (Psychoanalytic criticism has, of course, recently become fashionable again.)
2. As G. E. Bentley points out in *Shakespeare and Jonson: Their Reputations in the Seventeenth Century Compared*, 2 vols (1945) I, 128, neither the romantic comedies nor any of Shakespeare's female characters attracted much praise later in the seventeenth century: his brand of romantic comedy was considered old-fashioned, and the female roles are usually rather small, easily upstaged by comic characters such as Malvolio. Since the eighteenth century, however, Viola's theatrical and critical reputation has not been in doubt.
3. E. H. Gombrich, *Art and Illusion: A Study in the Psychology of Pictorial Representation*, Bollingen Series, XXV, no. 5, 3rd edn (1968).
4. G. K. Hunter sets these sexual transformations in the wider

context of Elizabethan staging in a stimulating recent essay, 'Flatcaps and Bluecoats: Visual Signals in the Elizabethan Stage', *Essays and Studies*, 33 (1980) 37–8.

5. John Fuegi gives some interesting examples of this principle at work in 'Meditations on Mimesis: the case of Brecht', in *Drama and Mimesis*, ed. James Redmond, Themes in Drama 2 (1980) pp. 103–12.

6. E. E. Stoll, *Shakespeare and Other Masters* (1940) p. 29.

7. Arthur Miller, *Collected Plays* (1957) p. 21.

8. *Shakespeare's 'Twelfth Night; or, What You Will': a Comedy. Revised by J. P. Kemble, and now published as it is performed at the Theatre Royal* (1815, repr. 1971).

9. A. D. Nuttall makes a similar point in 'Realistic Convention and Conventional Realism', *Shakespeare Survey*, 34 (1981) 37.

10. For a detailed and illuminating analysis of the speech of one of this very different class of characters, see Stanley Wells, 'Juliet's Nurse: The Uses of Inconsequentiality', in *Shakespeare's Styles: Essays in Honour of Kenneth Muir*, ed. Philip Edwards, Inga-Stina Ewbank and G. K. Hunter (1980) pp. 51–66.

11. M. C. Bradbrook, *Shakespeare and Elizabethan Poetry* (1951) p. 87.

12. E. M. Forster, *Aspects of the Novel* (1927) p. 93.

13. Ralph Berry, in '*Twelfth Night:* The Experience of the Audience', *Shakespeare Survey*, 34 (1981) 115, points out that '*Swabber* is one who swabs down decks – and is therefore pure metaphor – but contains the lingering hint that Maria was engaged in a similar activity, as *chambermaid*. The social insult is all part of what the play identifies as the fluid and shifting lines of social demarcation.'

14. I. A. Richards, *The Philosophy of Rhetoric* (1936), p. 94. See also William Empson, *Seven Types of Ambiguity* (1930) p. 32: 'Statements are made as if they were connected, and the reader is forced to consider their relation for himself. The reason why these statements should have been selected is left for him to invent.' I should only add that the invention is rather strictly controlled.

15. R. W. B. Burton, *The Chorus in Sophocles' Tragedies* (1980), p. 117.

16. V. O. Freeburg, *Disguise Plots in Elizabethan Drama* (1915); Bertrand Evans, *Shakespeare's Comedies* (1960). Evans's recent *Shakespeare's Tragic Practice* (1979) is, by contrast, merely eccentric: see my review in *Review of English Studies*, 33 (1982) 78–9.

17. *The Letters of John Keats*, ed. H. E. Rollins, 2 vols (1958) II, 205.

18. J. R. Brown, *Shakespeare's Plays in Performance* (1966) p. 211.

19. Schücking, *Character Problems*, p. 230.

20. E. H. Gombrich, *Meditations on a Hobby Horse* (1963) p. 10.

21. Dean Frye, 'Reading Shakespeare Backwards', *Shakespeare Quarterly*, 17 (1966) 19–24.

22. Kenneth Burke, *A Rhetoric of Motives* (1950) p. 13.

23. Schücking, *Character Problems,* p. 203.

24. 'A very natural scheme this, for a beautiful and virtuous young lady to throw off all at once the modesty and reservedness of her sex, and mix among men, herself disguised like one; and, pressed by no necessity, influenced by no passion, expose herself to all the dangerous consequences of so unworthy and shameful a situation' – Charlotte Lennox, *Shakespear Illustrated*, 3 vols (1753–4) I, 244.

25. George Stubbs, 'Some Remarks on the Tragedy of Hamlet', in *Shakespeare: The Critical Heritage*, ed. Brian Vickers, 6 vols (1974–81) III, 66.

26. Schücking, *Character Problems*, p. 110.

27. Evans, *Shakespeare's Comedies*, p. 141.

28. *Twelfth Night*, ed. J. M. Lothian and T. W. Craik, new Arden (1975) p. lxxvii n. 3 ('I distinguish between consistency and plausibility') and 2 (of another, similar inconsistency: 'the inconsistency will go unnoticed in the theatre').

29. Schücking, *Character Problems*, p. 96.

30. See Champion, *Shakespeare's Comedy*, pp. 118–22, for the difficulties created by our initial perspective on Helena. (I'm not myself sure that the ambiguity is a fault.)

31. Jonson, *Works*, I, 144.

32. For this distinction, see P. E. Easterling, 'Presentation of Character in Aeschylus', *Greece and Rome*, 20 (1973) 6.

33. Elizabeth M. Yearling has an illuminating discussion of this moment in 'Language, Theme, and Character in *Twelfth Night*', *Shakespeare Survey*, 35 (1982) 85.

34. Brown, *Shakespeare's Plays*, p. 211.

35. This is apparently how Richard Pasco, in the 1971 Royal Shakespeare Company production, interpreted Orsino: as an 'emotional masochist, whose "You uncivil lady" and "O thou dissembling cub" are rapier-thrusts which may scratch others but which are simultaneously deeper self-inflicted wounds' – David Isaacs, in *Coventry Evening Telegraph*, 9 Apr 1971; quoted in Stanley Wells, *Royal Shakespeare: Four Major Productions at Stratford-upon-Avon* (1977) p. 59.

36. Emrys Jones, in *Scenic Form in Shakespeare* (1971) p. 14, discusses the general principle by which Shakespeare constructs scenes (Othello's temptation, the gulling of Benedict) so that a

character's position at the end is the polar opposite of his position at the start.

37. Harold Jenkins, 'Shakespeare's *Twelfth Night*', Rice Institute Pamphlet XLV (1959); repr. in *Shakespeare: The Comedies*, ed. Kenneth Muir, Twentieth Century Views (1965) pp. 81–2.

38. John Dover Wilson argued that Viola originally sang the song, and that Feste was substituted in a subsequent revival, in which there was no boy actor available for Viola's role who could sing: see his New Shakespeare edn (1949) pp. 91–5. Like most recent editors I find this implausible: see the new Arden edn, pp. xvii–xxiii.

39. For the graver failures of dramatization in the play (to which Julia's are integrally related), see Stanley Wells, 'The Failure of *The Two Gentlemen of Verona*', *Shakespeare Jahrbuch*, 99 (1963) 161–73.

40. Edward Gordon Craig, 'On the Ghosts in the Tragedies of Shakespeare', *On the Art of the Theatre* (1911; repr. 1968) esp. pp. 276, 279. Casca's speech is itself preparation for the appearance of Caesar's ghost at Philippi, but the preparation has in this case (unlike the Soothsayer's) been poorly executed.

41. Ripley, *'Julius Caesar' on Stage*, p. 53. The distaste for Casca's catalogue of supernatural effects dates from the Restoration, and Ripley documents its persistence through nineteenth- and twentieth-century productions.

42. Dowden defended the character in a similar way, as a 'piece of higher art', Shakespeare showing 'the dramatic inconsistency of his characters'. Granville Barker replied, 'If this were so the thing would still be very clumsily done. What means is the actor given of showing that this is a dramatic inconsistency?' – *Prefaces to Shakespeare* (1958) II, 376.

CHAPTER FOUR: READERS AND SEERS: 'HENRY V'

1. By the time this book reaches print, Terry Hand's 1975 production will be almost a decade old; many of my readers will not have seen it, and most who did will have forgotten it. None of what follows depends on your familiarity with that production; nor shall I attempt to reconstruct it for you, or make you wish you could see it once more (or once). It interests me, for the moment, only as an example of the play's impact in performance, a data-base, and my selection of moments for analysis makes no attempt to be fair to the production, or to the individual performances.

Anyone who wants to know more about the production could

consult a variety of sources: Sally Beauman's *The Royal Shake-speare Company's Centenary Production of 'Henry V'* (1976), the actual prompt-book, the collections of professional theatre photographs in Stratford and London, the collection of reviews at the Stratford Shakespeare Centre, the director and the actors themselves. Beauman's book is occasionally misleading; it omits much; its selection of photographs seems somewhat haphazard. Nevertheless, I am immensely indebted to her work, not least because it has allowed me to concentrate upon the moments directly pertinent to my own inquiry, in the know-ledge that those interested in aspects of the production I have scanted will find a fuller description readily available. Richard David also discusses the production in his valuable *Shake-speare in the Theatre* (1978) pp. 210–14.

Such materials enable a reader to reconstruct, as far as pos-sible, the production itself. It would be rather more difficult to verify my account of the audiences' responses, so I should perhaps explain how that account was compiled. First, I have consulted the reviews of the original production, and of the 1977 revival. I have also spoken with the director and many members of the cast, often at great length. The actors, after all, can see the audience as well as it sees them, and are acutely sensitive to its reactions. I have personally seen the production eleven times (three, before the publication of Beauman's book), and these eleven performances are my main source of informa-tion. At the first of the eleven I was no more conscious of the other members of the audience that one normally is. But there-after I made it my business to watch the audience as closely as the actors, and by the end of this experiment, having virtually memorized the production, I watched it a good deal more than I did the actors. I spoke to as many spectators as possible, during intervals and after performances, and, though I approached these conversations with a mental list of carefully worded ques-tions, as much as possible I tried to let my interlocutors govern the dialogue, since what spectators want to talk about is often more revealing than their responses to direct questions. In all these conversations I pretended to be no more than an average spectator, seeing the play for the first time.

Other obvious sources of information about an audience are its applause, laughter and coughing. I compiled a list of all the lines, or bits of stage business, which produced laughter, distin-guishing between laughs which were only occasional and those which could be predicted night after night. One must also distinguish between kinds of laughter, it being fairly easy to tell genuine laughter from what Peter Thompson calls 'one of those compulsory laughs, which is no necessary reflection of an audience's good humour' – *Shakespeare Survey*, 28 (1975) 179. By sitting far front in a side balcony, it was actually possible to see most of the audience as the actors see it; by standing at the back of the stalls, I could watch other standing spectators, who not being confined to seats tend to express their reactions more physically, for instance by leaning forward or standing on tiptoe or clutching the rail at moments of tension or excitement, by fidgeting or shuffling their feet when bored. Though such observations do not produce quantifiable data, and cannot claim to be scientific, they do represent an attempt, more sustained and detailed than any of which I am aware, to watch the *audience* to a modern Shakespearian performance.

2. Beauman, *Centenary Production*, p. 84.
3. Sigmund Freud, *Jokes and their Relation to the Unconscious* (1912), trs. and ed. James Strachey, rev. Angela Richards, Pelican Freud Library 6 (1976) 189.
4. Beauman, *Centenary Production*, p. 65.
5. Vernon, *Psychology of Perception*, p. 110.
6. Hazlitt similarly complained that Edmund Kean as an actor depended too much 'on the expression of the countenance, which is a language intelligible only to a part of the house' – *A View of the English Stage; or, A Series of Dramatic Criticisms* (1818), in *Works*, ed. P. P. Howe (1930–4) v, 179–80.
7. There were however two exceptions: one a distinguished scholar, who had published an important essay on the play, and who found the production shallow and simplistic; the other a young woman who said she thought *Henry VI, Part One* much the better play (and indeed, the best of the *Henry VI* trilogy) because it was 'so full of action, and the ending was so hopeful', whereas *Henry V* was 'full of long speeches'. I have no wish to deny the existence of such spectators; but their views were clearly unrepresentative.
8. Beauman, *Centenary Production*, p. 153.
9. Ibid.
10. On 'sin', see Roy Battenhouse, '*Henry V* as Heroic Comedy', in *Essays on Shakespeare and Elizabethan Drama*, ed. Hardin Craig (1963) p. 180.
11. See Charles Beecher Hogan, *Shakespeare in the Theatre 1701–1800*, 2 vols (1952, 1957) I, 194–202, and II, 277–94. The absence of Alice from every surviving cast list in the century is better evidence than the scene's omission from Bell's Acting Edn (1774), since Bell also omits the Chorus, who was often acted. Conceivably, though, Isabel could have taken Alice's part. Johnson's own comment is in the past tense, probably

referring to the scene's presumed effectiveness in Shakespeare's lifetime.

12. Johnson, *Works*, VIII, 547.
13. BBC Radio 3, 18 Apr 1976, with John Rowe as Henry and John Gielgud as Chorus; Angela Pleasance played Catherine.
14. M. M. Mahood, *Shakespeare's Wordplay* (1957) p. 41.
15. Freud, *Jokes*, p. 80.
16. The Folio and modern editions actually read '*count*', which more directly suggests English 'cunt'; but this is almost certainly a misreading of 'coune', as suggested by the Quarto form 'con'. For a fuller discussion see my Oxford edn, p. 179.
17. M. L. Radoff, 'Influence of French Farce in *Henry V* and *The Merry Wives*', *Modern Language Notes*, 47 (1933) 427–35. J. H. Walter, in the new Arden *Henry V* (1954) p. 69, cites this article approvingly, as does H. J. Oliver in the new Arden *Merry Wives of Windsor* (1971) pp. lxii–lxiii.
18. Freud, *Jokes*, p. 146.
19. Ibid., p. 90.
20. Ibid., p. 141.
21. This bit of business ('Henry is about to kiss Catherine again, when he sees the French king') also occurs in Richard Mansfield's Acting Version (1911); quoted in Arthur Colby Sprague's *Shakespeare and the Actors: The Stage Directions in His Plays (1660–1905)* (1944) p. 121.
22. Aaron Hill, *King Henry the Fifth; Or, The Conquest of France, by the English*. For evidence Hill was poorly received, see *Shakespeare: The Critical Heritage*, II, 401.
23. Charlotte Lennox admitted that 'the Dialogue is not without wit, liveliness, and humour', but then pinpointed what was, for the eighteenth century, its unforgivable fault, that it was 'so utterly void of Propriety that we lose all Idea of the Dignity of the Persons who manage it' – *Shakespear Illustrated*, III, 137.
24. Hilda Hulme, *Explorations in Shakespeare's Language* (1962) p. 206.
25. Freud, *Jokes*, p. 283.
26. For the happy theatrical history of the leek scene, see Sprague, *Shakespeare and the Actors*, pp. 120–1.
27. Freud, *Jokes*, p. 241.
28. Ibid., p. 180.
29. Ibid., p. 282.
30. Johnson, *Works*, VII, 341.
31. Beauman, *Centenary Production*, p. 201.
32. This was true even of the RSC production. Mr Hands claimed that the death of Le Fer, a sympathetic figure, 'balanced' the Boy's death (Beauman, *Centenary Production*, p. 200), and in

an impartial moral reckoning this might be true. But the Boy was killed as far downstage as possible, in an otherwise empty scene immediately after his soliloquy, and his body lay there for some time, noted and spoken of by other characters. Le Fer died centre-stage, in the course of a busy scene during which he said nothing, during the confusion of a general exeunt, in the midst of a set cluttered by debris and bodies and a deliberately scattered and disorganized English army: as I said, in my first few visits to the play, I did not even see him die. The other victim, the Constable, was still harder to identify, and given a minimal emphasis. Our response to such deaths could not begin to disrupt the essentially comic structure of the play.

33. Emrys James in Beauman, *Centenary Production*, p. 63.
34. As the *Oxford English Dictionary* makes clear, 'cavalier' would not have been regarded as a 'French' word at the time of the play's composition: this was a detail which could only have worked for a modern audience.
35. Michael Goldman, *Shakespeare and the Energies of Drama* (1972) pp. 58–9.
36. Hulme, *Explorations*, p. 26.
37. Beauman, *Centenary Production*, p. 83.
38. Coleridge, *Shakespearean Criticism*, I, 160.
39. Beauman, *Centenary Production*, p. 211.
40. Ibid., p. 122.
41. Ibid., p. 69.
42. Ibid., p. 68.
43. Ibid.
44. Hunter, *Memory*, pp. 75, 79.
45. Ibid., pp. 58–9.
46. Ibid., pp. 58, 60.
47. William Babula, 'Whatever Happened to Prince Hal? An Essay on *Henry V*', *Shakespeare Survey*, 30 (1977) 47–59. Quotations from pp. 50 (nos 2, 6), 51 (no. 1), 52 (nos 3, 4), 53 (no. 5).
48. A. D. Nuttall, speaking of this tendency to hear echoes and repetitions, observes that 'among professional teachers of literature it can easily get out of hand. The teacher of literature is artificially directed, by the terms of his job, to elicit such repetitions' – 'Realistic Convention and Conventional Realism', *Shakespeare Survey*, 34 (1981) 34.
49. It will not do to argue that Shakespeare's audience had a better memory than contemporary audiences do (though that is probably true). See for instance Marion Trousdale's interesting 'Shakespeare's Oral Text', *Renaissance Drama*, 12 (1981) 95–116. Trousdale claims that Shakespeare's was an oral culture, and that as such it could be expected to perceive – even

on a first hearing – the kinds of 'spatial' patterns of imagery much loved of modern critics. But, if spectators noted such echoes, they should also have noted the many contradictions of detail or logic in the plots of the plays; the very abundance of such contradictions suggests that Shakespeare relied on his audiences not to perceive them. Moreover, the principles at issue here have nothing to do with memory in general, or with aural attentiveness, but with the specific phenomena of immediate memory span and directed retention, functions of human perception which we have no reason to suspect have deteriorated over the last four centuries. Finally, most of Trousdale's parallels are drawn from oral epic, a genre of dubious relevance to Shakespeare's plays. The point about oral style, and particularly the formulaic repetitions so characteristic of it, is that they testify to oral *composition*; Shakespeare, by contrast, and his contemporaries, clearly *wrote* their plays, even if they wrote them for an aural culture. The true parallels for Shakespeare's style should be sought in Athenian drama, not Homeric epic – and in that drama we find discrepancies of detail very similar to those in Shakespeare. See for instance the 'confusion' over the oracle in Sopocles's *Trachiniae*.

50. Beauman, *Centenary Production*, p. 76.
51. Ibid., p. 176.
52. Ibid., p. 111.
53. Ibid., p. 114.
54. There is some discussion of the distinction between focal and peripheral perception in Bernard Beckerman's 'Explorations in Shakespeare's Drama', *Shakespeare Quarterly*, 29 (1978) 140, and his *Dynamics of Drama* (1970) pp. 137–44.
55. Vernon, *Psychology of Perception*, p. 159; Miller, *Psychology: Science of Mental Life*, p. 62.
56. Beauman, *Centenary Production*, p. 68.
57. Ibid., p. 159.
58. Ibid.
59. Rudolf Arnheim, *Art and Visual Perception: A Psychology of the Creative Eye*, 2nd edn (1974) p. 63.
60. Beauman, *Centenary Production*, p. 210.

CHAPTER FIVE: REVOLUTIONS OF PERSPECTIVE:
'KING LEAR'

1. Thornton Wilder, 'Some Thoughts on Playwriting', in *The Intent of the Artist*, ed. Augusto Centeno (1941) pp. 85–6.
2. For recent challenges to the conflated text see Michael J.

Warren, 'Quarto and Folio *King Lear* and the Interpretation of Albany and Edgar', in *Shakespeare, Pattern of Excelling Nature*, ed. David Bevington and Jay L. Halio (1978) pp. 95–107; Steven Urkowitz, *Shakespeare's Revision of 'King Lear'* (1980); P. W. K. Stone, *The Textual History of 'King Lear'* (1980); Gary Taylor, 'The War in *King Lear*', *Shakespeare Survey*, 33 (1980) 27–34; Peter W. M. Blayney, *The Texts of 'King Lear' and Their Origins*, I (1982); and *The Division of the Kingdoms: Shakespeare's Two Versions of 'King Lear'*, ed. Gary Taylor and Michael Warren (1983). In what follows I generally quote (in modernized spelling) the Folio text, as representing Shakespeare's final version; however, relevant differences in the Quarto are discussed, either in the text or notes. (At the time this chapter was drafted, only the first of the above works was in print, and I was chiefly indebted to Peter Blayney for my awareness of the textual and bibliographical arguments for the distinctiveness of the two versions. The critical arguments in this chapter are, however, entirely my own.)

3. E. K. Chambers, *The Elizabethan Stage*, 4 vols (1923) II, 309. Though no one seems to have suggested this, the passage makes clearer sense if repunctuated: 'what a world are dead, / Which he revivd, to be revived soe / No more: Young Hamlett . . .'.

4. Thomas Davies, *Dramatic Miscellanies* (1783–4) II, 280; Joseph Pittard [=John Shebbeare?], *Observations on Mr Garrick's Acting: in a Letter to the Right Hon. the Earl of Chesterfield* (1758) p. 7.

5. *The Letters of David Garrick*, ed. D. M. Little and G. M. Kahrl (1963) II, 682–3 (letter to Edward Tighe).

6. Coleridge, *Shakespearean Criticism*, I, 60.

7. Marvin Rosenberg, *The Masks of King Lear* (1972) p. 70.

8. Helen Gardner, *King Lear* (1967) p. 13.

9. Randall McLeod, in an essay in *The Division of the Kingdoms* ('*Gon.* No more, the text is foolish.'), argues that the Folio presents a consistently more sympathetic picture of Goneril; in particular, he feels that the Folio cuts in I.iii remove lines of 'shrillness' and 'hypocrisy', so that in the Folio Goneril's actions are more 'measured' and sympathetic. The Folio cuts Goneril's

> Not to be overruled. Idle old man,
> That still would manage those authorities
> That he hath given away! Now, by my life,
> Old fools are babes again, and must be used
> With checks as flatteries, when they are seen abused.

These lines probably would alienate an audience, in a scene where Goneril makes an otherwise convincing complaint, and her strongest bid for our sympathy. But in the long run the cut does Goneril little good, because as a consequence the Folio puts a much stronger emphasis on the line just before the cut: 'Let him to my sister, / Whose mind and mine, I know, in that are one' – so that the impotence of Lear's later threats is the more likely to be noticed. Also, the Folio's omission of the description of Lear as clinging to the authority he had given away is crucial to our interpretation of the following scene (as indicated by the frequency with which critics quote or allude to it). If the line is kept, it strongly disposes us to criticize Lear's commands there, which we might otherwise be inclined to regard less ironically. After all, unless we are specifically told that Lear's conduct disregards his abdication, we have no reason to see anything unnatural in a father and ex-king still wielding considerable domestic authority. The Folio alterations to I.iii thus seem to me to help Goneril here, but to hurt her later. More generally, though I accept McLeod's contention that many of the variants (particularly in II.iv and after) do cohere in shifting our perception of Goneril, McLeod seems to me seriously to overestimate the structural significance of some such variants, in contributing to an audience's total image of Goneril's behaviour. This caveat applies especially to his analysis of Act I, which depends heavily upon changes to single words (hit/sit, not, then/thou, graced/great). Though he is right in claiming that the apparent patterning in such textual variants argues for their authenticity, it by no means follows that a handful of variants always radically transforms the larger structures common to both texts.

10. Emrys Jones makes this point in *Scenic Form*, p. 179.
11. For a fuller discussion of variants in the first scene, see the essays by Thomas Clayton and MacD. P. Jackson in *The Division of the Kingdoms*.
12. This variant might be no more than a case of misread minims. But, since the Quarto reads 'confirm' on both occasions, since the other variants are clearly deliberate, and since this variant fits the pattern of the others, I assume it is deliberate rather than accidental. (There is no parallel for the construction 'confirming ... on', but it is perfectly intelligible.)
13. S. L. Goldberg, in *An Essay on King Lear* (1968) p. 23, says that we first begin to feel for Lear and to judge Cordelia at 'But goes thy heart with this?'; H. A. Mason, in *Shakespeare's Tragedies of Love* (1970) p. 174, makes a similar claim for 'I

loved her most, and thought to set my rest / On her kind nursery'.

14. Coleridge, *Shakespearean Criticism*, I, 61.
15. Nahum Tate, *The History of King Lear*, ed. James Black, Regents Restoration Drama Series (1975).
16. Michael Long has also noted, for different reasons, the prosperity of Kent and Cordelia at the end of this scene – *The Unnatural Scene: A Study in Shakespearean Tragedy* (1976) p.167.
17. In the Folio (and conflated texts), Kent is silent until now; the Quarto gives him the line, 'He says, my lord, your daughter is not well' (I.iv.49); the next four speeches to Lear are spoken by a servant. The Quarto arrangement requires at least two people, Kent and another servant, to follow Oswald out, then return. No real purpose is served by splitting the speeches; one might even conjecture that Shakespeare began, thinking to assign the whole sequence to Kent, then realized in composition he needed instead one of Lear's train, but forgot to go back and alter the first speech prefix. The Quarto identifies this anonymous member of Lear's train as a 'servant'; the Folio, as a 'knight'. The elevation of social status seems designed to give the speaker more authority and dignity, while ensuring that an audience will identify him as a representative of the 'knights' Goneril finds so 'riotous'.
18. For a fuller discussion see Michael Warren, 'The Diminution of Kent', in *The Division of the Kingdoms*.
19. Leo Tolstoy, 'Shakespeare and the Drama', in *Shakespeare in Europe*, ed. Oswald LeWinter (1970) pp. 221–8.
20. Kent's phrase may be regarded as a certain reference to the proverb 'All fellows at football', glossed in seventeenth-century dictionaries as 'All alike, no difference'. See Hulme, *Explorations*, 74.
21. Coleridge, *Shakespearean Criticism*, I, 62.
22. Miller, *Collected Plays*, pp. 43–4.
23. Arnheim, *Art and Visual Perception*, p. 60.
24. A. L. Soens, 'Cudgels and Rapiers: The Staging of the Edgar-Oswald Fight in *Lear*', *Shakespeare Studies*, 5 (1969) 149–58.
25. 'Heroic hardness' is Rosenberg's phrase, describing Mikhoel's Goneril (*The Masks of King Lear*, p. 120). Sara Kestelman, in the 1982 Royal Shakespeare Company production (directed by Adrian Noble), consistently got a laugh on 'O the difference of man and man!' McLeod is particularly convincing in his account of the changes to Goneril in IV.ii and after (*The Division of the Kingdoms*, pp. 182–8). For a brief discussion of

changes to Edmund in the final scene, see Taylor, 'The War in *King Lear*'.

26. *King Lear*, ed. Kenneth Muir, new Arden rev. edn (1972).

27. I.v carries these techniques to new extremes, most strikingly in the sheer speed of the Fool's riddles, which in scene iv came in long speeches with considerable intervals between direct questions to Lear or Kent. Here the Fool demands answers without let-up. Most of his riddles in scene v are not as funny as those in scene iv; the advice and the assaults on Lear are more direct, the medicine is less sugared with wit. But then, too, sometimes the jokes seem entirely without satire, and quite funny. The Fool's joke about kibes, for instance, seems to me far simpler than commentators would suggest. 'If a man's brains were in's heels, were't not in danger of kibes?' This, coming immediately after Kent's exit, looks like the start of a joke at Kent's expense.

> *Lear.* Ay, boy.
> *Fool.* Then I prithee be merry: thy wit shall not go slipshod.

Since men wore slippers when they had kibes, the Fool means, 'thy wit is not in danger of kibes'. Why not? *Because his brains aren't in his heels.* We need not seek allegory in this, or allusion to the unwisdom of going to Regan, or sending Kent there. The Fool only means that, whatever his troubles, whatever mental anguish he may suffer, however great a fool he may be, Lear at least has this to be grateful for ('Then I prithee be merry'): his brains aren't in his feet. This is a simple and appropriate joke; Lear, for the only time, laughs. Why he would laugh at the moralistic glosses of commentators, I cannot imagine. The difficulty arises from the desire of commentators to seek a particular kind of relevance in everything the Fool says, when the Fool's whole technique depends on bewildering expectation, on unpredictability. In the kibes joke, in the stars and oysters riddles, the Fool's motives seem to be changing: where in scene iv he laboured to remind Lear of what Lear wanted to forget, he now begins to try distracting him from those memories and preoccupations. But this alteration in the Fool's motives only creates greater formal bewilderment in scene v itself, for it coexists with the earlier kind of satire.

The Fool's rapid shifts of audience also reach a climax in scene v, when after Lear's exit he directly addresses the audience. His final joke is simplicity itself, and it relates to his habit elsewhere of twisting the auditor's response into proof of the auditor's foolishness.

She that's a maid now, and laughs at my departure,
Shall not be a maid long, unless things be cut shorter.

A couplet innocent enough, till the word 'things'. Any woman who laughs at that *double-entendre* reveals that she knows more than she should, that she enjoys smutty jokes – and such a woman is not likely to preserve her virginity long, barring universal castration. This is in the line of sexually aggressive jokes men tell women, the woman's very willingness to listen and to laugh constituting proof of her sexual openness. It cannot be twisted into a relevance for Lear's situation – it functions by its irrelevance, by making us laugh. As Coleridge said, 'The Fool's conclusion of this Act, by a grotesque prattling, seems to indicate the dislocation of feeling that has been begun and is to be continued' (*Shakespearean Criticism*, I, 64). Without this couplet, Lear's premonition of madness is too powerful and too simple. The couplet will and should surprise and disorient us. But that disorientation is intended, and the content of the Fool's address to the audience only increases it.

28. Alexander Schmidt, *Shakespeare Lexicon*, rev. edn (1886), Go (1) and (2). Other dictionaries and glossaries add nothing to Schmidt's account.
29. Ibid., Learn (2).
30. Ibid., Set (vb, 7).
31. Ibid., Throw (vb, 1).
32. *King Lear*, ed. H. H. Furness, New Variorum edn (1880) p. 72. For the rules of hazard, see Charles Cotton, *The Compleat Gamester* (1674; repr. 1972) pp. 168–9; for its popularity, A. Forbes Sieveking, 'Games', in *Shakespeare's England*, ed. Sir Sidney Lee and C. T. Onions, 2 vols (1917) II, 468; on cheating, the pamphlets collected in *The Elizabethan Underworld*, ed. A. V. Judges (1930) pp. 27, 32–44, 50, 53, 57–9, etc.
33. On the necessity, for short-term memory, of grouping items in a sequence, see Miller, *Psychology: Science of Mental Life*, pp. 64–5. Interestingly, the number of unrelated items we can suspend in immediate memory is usually six or seven (p. 63).
34. *De Quincey as Critic*, ed. John E. Jordan (1973) p. 78.
35. *King Lear*, ed. G. I. Duthie and J. Dover Wilson, New Shakespeare (1960) pp. 163–4.
36. Tolstoy, in *Shakespeare in Europe*, p. 222.
37. Michael Long calls this speech 'a vindication of the rightness of the impulses which have unreflectingly taken his part' (*The Unnatural Scene*, p. 192).
38. I have necessarily simplified the Greek attitude, though not (I hope) distorted it. *Tyrannus* itself presumes an audience for

whom the archaic disregard for intent was no longer entirely satisfactory; this is also true of *The Oresteia*. But features of the archaic attitude survived into the fourth century and beyond: with revolutions of such magnitude, in ideas of such importance, periods of transition and overlap are to be expected. Plato, in his concern for the effect of evil on the soul, in some respects anticipated Christ, except that for Plato guilt, the soul's pollution, remains a *consequence* of the crime; for Christ the act itself becomes redundant. The stubbornness of Philoctetes or Oedipus at Colonus is a development of this insistence on the consequence of the crime, the indelible pollution: a wrong, once done, will not be forgotten. Thus, though Philoctetes refuses to return to Troy for reasons his opponents consider trivial, and Oedipus curses Polyneices for the lack of 'one small word', Sophocles's treatment of the trivial is radically different from Shakespeare's: it involves exacting the full price for an original wrong no one would consider trivial. In Lear's case it is the original wrong which is, objectively, trivial.

39. Burke, *A Rhetoric of Motives*, p. 70.
40. See for instance Honigmann, *Shakespeare's Seven Tragedies*, p. 106; and Mason, *Shakespeare's Tragedies of Love*, p. 200.
41. John Kerrigan discusses the effect of the Folio omissions and alterations in this passage in 'Revision, Adaptation, and The Fool in *King Lear*', in *The Division of the Kingdoms*.
42. The second of these functions is noted by R. H. Goldsmith in *Wise Fools in Shakespeare* (1958) p. 62; the third by Lawrence Danson, in *Tragic Alphabet: Shakespeare's Drama of Language* (1974) p. 175, where he says, 'the Fool's motives in these exchanges are perhaps less important than the sheer cacophony he helps to create'.
43. Emrys Jones, in *Scenic Form*, p. 167, compares this with a scene in *2 Henry VI*, when the Duke of Gloucester exits without warning or explanation, and upon returning excuses himself by saying,

> Now, lords, my choler being overblown
> With walking once about the quadrangle,
> I come to talk of commonwealth affairs.
> (I.iii.150–2)

Jones comments that 'The sudden exit and re-entry are visible signs of lack of self-control. *[King Lear]* contains exactly the same stage effect: Lear exits (I.iv.289) and abruptly re-enters, so making a similar impression of uncontrollable passion.' But, though the comparison is typically stimulating, it seems to me

that the two scenes create very different stage effects. Gloucester's exit at first seems unmotivated; his subsequent explanation
retrospectively motivates it. Both moments seem, as a consequence, contrived. Moreover, Gloucester's exit, and especially
his re-entry, testify to a *controlled* passion. Lear by contrast
leaves the stage not primarily in order to calm himself, but to go
to Regan's: Shakespeare carefully prepares an external as well as
'psychological' motive for the exit, so that it produces an effective 'moment' in itself, and then implicitly motivates the
re-entry, at once, with the news 'What, fifty of my followers at a
clap?' – thereby creating another effective 'moment', which like
the first does indeed suggest 'uncontrollable passion'.

44. Some have imagined a Goneril visibly pregnant in this scene,
which would of course radically alienate us from Lear and produce considerable sympathy for her. (It would also make
nonsense of the first six lines of Lear's curse – or does he suddenly notice she's pregnant, and correct himself by saying, 'If
she must teem'?) The only evidence for Goneril's pregnancy is
in II.iv, five scenes later, where, in Lear's further curse ('Strike
her young bones, / You taking airs, with lameness'), 'young
bones' has been taken to refer to an unborn child. Three parallels are adduced to support this usage; I shall add four more:

> These dead men's bones lie here of purpose to
> Invite us to supply the number of the living . . .
> Come, we'll get young bones and do't.
>> (Tourneur, *The Atheist's Tragedy*, IV.iii.172)

> poor soul, she breeds young bones,
> And that is it makes her so touchy, sure.
>> (*King Leir*, 844)

> If your fresh lady breed young bones . . . .
>> (Ford, *The Broken Heart*, II.i.122)

> And he took thee with thy belly full of young bones.
>> (Marston, *The Malcontent*, II.ii.15)

> . . . thou'rt breeding of young bones; I am
> afraid I have got thee with child.
>> (Middleton, *A Mad World My Masters*, III.ii.38–9)

> She breeds young bones.
>> (Middleton, *No Wit No Help*, II.ii.92)

> . . . you breed yongbones.
>
> (Dekker, *Blurt Master Constable*, III.iii.119)

It should be evident that, in each example, 'breed' or 'get', and the immediate context, make the specialized sense of 'young bones' absolutely unequivocal. But nothing in the *Lear* context encourages a listener to take the words in anything but their usual sense; indeed, Lear goes on to curse Goneril's 'eyes' and 'beauty', so that a curse upon her youth and health is entirely appropriate. Even if the reference here is gynaecological, Lear may only be cursing future children, as he did in I.iv.

45. Sprague, *Shakespeare and the Actors*, p. 287.
46. McLeod again sees the Folio variants at the end of I.iv working in Goneril's favour, showing her 'wrought in the extreme', yet 'self-possessed' and 'coming to the boil slowly'. In the Quarto, Goneril seems in complete and calm control of the situation after Lear leaves. But the Folio text, by adding lines 322–33 and altering others, presents a more worried, busier Goneril: calling repeatedly for Oswald, having considerable difficulty persuading her husband, even uncertain of Regan's response. These changes increase the tension of Lear's encounter with the third daughter, highlight Albany's importance and his reluctance, and make Goneril a fuller and more human creature. But against this fuller characterization must be set the new and palpable falsehood of her claims that Lear's knights are dangerous – after a scene in which Goneril has stood, alone, insulting Lear, on a stage full of his attendants, which he never even considers using against her, but simply dismisses.

Index

261